Chris Berlin

TOUR DE FRANCE

• THE HISTORIC 1978 EVENT •

COMMEMORATIVE EDITION
OF 75th ANNIVERSARY
BICYCLE RACE

by Robin Magowan

VELOPRESS • BOULDER, COLORADO

VeloPress
1830 N. 55th. Street
Boulder CO 80301
USA

An imprint of Inside Communications

Second Edition 1996
First published 1979 by Stanley Paul & Co. Ltd., London
1 3 4 5 6 7 8 9 10

Manufactured in the United States of America

Library of Congress Cataloguing in Publication Data
Magowan, Robin.
    Tour de France: The 75th anniversary bicycle race/by Robin Magowan. — 2nd. ed.
        p.   cm.
    Includes bibliographical references and index.
    ISBN 1-884737-13-7
    1. Tour de France (Bicycle race) — History.   I. Title.
    GV1049.2.T68M33   1996
    796.6 — dc20   —dc20
    [796.6'2'0944]   96-5519
                                                                                 CIP

All photographs copyright PresseSports. Cover photograph digitally altered.

    ♻ Text pages are 20 percent post-consumer waste
        Photo pages are 15 percent post-consumer waste

For Felix

also by Robin Magowan

Voyages

Persian Notes

Ecuador (trans. H. Michaux)

Looking for Binoculars

Triptych

Burning the Knife
And Other Voyages

Kings of the Road

Narcissus and Orpheus

Fabled Cities of Central Asia

CONTENTS

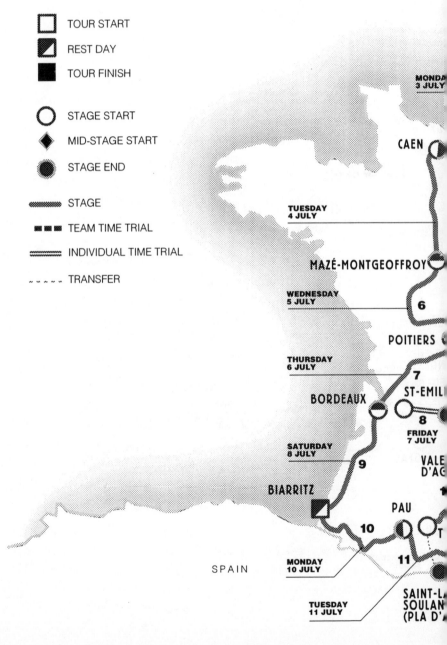

TOUR START

REST DAY

TOUR FINISH

STAGE START

MID-STAGE START

STAGE END

STAGE

TEAM TIME TRIAL

INDIVIDUAL TIME TRIAL

TRANSFER

MONDA
3 JULY

CAEN

TUESDAY
4 JULY

MAZÉ-MONTGEOFFROY

WEDNESDAY
5 JULY

6

POITIERS

THURSDAY
6 JULY

7

ST-EMIL

BORDEAUX

8

FRIDAY
7 JULY

SATURDAY
8 JULY

9

VALE
D'AG

BIARRITZ

PAU

10

T

MONDAY
10 JULY

11

SPAIN

TUESDAY
11 JULY

SAINT-L
SOULAN
(PLA D'

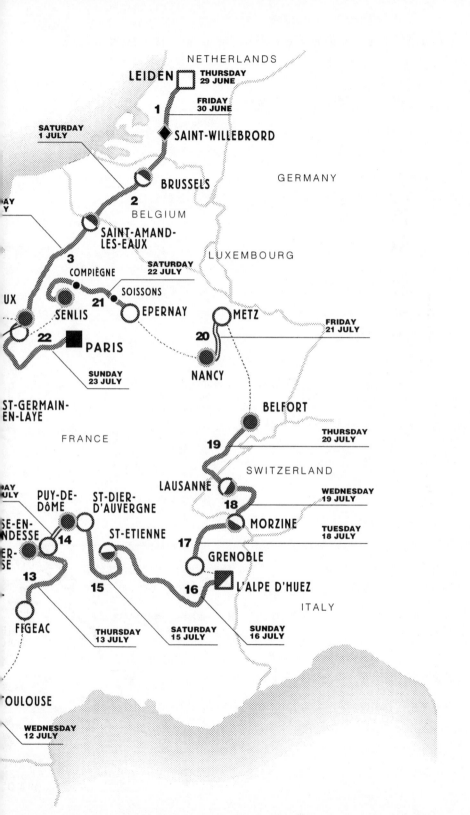

1978 TOUR DE FRANCE ROSTERS

Peugeot-Esso-Michelin
Manager: Maurice de Muer
1. Bernard Thévenet
2. Bernard Bourreau
3. Jean-Pierre Danguillaume
4. Régis Delépine
5. Jacques Esclassan
6. Yves Hézard
7. Michel Laurent
8. Régis Ovion
9. Guy Sibille
10. Jean-Luc Vandenbroucke   (B)

TI-Raleigh-McGregor
Manager: Peter Post
11. Hennie Kuiper   (NL)
12. José De Cauwer   (B)
13. Gerben Karstens   (NL)
14. Gerrie Knetemann   (NL)
15. Henk Lubberding   (NL)
16. Jan Raas   (NL)
17. Klaus-Peter Thaler   (G)
18. Aa Van Den Hoek   (NL)
19. Paul Wellens   (B)
20. Wilfried Wesemael   (B)

C&A
Managers: Rudi Altig;Joseph Huysmans
21. Lucien Van Impe   (B)
22. Joseph Bruyère   (B)
23. Jos De Schoenmaecker   (B)
24. René Dillen   (B)
25. Ward Janssens   (B)
26. Marcel Laurens   (B)
27. Ludo Loos   (B)
28. Jacques Martin   (B)
29. René Martens   (B)
30. Walter Planckaert   (B)

Kas-Campagnolo
Manager: Antonio Barrutia
31. Francisco Galdos   (Sp)
32. Julian Andiano   (Sp)
33. Enrique Cima   (Sp)
34. Faustino Fernandes-Ovies   (Sp)
35. Enrique Martinez Heredia   (Sp)
36. José Nazabal   (Sp)
37. José Pesarrodona   (Sp)
38. Juan Pujol   (Sp)
39. Sebastian Pozo   (Sp)
40. Jesus Suarez-Cueva   (Sp)

Miko-Mercier-Hutchinson
Manager: Louis Caput
41. Joop Zoetemelk   (NL)
42. Barry Hoban   (GB)
43. Maurice Le Guilloux
44. Raymond Martin
45. Hubert Mathis
46. André Mollet
47. Sven-Ake Nilsson   (S)
48. Patrick Perret
49. Christian Seznec
50. Charly Rouxel

Renault-Gitane-Campagnolo
Manager: Cyrille Guimard
51. Bernard Hinault
52. Jean-René Bernaudeau
53. Yvon Bertin
54. Jacques Bossis
55. André Chalmel
56. Gilbert Chaumaz
57. Lucien Didier   (Lux)
58. Bernard Quilfen
59. Willy Teirlinck   (B)
60. Pierre-Raymond Villemiane

Teka
Manager: Julio San Emeterio
61. Pedro Torres (Sp)
62. Bernardo Alfonsel (Sp)
63. Javier Elorriaga (Sp)
64. Eulalio Garcia (Sp)
65. Miguel-Maria Lasa (Sp)
66. Paulino Martinez (Sp)
67. José Martins (P)
68. Antonio Menendes (Sp)
69. Andres Oliva (Sp)
70. Pedro Vilardebo (Sp)

Lejeune-BP
Manager: Henry Anglade
71. Roger Legeay
72. Pierre Bazzo
73. Fedor Den Hertog (NI)
74. Patrick Friou
75. Joël Gallopin
76. Jean-Louis Gauthier
77. Daniel Gisiger (Swit)
78. Antoine Guttierez
79. Michel Le Denmat
80. Eugène Plet

Fiat-La France
Manager: Raphaël Geminiani
81. Jean-Jacques Fussien
82. Serge Beucherie
83. Alain Budet
84. Alain De Carvalho
85. Jacky Hardy
86. Gilbert Le Lay
87. Dominique Sanders
88. Philippe Tesnière
89. Didier Van Vlaslaer
90. Paul Sherwen (GB)

Velda-Lano-Flandria
Manager: Fred De Bruyne
91. Freddy Maertens (B)
92. Michel Pollentier (B)
93. Joaquim Agostinho (P)
94. Herman Beyssens (B)
95. René Bittinger
96. Marc De Meyer (B)
97. Sean Kelly (Irl)
98. Christian Muselet
99. Marcel Tinazzi
100. Albert Van Vlierberghe (B)

Jobo-Superia
Manager: Guy Faubert
101. Mariano Martinez
102. Dino Bertolo
103. Jean-Pierre Biderre
104. Dante Coccolo
105. Philippe Durel
106. Hervé Inaudi
107. Ferdinand Julien
108. Alain Patritti
109. Jean-François Pescheux

All riders French, unless otherwise noted: (B)=Belgium; (G)=Germany; (GB)=Great Britain; (Irl)=Ireland; (NL)=Netherlands; (P)=Portugal; (S)=Sweden; (Sp)=Spain; (Swit)=Switzerland

ACKNOWLEDGMENTS

This book would never have been written without the support and enthusiasm of the editor of the British edition of *Penthouse*, Gerard van der Leun. I also owe a debt which can never be sufficiently acknowledged to the staff writers of *L'Équipe:* Michel Clare, Noel Couëdel, Robert Silva, and, above all, Pierre Chany whose highly cerebral 2000-word daily column inspired me to want to see the Tour and, in a sense, translate his vision. Champagne these days is not often drunk over the breakfast table; but there is the particular *marque*, pale, sparkling Antoine Blondin, without whom rising would be very difficult for most of us Tourists. Sharing the same freewheel were Jean Eimer of *Sud-Ouest* and Reynaud Vincent of *France-Soir*, both novices like myself, but with better eyes. At every mile of the way I had Patrick Thillet to help initiate me into the finer aspects of Tourmanship; a more joyful, selfless, and loyal guide would be hard to imagine. Finally, both during the Tour and afterwards, I have profited from my friend John Wilcockson's considerable knowledge and unrelinquishing help. Photographs are reproduced by kind permission of Presse-Sports.

INTRODUCTION

News these days is sport, and war a species of sport. Not that there isn't much else worth reading about, just that newspapers make it increasingly seem that way. What advertiser wants you to concern yourself with political corruption, nuclear terrorism, and ecological holocaust? Not a single one. Society exists to sell, and entertainment sells, especially circuses.

It must be admitted that sports fit our daily entertainment needs quite nicely, thank you. A man robs a bank, commits the embezzlement of the century, and in some dark wood fathers sextuplets; that's usually the last we hear of our hero — unless he turns up prolonged in a Hollywood idyll. Unlike these unique and, at times, essential events, a sport rolls on and on over the long season with the same flotsam personalities bobbing up again and again in vast swells of newsprint. So the media spew them out for us: baseball leagues, hockey leagues, bowling leagues. No sooner have we heard that association football (rebaptized *soccer*) has taken America by storm, when here comes its blood brother, rugby! Will caber-tossing be next? Is the country of roller derby, rodeo and New York City big enough for yet more stadium violence?

Among the sports circuses, the Tour de France — the longest, most grueling and commercially rewarding of bicycle races — is unique. To be sure, there are bigger, longer-lasting events, such as soccer's World Cup and the Olympic Games, but these are stationary spectacles and don't require, in addition to the regular 1700 employees, a changing work force of 800 new personnel a day, 4000 police at the bridges, intersections and 'hot-point' sprints, 300 vehicles, 70 motorcycles (including 44 belonging to the motorized squad of the Paris Garde Républicaine), two helicopters buzzing away above the pack of riders, and an entire fleet of semi-invisible radio planes to relay the press and television reports. The media coverage, in the amount of personnel and miles of cable, is far greater than any during an international summit conference.

Coordinating the Tour is an organization that takes up the first floor of the *Équipe* building in the Montmartre quarter of Paris, with 22 permanent employees and an operation budget of about $2.5 million (see "Editor's notes," page 180). Watching this "Planet Tour" in operation, one American journalist confessed that the only comparable masterpiece of efficiency he had personally witnessed was the 1942 Allied landing in North Africa.

During the Tour, some 15 million fans line the 2500 miles of roads and 55 mountain passes to see the 110 riders go by, while 160 million others view the 22 afternoon finishes on television. This vast, mainly rural audience makes the race commercially feasible, as well as assuring the racers the exposure with which to obtain contracts for the lucrative single-day *criteriums* — 100km circuit races — of the remaining part of the season. Unlike most sport spectacles, it is the Tour that makes riders famous, and not the other way around.

In the America where I grew up, the bicycle was a child's toy. World War II and fuel rationing may have extended its clientele, but when the war ended the bicycle reverted to its essential function, of preparing you for a day when you would have a car. It was the right to drive that made you an adult. If at 16, by some bleak misfortune, you had that license suspended, you did not go back to pedaling about. You walked, even if it was three miles into town for a movie. You were an adult now with an image to maintain.

Though I often dreamed as a child of being a pro athlete, a baseball player, a touring tennis bum, it never occurred to me that a bicycle could be an instrument of sports competition. When that red, shiny, Raleigh two-wheeler came at a sixth birthday, I did not — unlike any European — automatically hunch down in some future champion's streamlined crouch. It was with genuine reluctance I accepted the natural evolution from my beloved tricycle, in my eyes a faster, generally more efficient vehicle. I knew nothing of the American involvement in the history of sport: Rynner Van Neste who, at 17, won the first Italian road race — a 35km Florence to Pistoia in 1870; Arthur Augustus Zimmermann, the Milwaukee Flying Yankee, an almost invincible sprinter on the Continent between 1890 and 1895; or Major Taylor, the black champion, his immediate successor. Nor did I know that all those continuous horse-like colors streaming around a flag, those six-day Madisons at the Vel d'Hiv that so enthralled Hemingway, for one, were again an American invention, the product of a country that cultivated the rawer emotions.

The first glimmer I had that the bicycle might have another use came when at

10 I saw my first racing bicycle. I remember being amazed by its lightness, I could pick it up in one hand! And the nickel-shiny beauty, the taped turned-down handlebars, the pointed saddle, and the complex gear mechanism, all fascinated me. But its owner, an ex-track rider, wouldn't let me fool around any further with it; and, beautiful or not, I could not see the point of a bicycle so specialized that it could cost as much as a new car.

There my interest ended until 1974, when I came to settle in the Burgundy countryside. I had been there almost a year when a friend I played soccer with for a railway town invited me to see the traditional Easter Monday race at nearby Pouillenay. The race involved three laps of a hilly 30-mile circuit, with different hamlets included each time. It was a charming way of getting to know the countryside, waiting on the various hilltops and looking down at the stone houses and zigzag roofs out of some old Book of Hours as seen against that unique light whirr of the advancing bunch's silver-flashing spokes. The conduct of the race itself utterly bewildered me. Struggling, panting, a breakaway group of four would arrive to dispute some hilltop prime. But the man dragging his tail in fourth position was just as likely to suddenly surge forth to win as those ahead of him. And the riders in the van at one hill were never the same as those at the next. I knew I was seeing an animated, highly fluid race, but I had no idea what was really going on.

Later that evening, I remember talking to a visiting Swiss architect. I was expressing my amazement at what I had just seen when he commented, "Most professions don't require any real decision, you just go on passing exams. But riding a bicycle in a race requires willpower." A willpower, he might have added, that the rest of us find immensely humbling.

Eventually, to be able to converse with my soccer teammates, I began reading *L'Équipe*. This is a widely circulated sports daily written in a style that has been called mandarin. Long paragraphs plentifully salted with epithets and classical allusions may not be to everyone's taste. But they do allow the scribe to register what may in fact be art, as 11 men on occasion collectively create it.

As a sometime reader of *L'Équipe*, it was inevitable I should discover the Tour de France. How could I not, when for a whole month its first five broadsheet pages were taken up with the event? But it was the writing that enthralled me. If *L'Équipe*'s soccer scribes are good, those covering the Tour de France are better. Reading them, I came to understand that the Tour is two things at once: a 2500-mile, 22-stage, decathlon-like endurance contest; and an epic spectacle, one that deliberately invites comparison with the "Iliad" and the "Song of Roland." This last aspect very much attracted me. I was not the sort of American likely to fly to the moon, or lower our sprint record through the Louvre. But a tour of France, the Netherlands, Belgium and Switzerland in three-and-a-half weeks seemed within my capabilities.

Trying to cover the Tour is very much like trying to cover a military exercise. If 15 million spectators are willing to stand half the day to watch the Tour flash past in half a second, one can imagine the limitless hordes who would love to follow the race from start to finish. The only possibility is to present oneself as a member of the working press. Just as the riders are human billboards, decked out from cap to pedaling toes in company and product names, so the vast commercial operation of the Tour lives and breathes on the daily dose of excited copy that the 300-man press corps spews out. As near as possible to each stage finish, a great hall must be turned over to journalists and the clackety-clack of their typing pool. Cattle showroom, Olympic swimming pool, convention center, sports arena or church, it is invariably equipped with a bar, since it's well known that the press would never meet a deadline without *some* incentive.

From the outset, it was clear that in the Tour's eyes I represented the very dregs of pressdom. Any neophyte reporter working for a monthly men's mag — and one not legally distributed in France was *persona non grata*. Only one creature might be considered worse — *a woman!* Women now and again turn up in the press room, but Tour rules specifically insist that no woman is ever to be glimpsed following a race. This is done partly to protect delicate sensibilities from the shock of seeing riders defecate; partly to preserve the sexual chastity that Henri Desgrange, the Father of the Tour, deemed essential to the cyclist's morale and stamina.

Finally, after some discussion in which I agreed to drop my visiting 15-year-old photographer and biker son, a green press card with my picture on it was issued. With that key around my neck, the gates of a new society flashed open. My place in it was clear: I was their token American. It hardly mattered that I had spent three of the last four years residing in France. To my colleagues, I was still that Noble Savage whose naïve eyes would somehow illuminate a sport in which too much was now taken for granted. In the course of the Tour, various souls made it their point to take me by the hand, offer me a bit of a banquet, interview me right, left and center, and even on the final day of the race stick me up on a five-minute spot of prime-time TV without giving any indication that it was my wonderful accent that so amused.

Doubtless, the Tour may have hoped for other things than mere understanding. The law in sport, as in much else in the modern world, is expand or perish. For years, there have been plans afoot to airlift the Tour to America, provided suitable municipal backing could be arranged. Bicycle racing may not yet be an American forte with only 16 velodromes and 10,000 racers. But a people who have been buying 10 million bicycles a year are not going to stand around forever pretending they are a lot of mailmen and health nuts.

Commercialism has been with the Tour de France since its inception, and · indeed goes back to the first road race, Paris to Rouen, run on November 7, 1869, and sponsored by the *Paris Vélocipede Illustré*. In this sense, bicycle racing has always been made a media event, designed to sell newspapers, bicycle accessories, and these days a whole host of other products from holiday flats and TV sets down to ballpoint pens, bottled water and ice cream. None of this has prevented it from developing a popular following sufficient to make cycle road racing even today the No. 1 continental summer sport.

This does not mean that there have not been and don't continue to be real conflicts within the Tour: between the newspaper organizers on the one hand and the commercial sponsors on the other; and between both and their proletarian subjects, the riders, and to some extent us journalists. The 1978 Tour may have been one of the most arduous and closely contested in recent memory — a true *tour de force*. But it was also one of the more farcical, enlivened by the first sustained riders' strike in Tour history, a peeing scandal, and some real commercial shenanigans. To understand them, one has to go back into that pioneering microcosm of sports and commercial history, so ably described by Pierre Chany in his book, *"La Fabuleuse Histoire de Cyclisme."*

By organizing Paris-Rouen, the *Vélocipede Illustré* was, in effect, inviting its readership to a party. All those changes in the guest list, new arrivals, cancelations, hints about costumes, medical advice, gourmet suggestions (beef and a light red wine were counseled), information on the states of the road and the accompanying maps, suggest what can be done when the organizing party has a virtual monopoly on the news. Bicycle historians remark on the total absence of coverage in the daily press. But how could their efforts seem anything but partial when compared with what a team of inside organizer-reporters might be able to convey? Through the weeks of build-up, the *Vélocipede Illustré* was able to create for its readers the illusion of a totally enclosed world where the tiniest detail could assume its own delicate resonance.

Spurred on by the notion of securing themselves a place in history, a hundred willing masochists showed up on their "boneshakers" for the start at the Étoile in Paris. Their number was such that the race had to be run in two heats, a half-hour apart. Besides bicycles, there were tricycles and quadricycles. There was even a petite nervous "Miss America," who, inspired by all the cheers, rose to the occasion and came in 40th. The winner was an English veterinarian living in Paris, James Moore

— the winner of the first-ever bicycle race in a Paris park in 1868 — who was the choice of three-quarters of the 40,000 betters. Riding a Michaux bicycle fitted with rubber-coated rims and equipped with ball bearings that were hand made by prisoners in a Paris jail, Dr. Moore covered the 123 actual kilometers in 10 hours 40 minutes, at an average speed of 12 kph. Forty-five minutes behind, equal second, were Bobillier and Castera. The English jockey, Johnson, the leader for most of the way, passed out at the Vaudreuil station at the 98km mark. He was revived with cordials, invited to a proprietor's home for dinner, and an hour later clattered off on his iron rims to Rouen, where he arrived at 9:50 p.m., good for seventh place.

Between Paris-Rouen in 1869 and the 1903 Tour de France, there remained two essential inventions: the transmission chain (already anticipated by Leonardo da Vinci); followed in 1888 by John Boyd Dunlop's inflatable tire. With this a new type of endurance race came into vogue, organized by the bicycle weeklies out to strike the reader's imagination in the manner of Jules Verne. The first in 1891 was the 363-mile Bordeaux-Paris run with pacers, which remains the longest single-day race. But this was topped, four months later, by *Le Petit Journal*'s 750-mile Paris-Brest-Paris, exploited by the Michelin brothers as a launching pad for their demountable tire, which took 15 minutes to change instead of the usual hour.

This is when we first hear of Henri Desgrange, the future founder of the Tour de France. While working as a clerk in a notary's office, Desgrange competed as a bike racer. This state of affairs lasted until one day a client complained about his exhibiting his bare calves in public. Forced to choose between the law and his unfashionable hobby, Desgrange opted for the Little Queen. Among his acquaintances was the head man at the Folies-Bergères, Clovis Clerc. Desgrange persuaded Clerc to plow his profits into the construction of a velodrome on the grounds where Buffalo Bill Cody and his Wild West show had held forth in 1890. At that Buffalo velodrome, Desgrange set the first official unpaced world hour record of 35.325km — to give, as he said, others something to aim at.

In the next years, Desgrange distinguished himself in a number of ways: program director for a group of Paris velodromes; a polemicist for the professional racers in their quarrel with those who wanted to keep the sport amateur; author of a series of articles on training methods collected in "The Head and the Legs." Among these, a piece on chastity reveals a streak of misogyny that goes a long way toward explaining the Tour's continued proscribing of women.

Desgrange's attitude toward the Little Queen was religious. To excel, a rider had to eat, live and breathe cycling. Desgrange did not care how this emotional commitment was attained, but once it was, he assured his readers, "from that moment on the rider was saved; he would have no more need of a woman than of his first pair of socks." Because women represented the only true self-denial, they became the test of a man's willpower. Desgrange was not against sex: natural needs were natural needs, provided it stopped there. "Oh, in the winter, with the tracks closed and the sun gone, go have yourself a ball with one, two, three, four, as many as you want. Make up for lost time anyway you can, so long as you don't act like my smoker friend who told me the other day, 'I'll give it all up March 11.' You know as well as I do that that's not something one cuts out from one day to the next."

This "trappist of the sport," as Chany rightly calls Desgrange, was doing part-time journalism while working as a promotion director for a tire firm, when a quarrel broke out involving the management of Le Vélo, a sports daily printed on green paper, with 80,000 circulation.

The France of 1900 was divided in two by the Dreyfus case, the story of a Jewish army captain falsely accused of selling state secrets to the Germans. On the one side were massed the army command, the Church except for an isolated handful, most of official opinion, and the entire press with the exception of Le Petit Journal. On the other side, along with novelist Emile Zola, were such figures as the dynamic future World War I leader, Georges Clemenceau, the great socialist, Jean Jaurès, and the poet, Charles Péguy. It so happened that Pierre Giffard, the editor of Le Vélo, did occasional assignments for Le Petit Journal. To what extent they put the screws on him is unclear. At any rate, Giffard seized on the occasion of a political demonstration at the Auteuil race track to write a pro-Dreyfus editorial condemning the Chief of Staff, Esterhazy, in literally capital terms. "For his sort of skullduggery there is only one punishment — the guillotine."

Giffard's editorial was picked up and exploited by his competition. It also came to the attention of Le Vélo's principal backer, the Count de Dion, who was unfortunately among the participants at the Auteuil demonstration. For some time, trouble had been brewing among Le Vélo's major advertisers, enraged at Giffard's "high-handed methods," his unwillingness to share authority, and, above all, his "unreasonable space charges." When they decided to form a rival newspaper, L'Auto-Vélo, to be printed on yellow paper, they hired as editor the very qualified Desgrange. But L'Auto-Vélo was more than a newspaper; as part of the continuing circulation battle it was expected to organize races. To this end, the backers appointed a velodrome comptroller, Victor Goddet, as the new organ's treasurer. Goddet's son, Jacques, today is co-director with Felix Lévitan of the Tour de France.

Although cut off by Count de Dion without a sou, Giffard did not roll over and play dead. He instituted a plagiarism suit against L'Auto-Vélo, which he won in

January 1903. Meanwhile, the financial situation of the yellow newspaper remained precarious. The circulation failed to rise above 20,000, and Desgrange knew the paper's backers would not forever pump money into a doomed cause.

With half his title legally amputated, Desgrange saw himself losing his bicycle clientele; one in those early years of the century which well outnumbered those interested in auto racing. It behooved him to come up with something sensational that would put in the shade such races as Bordeaux-Paris and Paris-Brest-Paris.

If Desgrange is the Father of the Tour, credit for the actual suggestion goes to Geo Lefèvre, the new journal's chief cycling reporter. It was Geo who, seated in Desgrange's large second-story office, suggested that *L'Auto* organize "a several-day race, longer than anything now going, something more on the order of the track six-day race, only this time on the road. All the major towns are begging for cycle racers, and they're bound to go along with the idea."

Someone else then said, "If I understand you rightly, Geo, you are proposing a cycling Tour de France."

"Well, *mon cher*, why not?"

The meeting then adjourned to a nearby *brasserie* for lunch. There, at the end of the meal, Desgrange queried Lefèvre, "You were talking a while ago about a Tour de France. Do you think the project can be pulled off?"

"I don't see that it's impossible."

"On our bad roads, in no matter what weather, thousands of miles bicycling! They'll all be killed, and even the best will take a beating."

"Not necessarily."

"How many stages do you reckon on? Have you thought about the overseeing, and the organizational costs?"

"This is the best I've been able to come up with. If we succeed, Giffard will have a stroke."

Desgrange stood up, patted Lefèvre on his shoulder, and after telling him that the idea personally intrigued him, promised that he would go see the man who held the purse strings, Goddet. Goddet also thought the idea excellent, and agreed to figure out the costs.

Four days after the news of the trial loss, *L'Auto*'s lead column of January 19 announced the creation of "the greatest cycling trial in the entire world. A race more than a month long: Paris to Lyon to Marseille to Toulouse to Bordeaux to Nantes to Paris."

At stake for these modern centaurs was the notion of a feat, a stretching of accepted ideas of human limits. The Tour de France would be as much a struggle

with the physical handicaps of dust and potholes and exhaustion as with fellow con-
testants. Not all of this was to the delight of the would-be entrants, and when only
15 had signed up a week before the scheduled May 31 start, Desgrange switched to
a three-week, July 1-19, formula, with smaller entry fees, and five francs a day
expense money for the first 50 entrants.

This carried the day and some 60 riders showed up on July 1, for the start at
Montgeron, on the southern outskirts of Paris. Apart from such known riders as
Garin and Hippolyte Aucouturier, most of them were itinerant out-of-work types,
butcher's boys, refugees from the mines, plus a few crazies. *L'Auto* gave them all
pedigrees. Paggie became "the prince of the mine," Pothier, the discovery of the race
with his second place, was the "fierce butcher of Sens." But *L'Auto* played down
the race, and rather than compromise his own reputation Desgrange deputized the
actual running of the race to Geo Lefèvre.

This low-key approach worked. Lefèvre controlled the course as best he could
by cycling alongside and slipping off by train to points further ahead. The rules were
flexible: a rider who dropped out of one stage could still start in another. In this way,
Aucouturier, a rider with a delicate stomach, the sort of thing no Tour de France
easily forgives, dropped out of the first 18-hour stage, but managed to win the next
two at Marseille and Toulouse. The overall winner was Garin, who carried off a
prize of 6125 gold francs. Twenty others finished, proving that human beings were
capable of linking the great towns of the French hexagon without succumbing at
the end, like the soldier of Marathon.

The next year, the Tour was run in similar fashion over the exact same course,
the one exception being that riders who quit one stage of the race were not allowed
to start again. Only this time the period of grace was over. In a sense, too much had
been learned, and by hook and by crook the riders and their manufacture-employ-
ers went at it.

Riders hopped trains. They rigged up ingenious systems with wires, cords, and
a cork plug held between the teeth so that they could be towed along without having to crank a pedal. Others had allies who dropped nails out of windows for a rival's
wheels. Riders took ill, and it was discovered afterward they had been poisoned.

But all this was nothing compared to the mayhem stirred up by defenders of
the home turf. Why stand passively applauding by the side of the road when, with
a club or a chain, a local lad might be given that needed edge? On the second stage,
outside St. Etienne, there was a pitched battle between fans and riders that ended
only when Lefèvre arrived in the official car firing pistol shots into the air. When
Payan was caught cheating and disqualified at Alès, his cycling club turned out 50

strong to appeal that bit of injustice. On the last stage, the Parisian mob dusted off those old tactics that had served them so well against kings and Prussians: with tree trunks and overturned carts they barricaded the road, strewing boxfuls of nails about for good measure.

Perhaps all the chicanery made it an exciting race. Aucouturier doubled his previous year's total by winning four stage finishes, but his constant punctures put him behind on overall time. Where a year earlier Garin had beaten Pothier by 2:49:00, this time at the start of the last stage he only led him by 28 seconds ... and three minutes at the end. But there had been charges of cheating before, notably in Bordeaux-Paris (again a night race), and after an inquiry by the bicyclist's union, the first four finishers in the Tour de France were disqualified. Garin was suspended for two years, and Pothier banned for life.

By now, the primary circulation battle had been won by Desgrange. Giffard declared bankruptcy, and was hired as an *Auto* reporter by a magnanimous Henri Desgrange. Now Desgrange could well afford to vent his spleen and announce that this second running of the Tour would be its last. "It has been killed off by its very success, the blind passion that it has aroused...."

It is hard to know how to interpret this fit of pique. Hypocrisy? Pure showmanship? At any rate, the rider disqualifications must have mollified him, for in November 1904, Desgrange announced that the Tour would be once more run as a "moral crusade for the sport of cycling." By this he signaled his own intention to step out and take personal charge in order to transform the Tour into a true sports competition.

To add to the Tour's following, he changed the itinerary, increased the mileage and the number of stages from six to 11, while cutting out the overnight cycling from which most of the 1904 disturbances sprung. As a further precautionary measure, the stage finishes were to be judged in secret outside the host town, with the riders brought into town afterward to compete for sprint prizes before the paying velodrome public (which did not look on all this inanimately). On the first 211-mile stage to Nancy, the Tour advanced on a bed of nails, with only half the platoon finishing within the permissible limits. Desgrange wanted to stop the Tour then and there, but was entreated not to by the riders themselves.

It was on the next stage that the first mountain climb made its Tour debut. In 1905, this was a single entity, the Ballon d'Alsace, and there was considerable speculation whether the riders would be able to pedal all the way to the top. In effect, only one man did, the unsmiling René Pottier, who went on to prove his mettle by winning the 1906 Tour, only to commit suicide six months later. Not that Desgrange was himself unsusceptible to the emotions that mountains arouse. After the Tour added, in 1911, the awesome Galibier to its previous conquests he composed an extraordinary *Acte d'Adoration*:

Today, my brothers, we gather here in a common celebration of the divine bicycle. Not only do we owe it our most pious gratitude for the precious and ineffable love that it has given us, but also for the host of memories sown over our whole sports life and which today has made concrete.

In my own case I love it for its having given me a soul capable of appreciating it; I love it for having taken my heart within its spokes, for having encircled a part of my life within its harmonious frame, and for having constantly illuminated me with the victorious sparkle of its nickle plates.

In the history of humanity does it not constitute the first successful effort of intelligent life to triumph over the laws of weight?

These sentiments were by no means unshared. After the Eiffel Tower cubists and those spoke-like nudes descending Duchamp's staircase, what could be more camp than the bicycle? The great pataphysicist, Alfred Jarry, called it "a mineral extension of our bone system, and one almost endlessly perfectible, being born of geometry." Jarry kept his own skeletal machine propped against his bed, since, after France, Italy, Belgium and the rest of the world, why "not a Tour of one's bedroom"? To prove this was not a passing fancy, he hopped on and proceeded to pedal about his room until everyone had left.

Among the roadside spectators of the 1912 Tour's penultimate stage was a *Le Matin* journalist by the name of Colette:

I saw three slight riders pass in front of us, to be immediately swallowed up in swirls of dust: black and yellow backs with red numbering, the three might just as well have been faceless, their heads down around their knees, their spines in an arch, under a white lining.... Very quickly they vanished, the only quiet people in all the uproar; both their haste in pushing on and their silence seemed to cut them off from all that was happening. One would not say that they were competing with one another so much as fleeing us, they who are the quarry of this escort among which one finds, all swirled together in the turbid dust, screams, horn blowings, cheering, and the rolling of thunder.

In 1919 came Desgrange's masterstroke — the creation of *le maillot jaune*, the yellow jersey — for the race leader. This was done without the slightest thought of Jason and the Golden Fleece. Desgrange just wanted to put his own proprietary stamp on the race leader, and what better way than to dress him in the color of *L'Auto*'s pages!

The Tour's very success brought out a new type of cheating on the part of the manufacturers, determined to influence the race results. As early as 1910, Desgrange had established the sag wagon, less out of humanitarian concern, than because it enabled him to survey the going-ons at the back of the race.

By 1930, the collusion, along with an apparent slackening of popular interest, forced Desgrange into a palace revolution. In spite of the threat of losing advertising revenue, he decided on a new system whereby riders would be selected on a national rather than a trade-team basis. In his own words, "The manufacturer wants to see his rider win, whether or not he is the best — the organizer would rather see the best man win."

At such short notice, no nation was ready to equip and provide for a team. So Desgrange decided to do it himself — lodging, food and transportation, all the way down to the yellow bicycles of unknown make. To finance it, he invented the publicity caravan, a sort of ambulating fair that to this day precedes the race by an hour, while offering a nightly show.

Of course what Desgrange did to the manufacturers could also be done to the Tour de France — why not nationalize *it*? Over the years, there have been a number of suggestions to this end, balanced in some way by those who wanted to extend the Tour, make it a *Tour de l'Europe*, a title the organization has taken care to copyright.

Desgrange died in 1940. After World War II, *L'Auto* emerged as *L'Équipe*. Since its new owner, the Amaury family, also owned *Le Parisien Libéré*, it was natural that the editors of the two papers, Jacques Goddet and Felix Lévitan, should take over the Tour organization. Their aim, Goddet wrote, "has been to adopt it to the intense rhythm of the period, while making it more social by putting all the riders at an equal advantage."

The last statement suggests the compromise formula adopted for the readmission of the 10-rider trade teams — which have been the rule since 1962, except for a brief hiatus in 1967 and 1968. While the national teams may have been popular, the countries able to afford them were too few, and they didn't fit the contractual realities of modern trade-team cycling.

The Tour now requires from each entering team a deposit of about $34,000 to cover lodging, food and transportation. The two main sources of funds, however, are the advertising sponsors and host cities. The advertisers supply 60 percent and the cities 25 percent of the $2.5 million budget. The cities recoup most of their outlay on bed and board, while advertisers can expect a 30-percent yearly sales jump.

To be sure, the publicity caravan is not what it was a few years ago, when the Tour riders could cycle from one end of the French hexagon to another on a never-ending carpet of promotion material. But in compensation for cleaning up their act a little, the sponsors have become more than a bunch of parti-colored wagons proclaiming their institutional support. A gala parade with floats and motorcycle clowns and a tubular tire man is one thing. But when the same tire man insists on embracing the daily yellow jersey winner on non-commercial TV it becomes obnoxious.

The supreme offender in this regard has been the Tour's No. 1 sponsor, Guy Merlin, the proprietor of a chain of mainly seaside holiday flats, and the man most often rumored to be in line to take over the Tour once septuagenarians Goddet and Lévitan retire. As far as Merlin is concerned, the satirical newspaper *Le Canard Enchaîné* says, no one can film the Tour unless they mention his chicken cages, many of which have gone up in highly questionable ways: without a building permit on state-protected dunes; by obtaining land expropriated to build a police station; or by buying land from the government that the government itself did not have title to. Finally some of this caught up with him and on June 29, the very day the 1978 Tour was scheduled to start in Leiden, Merlin the magician found himself arraigned in Caen on a charge of municipal bribery.

While the Tour's methods of funding its traveling circus of 1700 employees leave much to be desired, the organizers have had undoubted success in creating a race emphasizing all-around qualities in the manner of a track-and-field decathlon.

Obviously, 110 riders cannot be going all out each of the 2500 miles. But dangle enough incentives, and one can create a whole series of races *within* the race at both a team and individual level. In this way, not only is the battle stepped up, but the interest is spread. Each type of rider — sprinter, time-trialist, climber, general all-around *rouleur* — has something at stake, besides the triumph of finishing in Paris.

The Tour is a series of races, for each stage is a complete race in itself with its own prize money. Except for the time trials, all of these are conventional massed-start races at distances ranging between 100 and 155 miles. Each rider's daily times are added up as he goes along to create a general classification, and the rider who covers the total distance in the shortest time is the overall winner or *yellow jersey*. This year, the winning time was 108:18:00, beating everyone else by margins ranging from 3:56 to almost four hours. A rider can win the Tour without ever having won a separate leg.

The next most valuable race concerns the *green jersey*. This is a $4400 sprinter's points prize based on finish position plus a smaller number of points for each of the three intermediary *hot-points* sprints. This dates back to the 1905-12 era when, to keep the Tour from being dominated by a single mountain stage, the race was run on such a points basis. In addition to these official sprints, a number of prizes are put up along the way to honor a border crossing or a Tour official's memorial, or simply as an expression of a town's largesse.

The last main prize is the $2500 *King of the Mountains* with its red-and-white polka-dotted jersey. Sponsored by a chocolate company, it is awarded on a points basis according to the degree of difficulty: 20, 16, 14 for first category chunks; 15, 12 for second, etc. Again, each mountain prime line carries its own endowment.

Besides these prizes there is a *white jersey* for the best first or second-year pro, a time-trialist's prize, a consolation prize to suggest that a bank has a heart, a combativity prize for creating a breakaway, a teammate prize given by a maker of watch shock absorbers obviously intended for these human wind-absorbers, and, to make sure that everybody gets something, a pair of mickey mouse prizes for elegance and security.

Both the yellow and green jersey competitions have team equivalents with corresponding caps. These 10-man teams work on the order of a commando unit. Each has a leader, or in some cases a couple of co-leaders, who must be protected. Sometimes, the leader has his own designated squire who does nothing but wait on him, fetching him bottles of water, or passing him his wheel should he puncture. When a leader punctures, a number of the team may drop back and wait for him in order to relay him back into the pack. Besides these protected men, each team has a designated sprinter, who the others must try to place. To organize the various tasks, especially pursuit, each team has a road captain.

Road racing is basically an individual sport. But teams exist because of the inherent advantages of collaboration. The rider leading a group of cyclists is, because of the wind, at a disadvantage. By riding line-astern behind him (off of his back wheel), and using him and each other as wind-breakers, riders are able to conserve their energy. A rider leading at 30 mph cannot sustain such a pace for long, whereas those riding line-astern should be able to sit on his wheel almost indefinitely. The tactics of bicycle racing thus boil down to a matter of obtaining and withholding pace. Because a rider cannot win the Tour without the help of his team, it is customary for his prize money to go into a common kitty. The Tour winner, after all, can count on being rewarded from outside sources (endorsements, race contracts, and higher salary).

Besides these prize incentives, there are time bonuses, which are subtracted from the race time. This year's major innovation, the fourth stage's 96-mile team time trial, carries bonuses of 2:00, 1:20, 1:00, 0:40 and 0:20 to the first five finishers, enough to make an important difference at an early part of the race. There is also a controversial 20-second bonus for the winner of each hot-points sprint, provided the rider is in a breakaway group that contains less than a fifth of the pack. In a closely contested Tour, this margin can be enough to create a new yellow jersey.

The Tour itinerary is largely determined two years in advance, and announced in the autumn of the year preceding the race. Though the Tour has its traditional focal points — such as the Tourmalet, the Puy-de-Dôme, L'Alpe d'Huez — an effort within a 10-year period is made to include all of rural France (certain regions, such as Brittany, are slighted because they don't offer sufficient topographical difficulties). But the tour is limited as to terrain by the necessity of finding stop-over towns (or at second best a district) large enough to offer 2000 beds.

To eliminate dull flat stretches and widen the battlefield the Tour has increasingly turned to buses, trains, airplanes, even a Channel ferry in 1974, to transfer from finish to start. In the mountain week of this 1978 Tour, there will be two such hops on consecutive days, and another three in the last week as the Tour shuttles from Belfort to the Paris region. But early-morning transfers play havoc with the riders' minimum sleep requirements of 12 hours. As Hinault pointedly remarked in Leiden: "Dead legs don't make for an animated race."

For this 75th anniversary edition (and 65th running), the main innovation concerns the number of mountain climbs, which have been raised from 42 in 1977 to 55. Whereas in past Tours they have often been spread out, here they will occur in a single eight-day stretch as the Tour passes eastward across the Pyrenees, the Massif Central and the Alps. To balance the mountain diet and to limit the climber specialists, the directors have inserted three major time trials, all at distances exceeding last year's determining one at Dijon. With the addition of the team time trial, a brutal 96-mile leg against the wind between Evreux and Caen, we should have a Tour as arduous as any since the war.

Most prognostics see a drama in three acts: a long, nine-scene build-up from Leiden to Biarritz; then, following the rest day, come the mountain hostilities, which are expected to break out in earnest on the 11th stage and go on, with only one interruption, to the 17th stage's eight-pass jolt across the Alps. From Morzine comes the triumphant return procession to Paris, the key point being the 46-mile Metz to Nancy time trial that will decide whatever the mountains haven't.

For almost a year, all of France has looked forward to a duel, reminiscent of the

Anquetil-Poulidor era of the 1960s, between two-time winner Bernard Thévenet and the 23-year-old Breton from Yffiniac on the oil-marred north coast, Bernard Hinault.

A virtual unknown 18 months ago, Hinault survived a spectacular plunge into a ravine (voted France's No. 1 TV moment in 1977) to beat Thévenet in the Dauphiné- Libéré, the major tune-up to the Tour de France. When Thévenet went on to win the Tour, a race that Hinault was held out of because of his tender age, the stage was set. But this duel between the two Bernards is apparently not to be. Thévenet only courses well in the odd year — the French banquet circuit being what it is — while Hinault has won everything he has set his sights to, including the time trialists' Grand Prix des Nations, the season-long Pernod trophy, and this spring the Spanish Vuelta. Questions can still be asked about his ability to survive a high mountain climb. Last year, on the way to his Dauphiné victory, he conceded 2 minutes on the Forclaz pass. But he benefits from the most astute manager in the business, Cyrille Guimard, and from the presence of a Renault-Gitane team organized on socialist principles that, more than any other team, is truly a family. On top of all this he has the home-soil encouragement provided by the screaming, water-pouring throngs.

Co-favorite with Hinault is Michel Pollentier, a balding, sad-faced and highly intelligent (equally fluent in German, English, French and Flemish) 27-year-old Belgian. Until a year ago, this gnome was obscurely occupied riding as a *domestique* for Freddy Maertens, his neighbor and close friend. No doubt, this service had its rewards as Maertens won everything in sight including eight first-place stage finishes in the 1976 Tour, and the pots of money kept flowing in. Pollentier's trophy chest was not full, but life in Maertens's service was better presumably than chomping away at Freddy's heels. But after Maertens's victory in the 1977 Vuelta in which he took 14 stage victories — more than anyone in the whole history of the Spanish Tour — the cup began to run dry. When Maertens fell in the Giro, Michel stepped in to save the family honor. He not only won the Giro, but also took the very difficult Tour de Suisse a month later, as well as the Belgian national championship. And he might well have triumphed over Thévenet, Hennie Kuiper and Lucien Van Impe in last year's Tour had Flandria been entered.

Since then, Pollentier has not bided his time. Following a seventh clavicle fracture in the San Cristobal world championships, Pollentier has won the Majorcan Grand Prix, finished second to Maertens in the Tour of Flanders classic, and won this year's Dauphiné-Libéré. His only comeuppance was in the recent Swiss Tour. Pollentier's contorted position on a bicycle, all hunched over knees and elbows in the manner of a delivering obstetrician, may displease the sport's aesthetes. But as a time-trialist and climber he pedals as fast as Hinault.

The third choice is the 1977 Tour runner up — by half a minute! — blond, cherubic Hennie Kuiper. Kuiper is not in a class with Pollentier and Hinault either climbing or against the clock. His forte, rather, lies in his general all-around qualities, and his readiness to attack and improvise. Seconding Kuiper is a TI Raleigh squad that won last year's Tour, and which includes nearly every rider of note in the Netherlands.

The other main candidate is Leiden's native son, tall, pale, carrot-haired Joop Zoetemelk, a three-time Tour runner-up. Called by Merckx that most terrible of epithets, a wheel-sucker, Joop is now more charitably seen as the only one in those years able to have kept pace with Merckx. In Zoetemelk's favor is a Mercier team of very strong climbers.

The dark horse is 5-foot 6-inch, 141-pound Lucien Van Impe, the 1976 Tour winner, and the perennial king of the mountains. In a Tour as mountainous as this diamond jubilee's, this last of the winged angels would normally be a prime favorite. Unfortunately Van Impe fractured his shoulder this spring in a fall. That delayed his conditioning to such an extent that he has not been able to spare even the week necessary to have the plastic bracket in his shoulder removed. Like Thévenet, he plans to use the first seven days to harden his form — an easier matter for one of his size. He also benefits from the presence of the great Merckx team captained by Joseph Bruyère, a former yellow jersey. Van Impe, in fact, expects them to win for him the Evreux to Caen team time trial with the 2-minute bonus that he needs to make up for his shortcomings as a time trialist.

In a race meant to assemble a living hall of fame, the *dramatis personae* can never be complete enough. Among the absences the most acutely felt is Eddy Merckx, the greatest cyclist of all time and a five-time Tour winner. Baptized the Cannibal for his insatiable victory-gobbling maw, he owns a slew of Tour records, all by enormous margins: most days in the yellow jersey (96); most stage victories (34); fastest stage time (30.157 mph). Merckx is also the only man ever to capture in a single Tour the green, yellow and mountain jerseys. After last year's Tour, where he suffered from dysentery, he decided to team up with his long-time rival, Lucien Van Impe, under the C&A banner, feeling the combination might help free his improvisational genius from the tight, wheel-to-wheel marking that he has so long been subjected to. For a year, he has tried to train toward a single grand swan song. But his health never recovered and in early May, he announced his retirement to begin a new career as Van Impe's manager. Van Impe, pleased, said, "With

Merckx's head and my legs, I'll win."

The other notable absentees are the Italians, who for the first time since the war won't be represented. Up to the very last minute, the organizers had expected the 1977 world champion, Francesco Moser, and the SCIC team of Baronchelli, Saronni and Schuiten. But this year's hills do not seem to be to Moser's taste, while Baronchelli, a good climber, is leaving SCIC at the end of the season. For the Tour, the loss is unquestionable. The Italians are the recognized *seigneurs*, making the rest of the cycling fraternity look like the peasants they undoubtedly are. Other legs may churn faster, but a man who sits well on a bike is a figure not easily dispensed with.

Among the last-minute scratches is the only American rider on the pro circuit, 23-year-old Jonathan Boyer. Boyer contracted amoebic dysentery in Venezuela last summer, and rather than race in this year's Tour has decided to go home to be examined by a specialist. His place with Lejeune is somewhat compensated by the recovery of Swiss Daniel Gisiger. Only a fortnight ago, in the Tour de Suisse, Gisiger took a spectacular tumble on a descent, severing his ear and ending up in the hospital with a fractured skull. While short on condition, his prowess as a time-trialist will help one of the Tour's weaker teams, and one, like Jobo-Superia, faced shortly with dissolution.

On this score, one of the more amusing threats is Guy Faubert's to withdraw his Jobo-Superia team on the pretext that the press has not accorded enough consideration to Mariano Martinez's chances. This is an old complaint dating back to when Martinez stepped off the plane in Orly, fresh from a third place in the 1974 Montreal world championship (behind no less than Merckx and Poulidor) to find himself shunted aside by the press photographers wanting pictures of Poulidor only. That slight took two years to recover from, and now that Mariano is going well, having copped two successive king of the mountain prizes and a second behind Pollentier in the *Dauphiné*, he is inclined to flaunt his misfortune: his $420 a month salary; his nine months on the dole in 1976; his new Nièvre bicycle shop that sold just two bicycles in its first fortnight. Add glasses, bald head at 29, and prominent varicose veins, and one has a rider who is in some way a living reproach to the sport.

Backing up Martinez is a team culled from the same mainly immigrant substratum. Hervé Inaudi, Dino Bertolo, Dante Coccolo, André Romero, Alain Patritti, are not what one thinks of as French patronyms. But every society needs — and creates — its untouchables, and for the Jobos, all on social security relief last winter, riding in the Tour de France is the fulfillment of an impossible dream. They may not be able to do much to help Martinez win, but they have vowed to help each other survive to the Champs-Elysées.

On the Sunday before the Tour come the final heraldic notes. As Hinault and Pollentier won their respective national championships, Hinault will start off the race clad in a tricolored jersey, while Pollentier will be in black, red, and gold. Hinault will also be wearing a 51 *dossard*, the same number with which Luis Ocaña, Thévenet, Merckx and Anquetil pedaled to victory in their first Tour.

THE TOUR COMPETITIONS IN SUMMARY

Each stage of the Tour is a complete race in itself with its own individual glory and prize money. Except for the time trials, all the stages are conventional massed-start races over distances ranging between 100 and 155 miles. Each rider's daily times are added together to create the general classification; the rider who covers the 2500 miles in the shortest time is the overall winner, or *yellow jersey*.

The next most valuable race concerns the *green jersey*, a sprinter's prize determined by points based on finish position and a small number of points for each of the two or three "hot-points" sprints across a line drawn on the road.

The other main prize is the *King of the Mountains* with its red-and-white polka-dot jersey. This is a summit-line prize, points varying according to the degree of difficulty.

There is also a *white jersey* for the best first- or second-year pro.

Both the yellow and green jersey competitions have team equivalents with corresponding caps. Because all these competitions go on simultaneously, their results influence one another.

Leiden time trial

W ith no assurance I would be admitted to the Tour, or be able to find a place in a following car, I decided to arrive in Leiden a day before the opening 3.2-mile time trial.

As it turned out, I need not have worried about obtaining press credentials. I was a special case, but a green badge — similar to those flaunted at hotel conventions (with my photo on it) — was duly issued, along with a police pass good for the four frontiers. There remained the problem of securing hotel reservations. In addition to its own bank open 24 hours, ambulance service, bottled water dispensary, moving company, and Peugeot-leased fleet, the Tour has a press assistance (sponsored by Pernod) to cater to our every whim: stamps, cigarettes, flight reservations, typewriters, the odd lift, and hotel bookings. In a country where alcoholism is a major social problem, a liquor company selling syrups is not allowed to sponsor a sports event. But there are ways of expressing your solidarity with the beret crowd, and for making one's presence felt what better people to drool over than the sports media? So I booked for a spot on the gratuity trail and, as a first token, found myself supplied with a pale blue shoulder bag containing a ballpoint pen, an orange graph-paper notebook, and a first-aid kit.

Securing a seat proved more difficult. With the number of vehicles limited, I couldn't go out and rent a car. Moreover, rider safety requires that each car carry Radio Tour. This is a one-way, special band, $800 gadget bringing the voices of Messrs. Goddet and Lévitan. Most of the French media cover the Tour with a car-size, four-man team: sports reporter, color man, interviewer, plus a jack-of-all-trades chauffeur. And if a reporter dies, his seat may well be left vacant for a year.

My best chance lay in finding some small organization with a single reporter and in sharing costs with him. But often snags appear when dealing with such people; like the first person Louis Lapeyre, the courteous Tour press secretary, put me on to, who had to leave the race at 2 p.m. because he worked for an evening paper. Only on the eve of our setting out for Saint Willebrord did I finally secure a seat in an orange-and-white striped car belonging to Radio Sud, a private station that used to beam out of Andorra before moving to Toulouse. Its reporter, Patrick Thillet, had driven in the Tour once before, as well as in the previous year's Monte Carlo Rally. In the forthcoming weeks, I was to discover that his talents, far from being exceptional, were merely the rule for the Tour drivers — a fact that might go a long way to explain the prowess that often drew spectators to their cheering feet. As a car rally, the Tour was not all that dull!

These foreign starts are a post-World War II innovation. Except for 1926, when it started in Evian on the Lake of Geneva, the Tour — like French life itself — had always begun and ended in Paris. By 1951, that had come to seem anti-adventurous; why journey somewhere if it is only to return? So the directors decided to repeat the Evian experiment and start from Metz. From there it was a simple matter to cross into foreign territory.

In the years since, there have been six foreign starts: Amsterdam, Brussels, Cologne, The Hague, Charleroi … and now Leiden. One can imagine the pleasure with which the nation watched the Tour armada assemble for an invasion that had now one sovereign purpose — the pleasure of pedaling for an hour's trafficless bliss on the Champs-Elysées.

The city fathers had invited the Tour to Leiden in the hope of putting the birthplace of Rembrandt back on the tourist map, and encouraging use of the bicycle to save the remaining canals — most have been filled in since the war to make roads. The arrangements were entrusted to a bicycle race promoter, Riethaven. But the bad luck that has consistently dogged Leiden — the Spanish siege of 1573-4, the Mayflower Pilgrims, plagues and starvation under several French regimes, all culminating in 1807 when a gunpowder barge exploded, destroying three-quarters of the Netherlands' second largest city — was not to be averted. As the opening night ceremonies were getting underway in the Groenoordhal, a converted stockyard, I learned that Mr. Riethaven had just experienced a severe heart attack. He was still in the hospital in serious condition the morning of June 30 when the Tour left Leiden. These days, it's not every gathering armada that can claim a human sacrifice.

So with sponsor Merlin under threat of arrest and promoter Riethaven hospitalized, the Tour was off to an inauspicious start.

But better was to come. It rained. In the Netherlands, that's not so unusual; it's only when it gets to be 358 days in a year that it strikes local temperaments as excessive. As someone said, the Dutch are better at rolling back the sea than at keeping out what falls from on high. But racing flat out in a rain-drenched labyrinth of oily cobblestoned streets and over canal bridges with right-angle turns struck the team managers as risky. At 11 a.m. in a pouring rain, they met and decided to annul the prologue. The first day's race with its prize money would be run as scheduled. But the times would establish neither an overall pecking order, nor a yellow jersey.

At this piece of news, the good burghers of Leiden promptly sued to recover their out-of-pocket $80,000. Like much else in cycle racing, the prologue is a Tour invention. Financially, it allows the Tour to squeeze in an extra day of racing, while rewarding the host town with more of an overture than a mere parade. So the prologue came into being as a way of drawing a ring through a city and coloring it in — with numbers, pennants, jerseys, all taking off at precise two-minute intervals. A 3.2-mile time trial is no more than the distance of a track pursuit in which two riders start at opposite sides of a cambered oval and try to catch one another. But it helps get the theme of who is fastest stated early, while allowing the tribe of sprinters to grapple a few extra seconds at the expense of the goat-thighed mountain men.

Now instead of a preliminary classification and a yellow jersey as a mark for everyone else to shoot at, tomorrow's road race will decide all this. The problem here is that one might have a winner by a hundredth of a second, with some 30 or 40 bunched right behind. Then what happens if somebody else wins the second-half leg by a similar margin? Here the person most affected is Freddy Maertens, who had every intention of using his acrobatic skills to cut the glassy corners and win the prologue, as he had done in 1976. If so, he would have tried to defend that narrowest of margins all the way to Biarritz; remunerative for him, but hard on such teammates as Michel Pollentier and Joaquim Agostinho. In this sense, the yellow jersey can turn into an albatross around the collective neck, when a team is obliged to defend for many long hours what has been acquired in so few seconds.

The race run that afternoon in a gradually clearing liquid yellow sunlight is nonetheless compelling. As always in the Tour, part of the fascination lies in the gradual accumulation of details. First, the parade of the publicity caravan: mattress cars, rice-package cars, chocolate-bar cars, bottle cars; six jeeps in the form of a cigarette sticking out of a pack; another six white cars driven by embarrassed mannequins made up like drug-store sales ladies; then, more Kafkaesque, three enormous green flies, each suspended on a red car advertising the merits of an insecticide; next, a buffalo pawing impatiently away against the top of a truck; flanked in turn by three zebra-cars; then a fire engine out of a Buster Keaton film, with a wobbling white tire-man clowning up front; more ancient still, a 1903 Brazier, with a Prussian blue chassis and yellow wheels, goes by dispensing balloons; then, more Barnum & Bailey, eight equilibrists, in red and white, each standing on an apparently self-conducting motorcycle (later, one was to take a bad fall on his face); then, right behind the Tour's bank bus, a car with bits of wedding veil in the door handles to remind one of the advantages of a bank account in such circumstances.

As horror after horror blares by, wonderfully at one with shop and awning, I begin to notice the hawkers seated in the backs of their open station wagons: some dressed in the coveralls of garage attendants, lime green or brown; others in red outfits with a yachting cap. With that dignified gesture of a seedsman in a field, they toss out caps, posters, car stickers, lollipops — a cross between a huckster and a clown, "Daddies and mommies, make your child happy!" A hundred loudspeakers go by, sounding the first notes of a 2500-mile concerto; not quite a gala parade, and not quite a Fellini film, it must seem to the country folk like an invasion from outer space.

No one has bothered to tell the good burghers that the race would not count. So, there they all are, on the sculptured steps of the Town Hall, mounted on the tops of canal bridges and billboards, or sitting side-saddle with cameras across a window ledge; every lace curtain, seemingly, with a couple of faces behind it asserting their proprietary pleasure; while in the street below, at two-minute intervals, loudspeakers blare riders' names and times.

This sense of a visually layered theater — even in the rain, under the umbrellas — worked to bring out the best in the Dutch, who took the first four places, led by Jan Raas, tall, monosyllabic, spectacled perfection. Behind him came the future world champion, Gerrie Knetemann; then the carrot-haired native son, Joop Zoetemelk, pedaling his pink machine to a sustained, paper-showered clapping. Hennie Kuiper, who came in fourth, drew an almost equal ovation — as did the Raleigh team, which placed seven men among the first 14 finishers. In a Europe that is still highly sectarian, these figures show Bernard Hinault's advantage once the Tour reaches French soil.

Leiden to Saint Willebrord to Brussels

To the Dutch, the Tour's decision to invalidate the prologue seemed a cruel blow. Peter Post, the Dutch manager of the Raleigh team, who had most at stake, made clear that the decision to cancel was far from unanimous. Its only point, so far as he was concerned, lay in giving the cycling wounded — that is, former race winners Bernard Thévenet and Lucien Van Impe — an eight-day reprieve before the Bordeaux time trial. Others felt that the unprecedented decision had opened a can of worms. Did the Tour now intend to cancel the Tourmalet whenever there was fog? asked the Tour's only Dutch winner, Jan Janssen. The cancelation of the overall classification, however, wasn't what most rankled; rather it was the failure to do justice and to award the yellow jersey to Jan Raas.

With the current of feeling running high, Thévenet decided to renounce wearing on this first leg the yellow jersey, his traditional right as last year's winner. There he was, one more rider in his domino-patterned Peugeot jersey, looking bemused as he waited for the sound system to be repaired once again. In the torpid gray light, punctuated now and then by the shrill cry of a gull, most mysterious was the absence of an audience. It was as if, after yesterday's events, the whole city had decided to boycott the Tour and its works.

While the Tour dallied for over an hour getting underway, I strolled around, checking out this new breed of centaur. From the waist down, there is probably no handsomer athlete, with the vertical back-of-the-leg muscles descending into arrow-like points, set off against shaven, glistening legs.

Not that the upper body is lacking in its own superbly streamlined grace. Theirs is a sport where nothing can be in excess, each chest cavity making for its own kind of rider. All share the same closely cropped hair, only bangs differentiating them from soldiers. Its purpose is to help limit loss of water in the mountain glare.

In contrast to the medievally bright jerseys, shorts are uniformly black. Hands are protected against the taped handlebars by a golfer's sort of half-glove with perforated leather holes. More awesome are the huge wristwatches; less something useful, one suspects, than a reminder of where the battlefield lies. Shoes are a special heel-less slipper with cleated soles enabling the rider to grip the pedals — but obliging here a hesitant pigeon-toed walk. Perhaps that is why I see Zoetemelk, one foot propped against the stands, conducting an interview from astride his beaked saddle.

All by himself in the stands, and making weird snorting noises from time to time, is the broad-chested Portuguese champion, Joaquim Agostinho, at 35 the next oldest Tourman to 38-year-old Englishman Barry Hoban, riding in his 12th Tour. As the departure whistle sounds, Agostinho cups his hands to his mouth and shouts, "*Aux Champs-Elysées!*" It's the first real ceremonial moment we have had, and as everybody turns around and grins, I realize for the first time how far away July 22 and Paris really is.

So, here in the Groenoordhal parking area is the bunch: goggles; bright team caps concealing leather helmets; clumsy transparent rain capes; all stupidly waiting in the rain astride their mounts for a besashed matron with a huge pair of scissors to cut the symbolic orange-and-white umbilical cord so they can pedal off.

This wholesale departure from Saint Willebrord for the Champs-Elysées caught me unprepared. I had it on the authority of my landlady that the Tour was going to spend another night in Leiden; as I was led to believe, the run along the Zuider Sea coast to The Hague, then inland via blue Delft and Rotterdam to Saint Willebrord, was more in the nature of a reconnaissance before the Tour started out in earnest for Brussels tomorrow. In actuality, the day has been divided into two legs: a Dutch one and a Belgian one, starting in the afternoon and going on to Brussels.

My confusion took some time to clear up. By the time the Beach Club had been found, the landlady paid, and my bags sealed and dropped into the car, the Tour was on its way through The Hague, and Thillet was fit to be tied. In a flat drenched gray landscape of cows and tulips farms, we were able to stay more or less abreast of the race by keeping the two circling helicopters in sight. But in classic keystone cops fashion we missed our one chance to get ahead when we misjudged an overpass ramp and came down the wrong way just as the plastic-caped procession wheeled onto the Delft *autobahn*. In a futile attempt to catch up, we tried a number of side roads, only to find access blocked by spectators and their cars.

Finally, we gave up and hastened off to the finish line, the place, after all, where a radio reporter's work lies. As a nation, the French are too skeptical to trust a reporter's summary. They want to hear the words from Giscard D'Estaing directly. In the Tour that means a fantastic scuffle to get the mike placed under the winner's nose immediately upon his arrival. You can't do this unless you arrive some minutes in advance of a pack that is at this point pedaling at close to 40 mph. The essential done, you can then scurry about the grand hotels, culling interviews from your regional heroes.

In our own race to the finish, we missed the first moments of what was to become known as the Tour of the Crash. In the wetness, over the slicked roadways, riders dropped like flies, now and then flattened by some over-zealous member of the motorized press. The first mishap, involving five sprinters, was relatively harmless, the main victim being Thillet's regional friend, Jacques Esclassan, with a slightly sprained right thumb. The Green Fuse, as Esclassan was dubbed following his points victory in last year's Tour, managed to right himself to the extent of taking an eventual third place, but the next crash was rather more serious. A photographer's motorcycle following too close at the back of the pack skidded, bowling over some 10 riders, among them the future red lantern, Philippe Tesnière, and the Spaniard Julian Andiano, who became the Tour's first outright K.O. with a broken pelvis.

Last year's clown prince, Gerben Karstens, whose hilarious miming of a Tour crash won the 1977 Sports Picture of the Year award, has been formally warned of the most dire consequences should he try to liven matters up. But there is never a vacuum, and the race was hardly underway when Tour neophyte Jean-Jacques Fussien, a 26-year-old (with a wife and two kids) — who was tragically killed in a training accident two weeks after the Tour's close — twice sprinted to the front, feigning a breakaway. But with the yellow jersey at stake the pack quickly hauled him in.

What Fussien could not accomplish, the crashes did, fracturing the pack and forcing those dropped into a difficult chase in the face of the wind. Then, half an hour from the end, a real race began to develop, with a group of 31 riders in front and the rest of the field strung out in four unequal groups. The result was a sprint finish with 62 riders all bunched together, preceded by a highly motivated Jan Raas who, knowing the course, lit out 1000 yards from the end, to become by one second the first yellow jersey of the race. Second, with 24 green jersey points was Freddy Maertens.

Another drama lay further behind among those trapped in the three wind-fouled splinter groups: Danguillaume now 11 seconds behind; and at 18 seconds came another 30 riders, including such candidates for a high final place as Van Impe; the Kas team leader Francisco Galdos (fourth last year); the Teka leader Pedro Torres (the 1973 Tour King of the Mountains); the Swedish climber, Sven-Aake Nilsson (who many expect to be an eventual team leader); and the recent Tour of Switzerland winner, Paul Wellens. One can understand the reluctance of these climbing specialists to mix in the rough stuff of a mass sprint — witness René Martens riding in, 1:30 back, blood streaming from all over his face; but 18 seconds was to be precisely all that separated the three top riders at the end of the 16th stage. In a final group, 1:30 back, along with the two injured riders, Martens and Tesnière (who now wears two plastic pads around his left elbow and another on his right leg), is a Spanish quintet.

Doughty climbers to a man, these Spaniards lack any practical experience with this northern nuts-and-bolts phase of the discipline. Riding a bicycle over rain-slick cobbles may well be the next worse thing to trying to race one up a mountain. If this morning was bad, tomorrow afternoon promises worse with 30 miles of little else leading into St Amand. Taken at sprint speed that should provoke some casualties.

With a sense of justice done to Raas, I fight my way past 30,000 milling spectators and into the auditorium adjoining the church. A wonderfully complete box lunch has been prepared for us, and there is a free bar serving French wines. But for some, such fare may leave something to be desired. In the middle of us, with a champagne magnum, is the five-time Tour winner and now prosperous farmer with 275 head of cattle, Jacques Anquetil. Most riders are abstemious souls. A couple of glasses of mineral water, and the odd beer, totally suffices. But Maître Jacques, during his reign in the early 1960s, provided a whole other standard, and one not necessarily to the advantage of the lesser mortals who tried to follow him. It was not that champagne, caviar and late-night cards came first; it was rather that as an athlete he possessed an extraordinary constitution. His mechanic set him down on a bike and he was off, and, to the horror of the French public he usually won.

My first reaction as we set off in the afternoon for Brussels was one of disappointment. What was I doing in an event which with its publicity caravan and 562 vehicles looked more like a car rally than a bicycle race? Perhaps the one guaranteed way of *not* seeing the Tour de France is to attempt to follow it in a press car.

There are ways around the restrictions. It is possible to mount on the back of a motorcycle and enjoy a view of the race almost as intimate as the pedaling correspondents of the Geo Lefèvre era. Nothing very difficult about this. One simply borrows leather suit, helmet and goggles, and with a pair of cameras jingling about the neck enters the fray. Posing as a Tour photographer is probably as close as one is likely to come to assuming once more the rights of a Homeric god. This first day was certainly instructive in watching these press gods at work: dispatching one of the Tour's better climbers to the hospital; pausing at each skid, en masse, to admire their handiwork; finally, at the end of the afternoon, screwing up the Brussels sprint by their reluctance to be diverted.

All riders, no matter what their team allegiances, belong to a greater unit, the 110-headed Hydra of the pack, gobbling up each attempted escape. One might think of this *monstre sacré* as an air-sealed cask within which the members shelter from the constant wind. The presence of the pack gives the race its governing form. A rider's individual time standing may grow or diminish like a bank account; but one thing one can be sure of finding at the next day's starting line is the same old patched-up pack or *peloton*.

In a world where every turn of the road may yield a new Hercules, the sacred monster needs all the preservation it can get. There is very little one can do about natural disasters such as a tail wind or a mountain (a head wind loves a pack), other than deplore the helter-skelter, every-man-for-himself conditions they create. But one can try to give each of the 110 heads a feeling that it is needed.

To this end, each entering rider gets a medical check-up — to encourage him as to his fitness. Similarly, teams are discouraged from taking along people who may have to abandon once the mountains appear. For the pack to exist, a sense of a common purpose, of surviving to wheel *en masse* on the Champs-Elysées must be paramount. For the same reason, stragglers have to be nipped in the bud, and are disqualified if they fail to finish within a certain time percentage of the winner.

There are also physical needs. Riders puncture and crash. They may even have to detach themselves, however briefly, from the governing entity for a call of nature. At the rear, to help speed them back, are a host of support vehicles sufficiently numerous to drown out the siren song of the sag wagon.

This rear procession has its own hierarchy. Leading it are the two directorial chariots of Messrs Lévitan and Goddet. From their controlling vantage point, Radio Tour beams the news of attempted breakaways, punctures and crashes, to us blind ones of the press.

Behind come two lines. On the left, on the wrong side of the road, are the press cars, and, on the right, support cars who have, of course, priority. Leading them is the team car of the current yellow jersey, its rear right door cut away so that the mechanic can lean out with a screwdriver and make adjustments while the biker continues to wheel along. Behind the 22 team cars come ambulances, medic wagons, bicycle repair vehicles, all ending with the sag wagon (operated by a company that sells vacuum cleaners).

A rider who punctures, or needs to consult his manager, holds up his hand until spotted by Radio Tour or its motorcycle satellites. He saves confusion if he drops off on the right. If he is a person of eminence, much of his team will drop back to provide an escort, lest the *peloton* should suddenly accelerate. Five men relaying each other are faster than a single man in lone pursuit. Often, though, a puncturing yellow jersey may prefer not to call attention to his plight, hoping to slip back before his absence is noted.

These team cars, tops all spikily glistening with clamped-down bicycle frames and spare wheels, are more than mere repair vehicles. Each is a veritable treasure chest where, among the first-aid kits and water bottles, may be found ice cubes, American bourbon, Dutch cigars, excellent Burgundy or vintage Armagnac. Such pleasures are not hard to come by. One simply drives alongside, leans a hand out of the window, and asks Peugeot's Maurice de Muer, Fiat's Raphaël Geminiani, for whatever might slake one's thirst — why let dull time sit heavy on one's hands? So, like travelers anywhere, one shortens a long mile: there, inches apart, in the middle of a country lane; or perhaps both of you squeezed over to the left by a honking car that, with an expression of deep regret, slides by toward a punctured teammate.

While life in the wake of the pack has its evident charm (not the least being that one sees something of the riders, new water bottles in hand, scurrying back from piss or puncture), most journalists feel the better course is to drive in front. Even if you see nothing of the actual work of the race — the chance of a one-minute breakaway aside — you can still feel the sudden panicky accelerations of the pack, and enjoy the crowds that the rainy drizzle has brought forth like snails. Under their umbrellas, smiling from the curb, or alone with bicycle and club tunic on some forest bank, these are the famous Belgian hordes come to honor their Giants of the Road. You do not have to be black to play basketball, or gypsy Spanish to fight bulls, or English to play cricket, *but* perhaps you have to be Belgian — more specifically Flemish — to be a cycling roadman.

In the Latin countries, cycling is a sport practiced mainly by the socially disadvantaged, those who might otherwise go into boxing. Soccer players are a cut above, drawn from the trade union milieu. I am not sure to what extent one can talk, as French journalists do, of a school of suffering shared by these two sports; but there are temperamental affinities. Boxers may hit below the belt, and butt one another, and pull any number of shenanigans. But in private conversation you rarely hear them malign one another. They all understand that in a tough profession each does what he can with the means at hand. Cyclists know only too well that theirs is a sport in which events speak for themselves; on a given day, you either have it or you don't. When they speak, it is like listening to children; each proposal rings with its own refreshing frankness.

For the most part, the cyclists are the children of peasants, either landless day-laborers or small farm-holders. In France, they are more apt than not to be from Brittany, the one province where cycling enjoys an understanding akin to that in Belgium (cycling is also popular in the industrial north, which lies on the Belgian border). The rural background gives the cyclist a point of return should the adventure not work out. Brittany is pleasant, undulating country where peasants still prefer bicycles to cars. Hinault's parents, for instance, have never owned a car. But just as Bretons of earlier times have traditionally preferred going to sea to outright emigration, so they have adapted to cycling, another trade where the hours of long dangerous monotony are outweighed by the chance glory of a port of call.

Bretons like Hinault and Christian Seznec are often accused of being in the sport only for the money. But you have to begin by trying to support yourself, and it's only after you have succeeded as a professional that you start raising your sights. One good answer to these accusations is Hinault's: "I make money for my wife and son, I *race* for me." Hinault is no zombie. He does not train strictly, and many a nice day finds him, like a philosopher, busying himself with his plants in his Yffiniac garden. Biking, as he says, should not turn into drudgery. "If I thought I had to cycle every day, so many hours a day, I'd quit. It would be like going to the factory."

But the fact that French cyclists are by and large country people goes a long way toward explaining their current inferiority *vis-à-vis* the Belgians. For them, cycling is a personal hobby, something they do in the face of a society that has other concerns. In Belgium, cycling has all the fervor of a religion. The Flemish are, by and large, Catholics with consequently large families and a far higher urban density. As in many another land, sport has become a way of easing the problem of Sunday. The popularity of cycling is such that in a single age group in a small town like Tournai or Eecklo there are 150 registered cyclists. In France, you would have to scour a whole county to come up with that many. Over the years, the number of races (other than Sunday) has grown, so that now there is at least one every day throughout the year. Most of these are *kermesses*, organized in accordance with a religious fair. But they differ from a Latin criterium in that the promoters do not feel obliged to provide expense money. Instead, all the money (primes aside) goes to the first 20 finishers, which makes them all-out races conducted at speeds that the Tour generally approaches only in its last half-hour. For this reason, many English cyclists have expatriated themselves to Ghent, a celebrated medieval town only an hour from Brussels and Antwerp. There they can school themselves in the rudiments of their trade, while the easy access to races allows them to earn a meager living in this most strenuous of sports.

The trouble with Belgian races (and those of today and tomorrow) is that they inevitably are bunched affairs resolved by a sprint finish. In flat country, with unfavorable wind conditions, it is very hard for even a coalition of riders to escape from a motivated pack. This is especially true in the early stages of the Tour when any escape gives the winner the yellow jersey, and probably enables him to hold it all the way to Bordeaux at the very least. With the 20-second bonus adding a further impediment, it is rare to find a rider strong enough to impose his own law; even Raas, the only one able to eject from a pack going at a sprint finish speed of 37 mph, can sustain such a pace for no more than two miles. And he must work by surprise. Wearing the yellow jersey, he is a marked man, and any break will find a rash of Belgians clambering on to his wheel.

If one cannot see riders in direct action, a sprint finish is not so undesirable. French TV has worked out a system with cameras mounted on two motorcycles and an overhead helicopter so that something of the work of a sprint finish can be seen. Sprinting is an entire art in itself, and it's where most of the money lies.

While no two Tour sprints are alike, there are certain basic rules. For one, you have to be up there. This jockeying for position normally begins some 20 miles from the end of a leg that has seen you protected like fine wine in the vacuum-sealed rear of the pack. On a hot day, you may add to your vital fluid by popping some trinitin (on the theory that you'll be able to sweat it out before having to present yourself at the finish-line drug-control caravan — it's that tiger in the tank). Then, with a half-hour to go, you start moving up — nothing ambitious, mind you, just a place somewhere between 15th and 20th from the windward leader. These seats are hotly contested, and it may be wise to delegate an assistant to save you one, with another camped just behind to prevent a lone wolf from taking your wheel and sailing by in the last meters.

Then, as the pace picks up to something like 35 mph, you just try to hold that position behind the two men who will lead you in, the first launching the sprint from a mile out, and the second going all out in turn 200 yards from the finish. Then, as his effort fades, some 50 yards from the end, you rocket off, bearing down with 220 kilos of force on each downward thrust of the pedals, and then, which is very special, 20 yards from the finish line, re-accelerating. This thrust is such that a sprinter who depends on force rather than litheness, like Esclassan, requires an extra heavy chain to keep it from derailing.

The ability to sprint depends on morphology, the relation of bones to muscles.

In general, shorter people are more capable of quick acceleration than taller ones, who, however, can keep up a steadier pace. This ability to jump into a superior gear is the most mysterious of gifts, and one that few specialists possess, or possess for very long. How it is cultivated no one can say for sure, but one knows it applies to climbers as well, who don't jump so much as surge.

For the pure sprinter to succeed, the whole race has to remain tied up until the last 200 yards. This requires a certain amount of teamwork and mutual trust. In 1977, Belgian Rik Van Linden brought a whole Bianchi team to the Tour with the sole purpose being to help him in his sprinting battle with Esclassan and Patrick Sercu for the green jersey. Their job was to jump on the rear wheel of any rider attempting to break away, catching him on the downwind side. But while one rider is being nailed another is slipping off, which makes for a certain amount of jersey grabbing and saddle catapults, and now and then a spill (for some strange reason the *commissaires* don't watch the press's giant TV screen; nor, alas, does the commentator). At the end, though, the same personalities seem to emerge: large, and heavily perspiring, and perhaps solemnly weighing each word, like politicians, before the podium TV cameras.

One way to avoid falling into the clutches of these sprinter sharks and their pilot fish is to use Raas's device of attacking from afar. Just as track has its dash specialists and quarter-milers, so the Tour has its longer-range *rouleurs* who make up in stamina what they may lack in finishing kick. Theirs is a double game: on the one hand, they are playing their own victory card; on the other, by attempting to speed off, they are forcing the pack to accelerate and thus limiting the chances of anyone else intruding on the sprinter's final *mano a mano* (often literally that).

Raas's main antagonists in this initial phase come from the two local Belgian teams, C&A and Flandria, along with Peugeot's lone Belgian, Jean-Luc Vandenbroucke. But the yellow jersey has volatized Raas, who brings to cycling the stamina of a former "total football" right halfback. His glasses, with their famous ventilation holes, keep popping up all over, as he takes it upon himself to crush everything that moves. After René Bittinger (Flandria) and Roger Legeay have combined in an abortive breakaway, it is Vandenbroucke's turn to slot himself in front of the platoon, neutralized first by Knetemann, then on a second attempt by Raas himself. The next to find himself squashed is Joseph Bruyère, who tries to get away right after the Grimber ramp. As Bruyère is being nailed, Pollentier tries to pull off the same gutsy descending maneuver that five days before had won him the Belgian national road championship.

By the time Raas has caught up with Pollentier, the sprint is being launched by Peugeot's Jean-Pierre Danguillaume (fronting for Esclassan). But Danguillaume, with the 109-man pack thundering down behind him (all due to arrive within the same extended second of one another), finds himself bolloxed up in a swarm of stopped cars and police and TV motorcycles. Afraid of crashing, Danguillaume gives up. Nor is it to be Jacques Esclassan's day. Earlier, in the last mile at Saint Willebrord, he had his concentration broken by an unknown arm flailing against his jersey. This time, Esclassan has to slam on his brakes five times in the last 400 yards, and by the time he is at the bottom of the hill he has no more energy.

Meanwhile, Jobo's novice sprinter, Jean-François Pescheux, has made his own use of the motorcycles' slipstream to launch a sprint that opens a 10-yard gap with 400 uphill yards to go. That puts him in the sights of C&A's Walter Planckaert, a 30-year-old veteran whose main victory was over world-champion-to-be Francesco Moser in the 1976 Tour of Flanders. Aware of having Maertens on his tail, Planckaert lets Pescheux hold his lead, waiting for the 200-yard mark to surge by. Here, Maertens fatally miscalculates. Instead of attacking Planckaert and outspeeding him to the finish, as he would have two years earlier, Maertens prefers to wait and rely on his finishing kick and his 53-toothed chainring matched to a 12-toothed sprocket — which he alone of all the Tour riders is able to pound. But, just as he is about to take off, a red car gets in Maertens's way, and when he has extricated himself he can do no better than finish second behind Planckaert ... but ahead of Pescheux, Knetemann and French Renault-Gitane rider Jacques Bossis. Aided by Pescheux, and with five riders in the first 15, the unheralded Jobo takes the team challenge.

Brussels
to St. Amand-les-Eaux

aturday's trek from Brussels to the thermal station of St. Amand-les-Eaux (just over the French border) gets underway in the *Grande Place*, that most splendid of northern Renaissance squares. It's the first sunny day in two weeks, and a dense throng in summery sleeveless-ness has turned up along the barricaded sidewalks to see Eddy Merckx presented with the Tour's official medal. In the square, among the flags and pomp and milling interviewers, the riders go about their own daily ceremonials: signing, team by team, the race register; squeezing fresh grapefruit or lemon into their liquid food rations. Among the various Tour and city officials there is a certain jovial relaxation; as if today's pageant were more in the nature of a dry run for the 1979 extravaganza, when the Tour intends to paralyze the city with a 25-mile time trial in honor of the capital's millennium.

As at Leiden, today's departure in the Grande Place is mostly symbolic, giving the riders time to warm up for the real start in the suburbs. The old exhilarating starts and finishes in city centers have become increasingly rare, due to the expense of crowd control and the dangers caused by mass sprints through winding cobbled streets — at much faster than taxi-cab speed. What the race gains in rider safety it loses in public involvement, and it's maybe for this reason that the long tree-lined axial avenues with their parks and sumptuous houses seem so tantalizing. At the top of the last hill, we take our leave, with mixed regret, of the special brigade of Dutch police, lined up beside their motorcycles. From now on, we will be accompanied only by our 44-man escort belonging to the motorized squad of the Paris Garde Républicaine. They are all Tour veterans and less likely to cause the sort of pileup that disfigured yesterday's Brussels finish.

STAGE 2: BRUSSELS (BRUXELLES) TO SAINT-AMAND-LES-EAUX

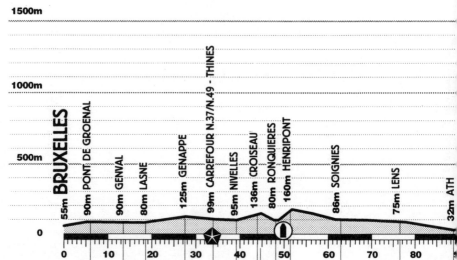

The early morning cavalcade through this triumph of city planning has got some of the Tour novices chafing at the bit. No sooner are we in our second mile of this 125-mile leg than a 14-man breakaway develops, led by the irrepressible Fussien. One can see these upstarts wanting to distinguish themselves, but, since only four breakaways in the whole history of the Tour have succeeded at that distance, their effort does look somewhat premature. Nor are Raas & Co. inclined to give them their head. Their lead never grows beyond a half-minute before yielding at the eight-mile mark.

Thereafter, the race quiets down for the next 70 miles, enlivened only by a sortie of the ex-Belgian champion, Willy Teirlinck, at the 30-mile mark. But the countryside is rolling Breughel-like hay and farm country, rather than the brick, fried-potatoes-and-beer mining-town gloom I was expecting. Few indeed are the miles on the Tour that are anything less than scenic, a tribute partly to a world where roads are still like rivers.

In the Tour, every regional rider has his day, and this is to be Teirlinck's. Not only does he cop a second $400 prime sprint at the Renaix feeding-point, but shortly after he takes a first and third on the first two hills counting for the Grand Prix de la Montagne. Neither is much more than 360 feet high, but what better way of inaugurating the 55-mountain calvary of the Tour than with a hill called Mount of

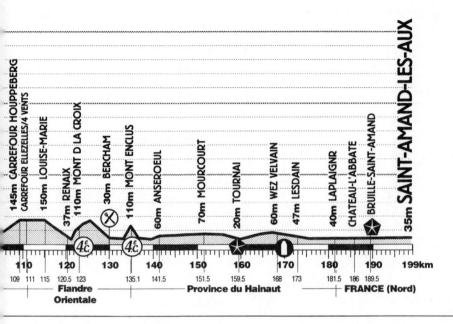

the Cross? Even so, the steepness is such that both José Enrique Cima and José Pessarodona find themselves twice shed by the pack, while the 1973 mountain king, Torres, crashes on the descent, sustaining a concussion and bruising his back. He continues, only to abandon the race 25 miles later, after a second fall on the French cobblestones.

At Tournai, a special hot-points sprint worth $2000 is judged right under the spires of its five-pointed cathedral, one of the authentic — and larger — jewels of the Middle Ages. This is enough to prompt Maertens into his 53x12 gear, and he cops it for his second so-called Rush victory of the day. Along with two second places yesterday, this gives Maertens a substantial early lead in his battle with Esclassan for the green jersey. But at this point in the Tour, Esclassan would rather coast along in the rear of the pack than be lured into contesting for these comparatively minor points. His thumb, injured in yesterday's crash, still smarts, and his form has not fully recovered from too much traveling in the four days between the end of the national championships in Saarebourg and his home in Goya's Castres outside Toulouse. Add to that yesterday's failure of nerve in the Brussels finish, and one might see why he must try to keep his reserves of energy intact for the final ordeal at Saint Amand on French soil.

After Tournai, the Tour jolts on to a new type of terrain — cobbles. These are not the famous foot-high ones of the similar frontier area near Roubaix, part of the "Hell of the North" of the greatest of all cycling classics, Paris to Roubaix. But trying to ride a bicycle along 25 miles of virtual cow track at pre-sprint speed is a bit like driving a Ferrari through knee-high water. Special bike-handling abilities — and good eyes — are of the essence, and it's not for nothing that Roger De Vlaeminck, the world cyclo-cross champion, has become Mr. Paris-Roubaix. As the tempo picks up, punctures are legion, especially among the less experienced Teka, Jobo and Fiat teams. Only now, late in the race, a rider may well lose five minutes on a flat. This is precisely what happens to Hubert Mathis, obliged to pass his wheel to his team leader Zoetemelk.

The last six miles into Saint Amand, thighs pumping, bicycles wobbling from side to side, are epic as sprints go. No sooner does one rider light up in the lead, than a puncture snuffs him out. After Zoetemelk, it is Maertens's turn. But rather than risk losing 20 green jersey points on a wheel change — or wrecking a teammate's chances — Maertens finds it more expedient to change bicycles, even if his new mount lacks his favorite 12-toothed sprinting sprocket.

With the battle for the green jersey paramount at this stage of the race, most eyes are on the Peugeot and Flandria teams. For several years, Maertens has had a favorite pilot fish in Marc De Meyer, a former Paris-Roubaix winner, and a good, if terrifying, middle-distance sprinter in his own right. At 6 feet 2 inches and some 190 pounds, De Meyer is the biggest man in the pack, and to see him bearing down with Maertens in his wake is enough in itself to give most of the opposition second thoughts. But De Meyer, like his master, is said to have lost some of his 1976 speed, and Maertens has taken on a second lead-out man in Irishman Sean Kelly, a rangy 22-year-old who outsprinted Merckx to win the Circuit de l'Indre in 1977.

Pollentier's work as Maertens's main shock trooper commands awe. Where an Esclassan properly saves himself, Pollentier is still doing most of the long-distance work, leading in the wind, etc. Pierre Chany says in his L'Équipe column that if Pollentier goes on at this rate, and winds up at Paris with the yellow jersey, the one thing he will certainly have proven is that he is not made out of flesh and bone. Pollentier's answer is that he needs 10 miles a day of sober exercising to tune himself up for the rigors ahead.

The final 1200 yards is very close and dangerous. The 1976 French champion Guy Sibille leads Esclassan in well, and although Esclassan manages to pick up a few wheelfuls of straw as he cuts the corners, he is able to keep his lead as Maertens's effort on his borrowed 13-tooth sprocket barely falls short on the line. In a post-race interview, the Green Fuse magnanimously attributes this, his fourth stage victory in as many Tours, to Maertens's puncture — catching up at all was a feat under the circumstances. Esclassan says that against anyone but Maertens he can take their rear wheel and in the last moment surge by; with Maertens, he would never get by. The only way to beat him is to get out in front with the help of Sibille and Danguillaume.

As one of 60 riders finishing in Esclassan's time of 5:21:31, Raas retains his yellow jersey by the most precarious of margins. Less lucky are the Spaniards, seven of whom straggled in at anywhere from 6:55 to 12:47 back. Between the end of the Vuelta and the Tour, they have had a month to ready themselves; their failure, all questions of weather aside, points to something disastrously wrong the other side of the Pyrenees.

Overall classification after Stage 2 (Yellow jersey)

1	JAN RAAS *(Raleigh)*	13:08:06		26	Zoetemelk *(Mercier)*	0:01
2	Maertens *(Flandria)*	at 0:01		27	Gallopin *(Lejeune)*	0:01
3	Planckaert *(C&A)*	0:01		28	Knetemann *(Raleigh)*	0:01
4	Esclassan *(Peugeot)*	0:01		29	Kuiper *(Raleigh)*	0:01
5	Pescheux *(Jobo)*	0:01		30	De Meyer *(Flandria)*	0:01
6	Bertin *(Gitane)*	0:01		31	Karstens *(Raleigh)*	0:01
7	Bossis *(Gitane)*	0:01		32	Laurent *(Peugeot)*	0:01
8	Thaler *(Raleigh)*	0:01		33	Seznec *(Mercier)*	0:01
9	Mollet *(Mercier)*	0:01		34	Bourreau *(Peugeot)*	0:01
10	Sibille *(Peugeot)*	0:01		35	Hézard *(Peugeot)*	0:01
11	M. Martinez *(Jobo)*	0:01		36	Bernaudeau *(Gitane)*	0:01
12	Kelly *(Flandria)*	0:01		37	Danguillaume *(Peugeot)*	0:01
13	Pollentier *(Flandria)*	0:01		38	Thévenet *(Peugeot)*	0:01
14	Delepine *(Peugeot)*	0:01		39	Wesemael *(Raleigh)*	0:01
15	Le Denmat *(Lejeune)*	0:01		40	Tinazzi *(Flandria)*	0:01
16	Lubberding *(Raleigh)*	0:01		41	Lelay *(Fiat)*	0:01
17	Gauthier *(Lejeune)*	0:01		42	Agostinho *(Flandria)*	0:01
18	Sanders *(Fiat)*	0:01		43	Villemiane *(Gitane)*	0:01
19	Bittinger *(Flandria)*	0:01		44	Dillen *(C&A)*	0:11
20	Hinault *(Gitane)*	0:01		45	Didier *(Gitane)*	0:11
21	Bazzo *(Lejeune)*	0:01		46	De Cauwer *(Raleigh)*	0:11
22	Bruyère *(C&A)*	0:01		47	Muselet *(Flandria)*	0:11
23	Ovion *(Peugeot)*	0:01		48	Le Guilloux *(Mercier)*	0:18
24	Legeay *(Lejeune)*	0:01		49	Nilsson *(Mercier)*	0:18
25	Vandenbroucke *(Peugeot)*	0:01		50	Quilfen *(Gitane)*	0:18

St. Amand-les-Eaux to St. Germain-en-Laye

After St. Willebrord and St. Amand, Sunday's 152-mile jaunt was to take us from the Belgian-French border across Picardy to St. Germain on the outskirts of Paris (later the starting point of the last day's leg). While the riders prepared for the Tour's longest stage under the eyes of the station's paraplegics, I chatted with pint-sized 22-year-old Englishman Paul Sherwen. Naïvely, I began by asking him how he fitted into the overall Fiat picture. "Search me," Sherwen answered. "On our team, there are riders who are faster than me, and others who are better climbers. I'm, I guess, what you call an all-rounder." An all-rounder, I later learned, with far from modest credentials, who last year finished second in the leading French amateur race series with four major victories.

I asked Paul what the difference between riding with the amateurs and with the professionals was. "The pros speed up at the end of the race," he replied. "They're going at speeds we never dreamed of. That's why I took 20 seconds yesterday. Also, the sense of fair play. In the amateur ranks, a crash is always a signal for the bunch to take off — whew, there's a couple less to worry about. Here, that's not done. Still, there are things I have to keep working on — like staying up and not getting caught in a back wave, especially when the wind is behind us."

On the Tour, each stage is subtly calculated for its sapping effects. Even if the race is to be decided in a round of wheel-to-wheel duels in the mountains, still there has to be some prior softening before the flutter of capework, all those jagged passes, can be allowed to have their effect. Cobbles, dysentery, crashes, may not be what a picador can do with a long pole, but they serve somewhat the same end, of setting up the beast for its eventual dismemberment.

Within this gladiatorial perspective, today's marathon run across Picardy seemed intended to pound riders' organs a little further into submission. To the usual aggravations were to be added those of the foul weather, making for conditions much closer to All Soul's Day than July 2. A Merckx might have exploited these conditions to steal a march on the climbers. But then Merckx was not one to mind earning himself the hatred of his fellow pack members by making an already long day that much more odious.

As it was, the riders refused to let themselves be panicked by all this pole-twisting in their guts. How were they supposed to go all out when they had four to five hours' work ahead before they could begin plotting a successful breakaway? So they adopted a tactic of passive resistance, one for all, and all for one: "Twist that knife in my guts as you will, M. Goddet, but I shall not be moved." As the day went on the pace decreased, reaching an average of a little more than 18 mph for the first 105 miles, a speed not much faster than a good touring cyclist.

As the afternoon wore on and the rain hardened, I became amazed, not at the racers, but at all those spectators patiently lining the road in such inclemency. I watch them there, cringing, all hooded under their umbrellas, caressing each other for warmth, and think, "Oh yes, that's the Tour." But even in this flat wheat-and-corn country, enlivened only by the odd unicorn of a church steeple, such madness is not all that easily explained away. "Nothing changes," I can see some Tour rider thinking after two-and-a-half hours of purposeless pedaling, "it just gets longer." But in this age, such green fertility has its own succor, and even in a car I sense this, just as I sense the beauty of these pink-cheeked, red-nosed, blue-denimed countrymen waving out to us with the same delight that in olden days we all waved at absolutely anything passing.

Now that we are in France, I realize that riding ahead of the pack serves other purposes as well, such as leaving one free to get to lunch on time. Throughout the country, the midday meal remains the ecstatic point of the day, and there are very few Tourists who could get through the strains of a seven-hour race without the usual four-course repast. Now and then some interloper from the foreign press hastily enters some café for a glass of wine and a sandwich. But a Tour de France has its *gourmand* overtones, and after a look at some of these 270-pound French journalists with seven, or 34 Tours showing under their belt, Thillet and I decided to throw our own paunches into the fray.

By sitting down a little before noon in a restaurant and briskly indulging, you are missing no essential cycling action. Breakaways are wonderful, they allow you actually to see something — riders pedaling — and thus size up the various motivations present in the teams. But since the moves have to do with winning, and the race itself is going at something like 35 mph during the last half-hour, it

STAGE 3: SAINT-AMAND-LES-EAUX TO SAINT GERMAIN-EN-LAYE

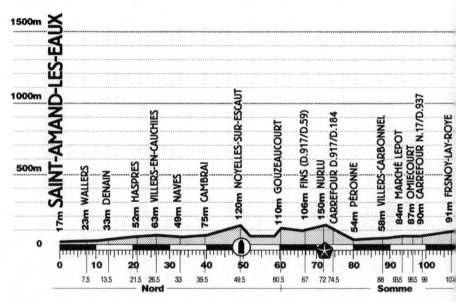

is not always possible to give the escapees more than a cursory glance before beeping by in your own mad, if well-applauded, rubber-squealing dash.

While we were resigned to yet another absent spectacle, the organizers had some reason to feel miffed. Intemperate weather was no excuse for a performance that, by early afternoon, was running a half-hour late on even the most pessimistic schedule.

"To what end were so many inert riders pedaling?" Goddet raged next day in his editorial. "Were they all blindly willing to accept a fate that would soon see them snuffed out by the climbers in the mountains without ever having made the least name for themselves?" Here was super-start Raas's yellow jersey up for the grabbing, and all anyone was thinking about was the cramped legs from any long attempted breakaway. With a group event, the Evreux to Caen team time trial coming up tomorrow, such fears could well seem misplaced.

Finally, in an effort to pull some chestnuts out of the fire, Goddet dispatched the head official, Jean Court, to each of the team managers. He reminded them of Tour rule 34, which absolves the Tour of having to bestow prize money when the average speed falls below 21 mph. (Non-distributed prize money goes into a weak-and-crippled fund, to be distributed among the Tour's laggards.)

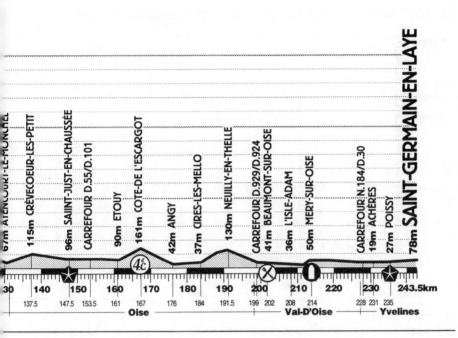

What effect these remonstrations had on the sluggard pack is unknown. It was shortly after the aptly named Snail Hill, the only fourth-category obstacle of the day — where Raas, for one, found himself left briefly behind — that a massive 36-man escape got underway, led by Legeay, Lelay, and Zoetemelk, who had just contested the Grand Prix de la Montagne sprint. Spurring them on was the new Tour provision that attributed a 20-second bonus, and thus automatic possession of the yellow jersey, to the first member of a breakaway group sprinting across the hot-point prize line at Poissy, then 40 miles away, and five miles in turn from St. Germain.

The *peloton* would not take easily the escape of such riders as Pollentier, Zoetemelk, Maertens, and *seven* Peugeots, Thévenet among them. With the destiny of the whole Tour at stake, an energetic pursuit developed. Led by Joseph Bruyère and the Raleighs, and helped by a certain number of punctures and withdrawals, it finally culminated successfully 12 miles later.

As the waves of overtaking riders come together, an air suction frequently develops that can help the unleashing of an attack. With attentions not concentrated, and everyone out of breath, a rider from the chasing group may decide to pursue his effort. This is what Patrick Friou did, a first-year pro who won 118 races as an amateur (that's more than Hinault ever entered). He was joined by Gerrie Knetemann, in what proved to be the decisive break of the whole Tour.

Decisions happen quickly in a road race. As the Friou-Knetemann wagon took off, eight riders, for their own diverse reasons, saw fit to hop on: Bruyère, Sherwen, Jacques Bossis (Renault), Klaus-Peter Thaler (Raleigh), Maurice Le Guilloux (Mercier), René Bittinger (Flandria), Jean-Pierre Danguillaume and Régis Ovion, both of Peugeot. Many of these might not have been willing to take part in a 45-mile long, two-man commando raid. But a platoon effort is something else, because the work of leading in the wind is shared.

The first rule of an escape is to create a hole. After that you can sit back and take stock to see just how interested you are. With Bruyère doing much of the early hauling, abetted by Sherwen, Le Guilloux and Friou, the lead grew quickly, reaching 3 minutes in the 10 miles between Le Tillet and the Beaumont-sur-Oise feeding station. Ten minutes later at Isle-Adam, with St. Germain 22 miles away, it had attained 4 minutes, in effect its apogee. But by then, as we ourselves could see, having pulled off the road and squeezed into the blaring file of opportunist press cars, only Sherwen and Le Guilloux, with occasional help from Friou, were doing any pacesetting. As it was, an advance that could have attained nine minutes, enough to have won the Tour for Bruyère — shrank to a far less determining 3:05.

The success of this breakaway had much to do with its eight-team composition. Had the advance reached 10 minutes, the peloton might have reacted. But with all the supposed aces left behind in hostage a *dolce far niente* developed. Why draw fire on your own troops?

The miscalculation of the danger Bruyère represented had something to do with the fact that in his six previous Tours he had never got through the mountains without one day coming a cropper and losing 15-20 minutes. At 6 feet 2 inches and 180 pounds, his build falls outside that of the rangy climber, all legs and no chest, represented by Christian Seznec. But the number of authentic climbers in the Tour is not large, and among the others Joseph can more than hold his own. His victory this year in his local classic, Liège-Bastogne-Liège (which he also won in 1976), was earned in the course of a long escape over two hills.

Great cyclists are obsessed creatures. Merckx, commenting on the strange situation in which he finds himself, free at 32 to do anything he wants, said in Brussels during his retirement ceremony, "When a man has dreamed about one thing, and one thing only, all his life he finds it very hard to know what to do with his sudden wealth of choice. Even on the podium as I was collecting my trophy, all I was seeing were the curves of the next course."

Bruyère's is a flakier temperament. For him, cycling is not a passion, but a job, and he has made clear that he can take it or leave it. Promoted to leader of C&A, after Merckx's retirement and Van Impe's crash, he failed to show up for the start of the Tour de Romandie (in French Switzerland), leaving his team no other course than to withdraw. Merckx's comment was, "That's typical Joseph," suggesting at the very least a certain history.

Bruyère's loyalties are not to teams, but to people. As far as cycling goes that has meant Eddy Merckx, whom he has served since 1970. Many observers have wondered how a rider of Bruyère's class could be satisfied with the obscure joys of servitude. But then Merckx is no common boss. Meeting him in a hotel elevator, it is immediately clear whom one is in the presence of — a god. Merckx has the sort of personality that radiates both on and off the field — like a Willy Mays — nor is it an accident that Merckx's Red Guard during his Faema days was the greatest of all modern road-racing teams.

Now and then, when circumstances were favorable (early season, rainy, misty), Bruyère was encouraged to win. Twice in successive years he took the first of the season's classics, the Het Volk, and his 1974 three-day tenure in the yellow jersey included the Tour's one séance on British soil. As a time trialist and all-around *rouleur*, he can be as good as anyone, Hinault aside. His problem, as Bruyère keeps pointing out, is a lack of consistency. It's impossible to ask others to serve you if you are bound to have one bad day.

With the rest of the old Merckx Red Guard — De Schoenmaecker, Ward Janssens, Jacques Martin, all broad-shouldered, strapping St. Bernards — Bruyère enlisted this year for what was meant to be Merckx's last campaign. With Merckx's transformation to a *de facto* team manager, Bruyère's commitment has been considerably lessened. His failure to show up at Lausanne speaks for itself. In the Tour, he has been charged by Merckx with one basic mission ·— conveying Van Impe in safety to the foothills of the Pyrenees. There his responsibility ends. He would like to win himself a stage victory before Biarritz; even so, he has let it be known that he intends to quit the Tour at that point and go home to his wife. For a handsome, courteously spoken man of his sort, 10 days on the monastic road may well mark the limit of his obligations.

The imponderable here is not Bruyère, but Merckx. Bruyère may be incapable in a race of this length in going all out for himself, but there is no reason why he might not suddenly decide to win the race by proxy for Eddy Merckx.

All it will take then is a phone call from his old roommate. Unlike most, Joseph has not over-raced this season, and is consequently in very good condition; the sort of condition that makes one think he could singlehandedly have taken nine minutes had not other considerations — loyalty to Van Impe and his obligations in tomorrow's trial — overruled him. The problem will be if he runs into hot weather in the mountains, since he has not had the chance to acclimatize himself. But if the unseasonal cold keeps up, and he decides to play his card, the three minutes he had garnered here could be a real factor.

For Le Guilloux, the failure of everyone but Sherwen to help shoulder the breakaway was very bitter. If he and Sherwen were willing to go all out, why didn't the others? One answer lies in Sherwen's subsequent failure on the long ramp between Poissy and St. Germain, when he dropped off and lost 1:38, or half of what he had gained in the previous 40 miles. The same explanation could have been volunteered for Bruyère. Riders know their limitations; if you do too much of the work, the others will profit and leave you behind.

At St. Germain with 100 yards to go Danguillaume was well placed in third position behind Bossis and Thaler. But he skidded on the rain-slickened asphalt and fell, taking down Ovion and Bittinger. Thaler survived to win the sprint ahead of a radiant arms-raised Bossis, who with the help of the 20-second bonus becomes the new yellow jersey. For Thaler, it is his first victory of the season, and it puts the German in a position to be the next yellow jersey, should Raleigh win tomorrow's time trial.

Overall classification after Stage 3 (Yellow Jersey)

1	JACQUES BOSSIS *(Gitane)*	18:33:29
2	Thaler *(Raleigh)*	at 0:20
3	Bittinger *(Flandria)*	0:26
4	Bruyère *(C&A)*	0:26
5	Ovion *(Peugeot)*	0:26
6	Knetemann *(Raleigh)*	0:26
7	Danguillaume *(Peugeot)*	0:36
8	Le Guilloux *(Mercier)*	0:43
9	Sherwen *(Fiat)*	2:20
10	Raas *(Raleigh)*	3:24

STAGE 4

Evreux to Caen
team time trial

July 3's 96-mile team time trial from Evreux to Caen revives an ancient discipline first seen in the Tours of 1927, 1928 and 1929. As such, it marks a fitting place to talk about the group aspect of what often just seems an individual sport.

Cycle racing is not and never has been a cheap sport. For this reason it has always required trade sponsorship to pay the salaries of the riders and their various supporting personnel — managers, mechanics, masseurs, soigneurs and doctors — as well as provide the equipment. Besides the bicycles, which cost between $1400 and $3000, there are the expenses of two or three team cars and an equipment bus. Add things like entry fees and transportation costs, and one gets a figure of $600,000 for a team such as TI Raleigh.

In bike racing, trade teams have always been promotional vehicles, run out of a publicity budget. This means that the sponsorship follows the fortunes of the business cycle: a team is dropped as soon as its cost outweighs the rise in sales it may bring.

Until 1955, cycling teams were run exclusively by bicycle or bicycle accessory manufacturers. But the change-over to cars brought a retrenchment when it looked for a moment as if bike racing, and not the oil-driven car, was headed the way of the dodo. In desperation, riders turned to sources outside the trade, although this was against French cycling legislation at the time. Some sought to capitalize on their names. When *Apo* Lazarides found backing from Apollinaris mineral water, it was natural that *Raphaël* Geminiani — a second-generation Italian from the Auvergne — should head a team dedicated to St. Raphaël aperitif. When St. Raphaël ran afoul of the new anti-alcohol law restricting sports advertising, "Gem" turned to Ford-France — if Peugeot (which manufactures both cars and bicycles) had a cycling team, why shouldn't Ford?

With Geminiani managing a team headed by Anquetil, Ford won most everything in sight in 1965-6. There were even plans to have Anquetil paced by a car on the San Francisco to Los Angeles freeway, where he would have exceeded the 50-mph speed limit and presumably gone past a car or two. But plans for such publicity gimmicks had to be scrapped when the American branch of the company suddenly triumphed in the Le Mans 24-hour race with a Ford Mk II seven-liter piloted by Amon and MacLaren. With the French subsidiary now obliged to devote 80 percent of its budget to motor racing, Geminiani and Anquetil were back on the street ... where they managed to be picked up by the Bic ballpoint company.

As the price of success, Bic was on the verge of becoming a household name and of losing its trade identity, as happened to Hoover in England and Raleigh in Nigeria. To Bic, a cycling team seemed the best means of establishing a distinct company name with a product intended for the public pocket.

Since Bic's pioneering days, a number of firms have sponsored cycling teams to make inroads on the mass market. The current fad lies with teams sponsored by ice-cream makers, each aimed at its own national market. But the market can be even more locally restricted, and pay off. Flandria's French associate, Jean de Gribaldy, has for years sponsored a team solely out of the profits of a single furniture and appliance store in Besançon.

When Belgian company Zeepcentrale backed a cycling team in 1978, its sales jumped an immediate 30 percent in the first two months. The success of TI Raleigh has been more spectacular still and bears, I think, important consequences for the commercial exploitation of the sport.

Raleigh is no newcomer to cycling. By the early 1900s it was already serving world markets, and its business even then was large enough to supply its own components. This vertical integration distinguishes the company from most other large cycle manufacturers that, as in the car industry, tend to be assemblers of bought-in components. Control of the product enabled Raleigh to emphasize quality and produce 4 million bicycles a year — about 10 percent of world sales.

Trouble came in the 1950s as developing countries such as India and Malaysia began to industrialize, forcing Raleigh either to build bicycles locally or grant licenses. Caught in the post-war recession, Raleigh was obliged to merge with its chief rival, the British Cycle Corporation, owned by the conglomerate, Tube Investments (TI). Together they now account for 60 percent of the United Kingdom bike market.

While rationalization proceeded, the merged company turned its attention to the American market. The first real dent in it had come when Peugeot gave a bike to Ike after his heart attack. But the real boom came in the early 1970s when bicycling caught on as a leisure and health craze. In one year alone, 1973, Raleigh's own sales more than doubled to $30 million. But the U.S. boom collapsed a year later, and it has taken four years for sales to recover to a more sane level. In the meantime, Raleigh had to find a new market for its overextended plant capacity.

The British manufacturer's strengths had been in the Commonwealth and U.S. markets where trade followed the flag. But Britain's joining the European Common Market suddenly created new options. As trade barriers came down a new market opened for the 2 million plus bicycles that Raleigh manufactures every year at Nottingham.

As opposed to the disadvantages of the overseas market — high labor input and the cost of transporting frames — the Continent offered three distinct advantages. It was near; Britain's labor costs compared favorably to those of her more prosperous neighbors; and the EEC provided external tariff protection. Hence the decision to expand within the Common Market.

But it does no good to enter a market unless people know of you. Raleigh's research showed that its name was not widely known in the EEC countries, and where it was, it was associated with the stodgy clunkers of another era. For its marketing tool, Raleigh chose to form a racing team "good enough to win the Tour de France." The mount that carried a hero over the Tourmalet would cast its glory on every Raleigh that kids pedaled around the park.

It was precisely Raleigh's weakness in the nearby Benelux market that led them to choose as manager Peter Post, a talented road racer (winner of Paris-Roubaix) and the all-time king of the six-day circus. Post assembled a mainly Dutch team that included British, Belgian, and German elements. The cost of the team since then has been about $2 million as opposed to $40 million using regular advertising channels over the same four years — and nobody within Raleigh will argue that it has not been money well spent. In the 1977 Tour, the team took second place with Kuiper, won eight stage victories, the white jersey with Thurau (after holding the yellow jersey for 16 days), along with the team prize. That got Raleigh's name in the headlines and on the television screens, and sales on the Continent increased by 30 percent.

In France, where Raleigh had only begun to market in earnest in 1976, sales rose to 14,000 bikes last year, and the number of dealers jumped dramatically from 250 to 600. The company didn't have to approach these dealers; after the

Tour success, they came to the Raleigh exhibit at the Paris bike show. But the spin-off in goodwill and new opportunities has been wider still.

Where Raleigh wanted to expand its sales on the Continent, the Fiat-La France team seems intended to give Fiat access to a much more specific market. Fiat's problem was to convince a young French working-class market that it was a French, and not an Italian, manufacturer. The pairing up with La France cycles could not, as a hyphenation, have been better. For its team manager, Fiat picked that obvious Frenchman: Geminiani. On the notion of going with youth, a novel concept in French cycling, Geminiani recruited a team of mainly first-year pros, all of whom were French except for Sherwen. That their salary structure was low allowed Fiat to be patient. An outsider seeing the team would have difficulty convincing himself that Fiat was not a French outfit that had style and was willing to take a chance on youth.

Even more interesting for the socializing of the sport is the Renault-Gitane team of Bernard Hinault, managed by 31-year-old Cyrille Guimard. An ex-head of the riders' union, Guimard was able to convince the nationalized and immensely successful Renault company to form a team that would be a notable model of socialist principles.

The starting point was to recruit a somewhat smaller team of 15 riders than the usual 20 to 25. The extra money could then be spent on support personnel, medical and administrative. Guimard is the only team manager who is free to devote his time solely to the preparation and guidance of his team. Guimard is generally conceded to be the most astute tactician of all the team managers (single-handedly responsible for Van Impe's 1976 Tour victory). Guimard has an administrator to control the financial details, including his riders' outside advertising arrangements and the post-Tour criterium contracts — all negotiated this year in advance of the Tour. This sophisticated in-house bargaining service makes Renault the one team able to bypass the sport's middlemen — an isolating position, and one that at times in this year's Tour looked as if it might backfire on Guimard.

The general health preparation has been equally thorough: an in-depth hospital service in Nantes directed by a professor of sports medicine, Dr. Ginet, where the riders go several times a year; a mountain training camp in the south to help develop ambiance; a sea-water treatment center in Brittany. This list could be extended, but it shows Guimard's own priorities and his trust in an advancing science to help with a grind as physically taxing as the Tour de France. In this measure it helps Hinault to know that Gitane does not require him to win each race he enters. Unlike most stars, he has been able to prepare his objectives, the Vuelta a España, the Tour de France, the Grand Prix des Nations. This has given him the rare luxury of being able to treat these events as appointments — with his own destiny, his social truth. When asked on the eve of the mountains what he felt was his strong point, Hinault replied very succinctly, "My health, my ability to recuperate."

On this score, it is interesting to note that Fiat-La France, Renault-Gitane and TI Raleigh all have rider contracts allowing them to dismiss a man caught taking illicit substances. One understands the companies' point of view. Why spend all that money promoting a team if the public is going to believe that it is not the bike, but a magic pill that has carried a rider over the Alps?

A Tour team's official personnel includes, besides the 10 riders, two team managers who drive the repair cars, three masseurs and three mechanics. To a biker, a masseur is what a hairdresser is to a Sophia Loren. Freddy Maertens's masseur accompanies him to each race. It is perhaps the masseur-trainer-witch doctor (the para-medical roles being inevitably added) who alone allows a star to survive some of the effects of an overcrowded season, and such long stages as yesterday's.

Besides the mechanics in the team cars, there are the assistants who man the feeding-station posts and work long into the early morning cleaning and repairing the bicycles. Chains have to be cleared of every particle of grit, tires checked for cuts and replaced if necessary, and gears changed in accordance with the requirements of the next stage. Among the poorer teams such as Jobo, many of these posts are filled by volunteers. If Russians spend their vacations on the Trans-Siberian Railway, others presumably might want to spend theirs on the Tour de France.

It seemed gastronomically fitting that the Tour should make its visit to Caen on a Monday, the day when the only butcher stores traditionally open are the *triperies* specializing in innards. After a night in Paris *tripes à la mode de Caen* might seem a worthwhile restorative for an overtaxed Tour system. Culturally, the town promises to be somewhat meager, as three-quarters of its patrimony was destroyed in the bombardment and heavy street fighting following the Normandy landings.

Caen has since turned its attention to trying to recover its former prosperity. Here the Tour de France fits very well. The $20,000 it costs is no more than what the town would have had to shell out for the now canceled July 14 Bastille Day celebrations. In return, Caen gets both a fair (minus fireworks) and the solace of immediate patronage.

Along with St. Amand's cobblestones, the Evreux to Caen team time trial belongs to the organizer's efforts to transform the Tour de France into a more varied, decathlon-type event. As a homage to the team principle, as a resurrection of a lost art, the experiment has much to recommend it. However, a plunge into the unknown is not lightly undertaken, especially in a discipline that last figured in professional races in the early 1970s and then over very short distances of 10 miles or less (the Olympics still feature a four-man 100km team trial). Ninety-six miles may not seem very long, as Tour legs go. But in a four-hour race with every rider obliged to go flat out at a speed equal to what is normally seen only at the end of a stage it could cause serious time spreads.

Rather than lower the distance and compromise the gravity of the event, the organizers chose a bonus system (2:00, 1:20, 1:00, etc.), with times based on the fifth-placed rider. To many, a proportional system based on the real time differences between teams would have been more in the spirit of the Tour.

In the late 1920s when team time trials were a regular feature of multi-leg courses, preparation would begin at the end of winter with each member obliged to lead his mile. Mainly this served to get you used to the rotation, of having always the same rider in front and behind you throughout the season. When you are only inches off another's wheel, you have to know his reactions, when to take over the relay and, what is *most* difficult, how to drop off without creating, or getting caught in, the air pockets caused by the extra movement. This is why some people feel that the four-man Olympic system is more manageable, because the air pockets are more easily sealed. The rotation is rapid, since it's not possible for a rider to go flat out for more than 100 yards without leveling off. Also, the concentration required by the wheel-to-wheel closeness — both hands on the handlebars — makes feeding somewhat problematical, although there is a feeding station at the base of the Livarot hill. It will be interesting to see what accidents we get there and on the way down.

In the pre-race speculation, there is a marked debate over how to run the race. If a rider punctures, or has an accident, the normal thing is to wait for him, except perhaps in the last few miles of the race. But if he is too weak to take his relay effectively, then he must be dropped, even if it cuts him off from a share in the prime bonus. (This decision is more difficult morally in a race based on real time differences, as the dropped racers still have to finish. Then a team has to decide whether it is racing to win, or racing to pull everybody through in the best possible circumstances.)

For their own reasons, a number of teams, including two main contenders, Renault and Peugeot, have announced that they will do everything to finish all together. To this end, Renault plans to start off at a moderate pace and step it up from the Livarot hill onwards. Others will demand as much as they can of their weaker members up to that point, and then gradually begin shedding them. The only certainty is that the last half-hour of a continually adverse wind will be very hard on everyone.

With the teams starting off at six-minute intervals, we are able to tag along behind a team for a while before pulling off the roadway to await the next. It's a bit like watching a long decisive escape. The riders are all alone in the wind and one catches the play of the colors, the gold of the mustard plots as it blends with the Renault jerseys. The rotation flows like a well-oiled chain, with the riders coming up and dropping back in two parallel lines of five each, the time of each man at the head for his hundred yards burst lasting but a few seconds. This whole brotherhood of a team pulling each in turn forward on the rope of the wind, makes for an impressive spectacle. There is also the time element for the amateur chronometrists, armed with stopwatch and pad and shouting out their encouragement. In spite of the gusty wind, there is the feeling of a holiday afternoon: checked tablecloths, people huddled over radios inside trailers, even a man sitting aloft in an official timekeeper's booth, playing the accordion as if at a village ball. This is what I was continually astonished by — the gaiety of the Tour's fans in conditions that require a certain patience. This is not a Be-In with bands, semi-costumed participants, Bat Man dropping out of the sky, folk dancing on the walkways, but the ambiance, the vibrations given off, certainly approaches it.

We have dropped behind the Peugeots when all of a sudden on the brow of a wheat field we catch the red and gold of the charging Raleighs steamrollering down on us. The Peugeots themselves seem hardly able to believe it; in spite of the risks each must twist in the saddle and sneak a look. For a team of aces it must be hard to think that another team could have taken six minutes off them in less than 60 miles. Although their domino-colored jerseys and gray bicycles are in the Raleigh sights, the Peugeots manage to keep from being overtaken for five more miles before finally succumbing to a team more highly motivated, and better organized. When Michel Laurent punctured, we watched the whole Peugeot team wait for him, getting their breath back and feeding themselves, but losing a good minute and a half. When Hennie Kuiper punctured, we saw only one Raleigh rider left with him.

Peugeot had its alibis. Both Danguillaume and Ovion were clearly handicapped by their fall yesterday. Nor was Thévenet, the victim of a fall and a puncture, able to take his full share at the helm. The efforts of Yves Hézard, Bernard Bourreau (Thévenet's personal caddy), and now and again Michel Laurent to take up the missing slack, merely proved that you can't run a team race on one or two cylinders — especially when you need group momentum to make headway in the wind.

The Peugeot morale deteriorated to the point that riders were no longer willing to relay. In the next 35 miles, they lost an additional seven minutes while they screamed at one another, and Thévenet was able to rally the Caen stadium only with the help of a supplementary food hand-out in the last mile. At the finish, he looked utterly shattered, and it is clear that the Tour is over both for him and his team. That's a singular way to have fallen in just a year.

Unluckiest of all was Flandria with Michel Pollentier taking a horrid fall, and three others puncturing. Pollentier's crash occurred at the 25-mile mark, at a time when Flandria was still running second to C&A. He had surged to the front to take the relay when a sudden gust of wind caught him on the white line. Through no fault of his contorted style, Pollentier skidded and fell heavily, suffering severe abrasions along his left shoulder and elbow and painfully bruising the lumbar region of the lower spine.

During the next 12 miles, with Pollentier being treated from his team car as he pedaled along, Flandria's rhythm suffered, as the team could not go flat out with Pollentier unable to take his place in the rotation. From there, with Pollentier, Bittinger, Maertens and De Meyer taking the longest relays, Flandria turned it on to such an extent that they had to drop Beyssens after the Livarot hill and three other riders including surprisingly Agostinho, between the 70th and 71st mile. Then, a mile later, with Flandria in third place behind Raleigh, but ahead of Mercier and Renault, came further bad luck as Maertens punctured. At that point, with slightly under an hour still to go, Flandria might well have dropped Maertens, leader that he was, to preserve Pollentier's chances. But with time based on the fifth finisher that would have meant further risk, and the team chose to wait for Freddy *en masse*. The depleted six-man squad came in fifth, earning a 20-second bonus.

As expected, the real battle was between Raleigh and C&A, who both finished four minutes ahead of Mercier, their nearest pursuers. Here the advantage of starting last worked in Raleigh's favor. Trailing by a half-minute at the 50-mile mark, the Dutchmen knew what they had to do and did it, shedding

Wellens 15 miles from the end, and two others shortly thereafter, to defeat C&A by a bare seven seconds. But Raleigh's victory was not exactly stolen, as they had an extra puncture to contend with.

The main beneficiaries of the operation are Hennie Kuiper and Klaus-Peter Thaler. And it is the German who becomes the new yellow jersey, although he too barely made the finish line race track. Thaler hopes to hold on to his precious jersey until Friday's wine-country time trial. But Knetemann, now six seconds behind and by all agreement Raleigh's strongest rider at this stage, may not feel like waiting much past tomorrow's American Independence Day. The Dutch bitterly remember last year when they were duped into serving the personal ambitions of Thurau; they would feel more secure with one of their own in the yellow jersey. Meanwhile, the whole team will divvy up $6000 as their reward.

The other net beneficiaries are Van Impe and Bruyère, though they are apt to feel short-changed by a bonus system in which a seven-second defeat registers as if it were 40 seconds. Also, C&A is only 20 seconds ahead of a team that was actually 4 minutes behind them. Bruyère's saving himself on the latter part of yesterday's escape almost paid off, as it allowed him to be the main C&A locomotive in the near gale-force wind. By these efforts, he leapfrogs over Sunday's yellow jersey, Bossis, into third place, 40 seconds behind Knetemann, while Van Impe's 1:20 bonus will help cushion him against the expected ravages of Friday's individual time trial.

For the other teams, with the possible exception of the Merciers and thus Zoetemelk, the long haul to Caen may not have been worth more than the proverbial load of tripe. Even the Merciers had their moments of panic as Seznec punctured at 50 mph descending the Liverot hill and crashed off the road. As a result of not eating, Seznec had a bad attack of the bonk in the last miles, and looked truly agonized as he crossed the line. For most, the time trial seemed unnecessarily long, and many wonder what the effect of dragging these 13- and even 12-toothed sprockets is going to have on the long stints promised for the next couple of days. If today's northerly wind holds, we and our almighty Thaler could be in for some battering.

Caen
to Mazé-Montgeoffroy

After Monday's incursion westward into Normandy, the Tour turns directly south on a course it will hold all the way to the Spanish frontier. July 4's part of this phase takes us across the famed apple brandy region of Calvados, and thence through Brittany to Mazé-Montgeoffroy, a small town on the Loire River midway between Angers and Saumur.

But yesterday's northerly has shifted to a more customary southwesterly wind, so it looks as if we won't have an Independence Day upheaval. Instead, the day promises a transitional leg, with a breakaway possible in the last 40 minutes of the race after the Beauvau hill. In distance, it is virtually the same as Sunday's from St. Amand to St. Germain-en-Laye, only the bad weather may make it brisker. Dampness helps the riders' intake of oxygen, and the Novemberish chill may encourage riders to pedal faster to keep their blood circulating and their bodies warm.

The first part of the race is across a rich plain. Here among wheat and corn and red poppies are occasionally fields of delicate flax, all wavering eye-like blues. This soon changes into a long cedar forest set with wild ponds and black-earthed bogs. Along the road here it is the feast of the bicycle. Whoever has one seems to have brought it out where he can be alone with his machine to gleam it back to them. Jean-Jacques Fussien launches one of his matinal breakaways. A short-lived affair, it succeeds to the extent of allowing him to carry off the hot-point sprint at Falaise with its 20-second bonus, enough to push him up from 85th to 81st in the overall standings. Behind, Maertens serves notice of his intentions by copping the pack sprint for second place with its two green jersey points. Besides denying anyone else the points, it helps protect him if there is a breakaway or a missed finish.

The landscape reminds me of Virginia or Eastern Tennessee — names one throws out before stiffening at other sides of the rural equation. But France has kept its rural heritage in a way that the more-crowded European countries haven't been able to. The Green Revolution has not kept two-thirds of the 1945 rural population from migrating to the cities. But it has stayed the loss, while preserving a viable point of return, should city life succumb to the predicted horrors. Meanwhile the Frenchman keeps his foot rather successfully in both camps. There are more second homes in France than any other country, and polls continually confirm the almost unanimous veneration with which the Frenchman regards the countryside. It is into this rural cadre that the Tour de France fits so admirably.

We've bolted down the most succulent of tripe stews at the Carrefour posthouse when word comes of Perret and Pollentier falling in a 10-man collision. Later, at the 120-mile mark, Kuiper takes a tumble. None of these falls, fortunately, are serious, but they point up the difficulty the Tour pack is having in staying out of each other's spokes. In the drizzle, the white stripe in the middle of the road — the cause of Pollentier's accident in the team time trial — is like a bar of soap. Once you start sliding there is no way to right yourself.

While most serious accidents occur in the high speeds of the last hour, the slow pace also takes its toll. Riders are bored, attentions are not concentrated, and the deliberate eccentricities of the clowns must be contended with. Also, this year the pedaling community has had to assimilate more than its usual share of new faces. Among the established riders there are those, like Agostinho, who weave a lot; hence the crashes that have plagued his career. Basic bike control can be acquired through such exercises as picking up balls on a track with alternate hands. If all else fails, a pack menace may find himself sentenced to the Siberia of cross-country.

So many crashes involve the leaders perhaps because they tend to compete for the same pack seats. Somewhere between 15 and 20 seems the most sought-after position — as they are also for very different reasons with the sprinters. The rider is sheltered, and at the same time safe from surprises. But most of the leaders have their faithful squires whose business it is to carry supplies, crack jokes, surrender their own wheels, and do whatever else is required to keep the poor knight from feeling the loneliness and vulnerability of his great office. With these knights and squires, and the furtively arriving sprinters, life in the leadership block can get rather congested. It's why a tall awkward rider such as Christian Seznec prefers to ride outside and take his buffeting from the wind rather than risk his livelihood in a pack accident.

Midway between the Pollentier and Kuiper falls, and with 40 miles of open, windy pampas country still to cross, the race all of a sudden flares up. As so often happens, the attack comes just after the second feeding station at Sablé-sur-Sarthe. Everyone must eat sometime to avoid what riders call the knock (or bonk), a nauseous weakness caused by hunger cramps. Because of the energy demands, these stations often precede a climb. Every few yards for a mile or more there are team helpers holding out a little cotton satchel called a *musette*, which is filled with fruit, rice cakes, nuts, chocolate, honey sandwiches. The rider grabs it and slings it around his neck, before divying it up among his jersey pockets for later consumption. But since getting the food is essential, these feeding-points make a good place for attacks, especially if it precedes a climb. Here the climb is only the 300-foot Beauvau hill, but still enough of an obstacle to daunt the pack from undertaking a pursuit until over the top.

The first to try his luck is Jean-Pierre Danguillaume. The next attempt by Planckaert, the stage winner at Brussels, catches everyone but Bazzo napping. Planckaert is too large and heavy-chested to be thought of as a climber of anything but a 300-foot hill. His *forte* is sprinting, rather than the long solitary effort. Still, with Planckaert doing all the initial hauling, they manage to get a 24-second advance going, when Teka's Javier Elorriaga sets out to make it a threesome. The sight of Elorriaga steaming up must have prompted Bazzo, who earlier in the day has learned of the end-of-season disbandment of his Lejeune squad, to thrust caution aside and cast in his lot with the Belgian. *He* knows Planckaert is very fast, but Planckaert has no reason to know how fast this 24-year-old second-year pro is. Planckaert may be underestimating him, and get a surprise.

With the two loyally relaying one another, the advance quickly grows, reaching 1:04 at Durtal. Bazzo takes the Beauvau hill sprint seven miles later, while Planckaert garners the 20-second bonus that goes with the hot-points sprint at Jarze. With 14 miles to go the breakaway pair has a 1:38 lead, which in effect means Planckaert has vaulted into sixth place. Shortly thereafter, alas, a puncture immobilizes Bazzo, leaving Planckaert to the voracity of a pack led by the Flandria, Raleigh and Peugeot teams, all driven by a like ambition. Planckaert's flight endures for another eight miles, only to be caught six miles from where the pack is to enter Mazé-Montgeoffroy and the final three-mile circuit.

With Pollentier indisposed, his normal task of keeping a taut, escape-proof pace falls on three other Flandria work-horses: Bittinger, Albert Van Vlierberghe and Marcel Tinazzi. The three prove more than up to their mission, silencing a first move of Raas's that leads in turn to an attempted breakaway by the Breton Le Denmat as the 99-rider palette-pack bursts like so many tropical fish into the streets of Montgeoffroy.

Here, for the three miles of the circuit, attack follows attack as the Breton's effort is prolonged by Nilsson, then by Teirlinck, then by Lubberding — who gets catapulted off by Karstens in the now-illegal six-day hand-sling fashion. But the Flandrians blanket Lubberding, only to see his teammate, Jan Raas, sprint away — with such dispatch that he misses the curve and ends up among the crowd! Then it is Teirlinck's second turn, which ends only when Guy Sibille leaves Esclassan's side to rein the Belgian in.

By now, Maertens has anchored himself on Jacques Esclassan's wheel, a mark of the highest respect, if inhibiting for the Frenchman. Beaten by Esclassan and Bertin at St. Amand-les-Eaux, by Planckaert at Brussels, and by Raas at St. Willebrord, he is now finally in a position to set matters right as to his own relative weakness — eight stages won in 1976 and nothing so far. As De Meyer, with Sean Kelly in his immediate wake, launches the final sprint Maertens drops into his 12-tooth sprocket. What happened next is a matter of some conjecture. Did Maertens use Kelly to launch himself, pushing off against his chest, as Planckaert claimed? Or were those flashing hands Maertens's way of pushing his lead-in man aside, Kelly perhaps not aware that he was in Maertens's way? In the next instant the lime-shirted Maertens overtakes Karstens to win by two bicycle lengths for his 11th victory of the season and his first of this Tour. In the green jersey competition, he now leads Esclassan by 32 points. But sprinters are perfectly capable of dealing out their own justice, and Maertens is going to have to keep a sharp watch on Karstens. The Dutchman's speed may not be what it once was, but in putting a wheel ahead of another and blasting him into the straw barricades, Karstens is in a league by himself.

Mazé-Montgeoffroy
to Poitiers

With some 700 souls, Mazé-Montgeoffroy is the smallest of our host towns. At the end of the race, most of us are scattered to the four winds — in a Loire of white stone castles, poets and the purest spoken French, a hardly unpleasant prospect. After following the teams into Richard the Lionheart's Angers I wound up, for lack of a bed, taking a train to Saumur, where I found an old hotel on the river in the Renaissance quarter. Good local wine, fish for dinner, a chance to stroll around among limestone buildings in a serenely gray summer evening, all proved a welcome change after the industrial blight of Valenciennes and Caen's sterility. Nonetheless, I felt, as I often would, banished. Races don't completely stop at the stage finish line. Rather they go on in the restaurants and bars and hotel lobbies long thereafter, and you have to be present if you are going to make any sense of them.

The main reason the Tour had been invited to Mazé-Montgeoffroy was so that the Marquis de Contades might have the pleasure of hosting a Tour start and help put on the tourist map a castle boasting a complete set of original Louis XVI furniture. With only a 100-mile race on the day's agenda, the feeling on the great lawn leading up to the château was unhurried enough that I had time to talk to Sean Kelly, Flandria's Irish sprinter.

Born in Ring on the southernmost tip of Ireland, Kelly grew up in Carrick-on-Suir in Tipperary before pedaling off to Metz, France, at the age of 19 to try his luck. At the end of the 1976 season in which he won the amateur Tour of Lombardy, he was recruited by Jean de Gribaldy, the Besançon furniture dealer. While not paid expressly to win on his own, he has managed to cop victories at the expense of such accomplished fast finishers as Merckx, Patrick Sercu and

Marino Basso. Also unlike most sprinters, who work out of their lung intake and are consequently deep-chested, Kelly is of a rangy build, which helps him in the mountains.

Fast as Kelly is, he is not yet as fast as Freddy Maertens. "That's why I work for him, it's better than getting beaten all the time," says Kelly. He is particularly good at guard duty. Being so swift, riders can't drop him when they try to break out of the pack, as Merckx discovered during the San Cristobal world championships. Kelly tells me that in organizing a defense the usual Flandria tactic is to let a breakaway develop until it has a 30-second lead. Like the other young Flandria recruits, Kelly likes the ambiance: "Michel and Freddy don't boss us around, the way other leaders do. And they encourage us to take our own chances." At this point, with Agostinho being saved for the mountains, it is up to Kelly and Bittinger to jump on every breakaway wagon. As Kelly says, "If we keep jumping on them all we're bound some day or other to catch a good one."

With an informant of Kelly's English-speaking sort, I have to keep going. So I ask him about Freddy Maertens, who is, at least physically, the Micky Mantle, the Marilyn Monroe of the sport. Blond, young, curly-headed, with blue friendly eyes and no more than 5 feet 10 inches high, Maertens differs in that he so succeeds. Or did until the middle of last year, when it began to look as if he was already at the age of 26 burned out. What intrigued me was a photograph that appeared in the *Équipe* at the time when Maertens was sweeping his way, stage by victorious stage, through the 1977 Vuelta. The photograph showed Maertens doing yoga calisthenics. Aware of the value yoga might have in a sport so dependent on willpower, I ask Kelly if Freddy still practices yoga.

"No," Kelly answers. "Yoga is something Freddy does only at the beginning of the year. During the season there is no time for it."

"Any other questions?" Kelly asks.

"Yes. During the Dauphiné-Libéré, I read that Pollentier does not suffer from hunger cramp exhaustion because he is a vegetarian. How does he get his protein then?"

"That's wrong, Michel is not a vegetarian, he just doesn't eat red meat because of the supposed soporifics it contains. But white meat, chicken, veal, that's all right."

The stage started promisingly: an escape in the first mile led by Planckaert, Charly Rouxel and Raleigh's Aad Van Den Hoek; then another two attempts some 14 miles later. In the hectic going, Ferdinand Julien and Joël Gallopin collided heavily, Gallopin sustaining a very painful shoulder dislocation, but something less than the broken bone originally feared. Bicycling courageously, he managed to rally Poitiers in the same brisk 4:02:27 as the 104 others, though whether Gallopin can survive one-handed in the mountains is to be doubted.

The rest of the action up to the 85-mile mark shimmered around the three hot-points sprints. Esclassan chose the first at Onglée to try out for the first time in his career a 12-tooth sprocket, beating in the process, Maertens, Kelly and Planckaert, which must have been reassuring. But forearmed is forewarned, and with Maertens dogging Esclassan, the next two sprints went to Danguillaume and Bossis with Kelly second each time, a sign that something Irish was in the wind.

Here, at the last hot-points sprint, with 15 miles left to go, the usual end-of-race fireworks flared up. Minutes earlier, Fussien had broken away in the hope of garnering — or at least sabotaging — the 20-second bonus. With him, to help shut out Esclassan, was Maertens's teammate Van Vlierberghe. It fell to a second Flandrian, René Bittinger, clad temporarily in the white jersey of the best youth, to try to head them off. Once the junction was made, and the risk averted, Willy Teirlinck tried his chance, only to be countered by an omnipresent Bittinger. A second later Bruyère, in his perfect flowing style, jumped, only to have his own wheel sat in on (just barely) by Knetemann. The sight of these two spurred Bittinger and Kelly to play their own team card: a Flandria victory. While they were about that, Sven Nilsson (Mercier) saw a chance to snatch a few seconds in the overall classification.

These attacks all came at a particularly favorable moment that found Peugeot caught short-handed by Thévenet's puncture. With Sibille, Ovion and Bourreau deputized to the rear, that left the Renaults and Flandrians alone to organize the pursuit of Bruyère, whom they now justifiably feared. By the time the four Peugeots had remounted the 106-man line, the fleeing quintet had a half-minute lead. Possibly this might have narrowed had the sprinters been willing to relax their customary watchfulness, and allowed their heavy artillery to be wheeled into the fray. But heavy artillery is heavy artillery, and there are rules in the trade as to when each piece is to be detonated: as close to the finish line as possible to yield that maximum bang! Hard to convince a Bertin lurking on Maertens's wheel, and Esclassan timorously crouched behind Danguillaume, that others were not willing — nor capable — of doing their work for them; that if they didn't bestir themselves they would be sprinting for sixth place.

That Knetemann might turn into Bruyère's ally of circumstance seems more unusual. Normally, you don't strip your own teammate of his yellow jersey, nor do you help the enemy obtain a position to the detriment of another of your own men, Kuiper. But Kuiper's chances in this Tour may require all the psychological ballast they can get. By establishing Bruyère as a rival, he draws attention away from himself, while making life all the more complicated for Hinault, Zoetemelk and Pollentier. Kuiper may not be able to match his main rivals wheel for wheel, but he may be able to out-think them. Admittedly, it's playing with fire, but then an extra 27 seconds should not mean that much in the mountains, even if it does properly annoy Hinault.

In a Tour where maneuvers are never merely individual, the time gains made in a five-man break of this sort ramify over a whole series of categories. Also, any single day's result has its distant offshoot, each performance conditioning in some way the future. Bruyère's offensive, supported by Knetemann — all questions of the yellow jersey aside — fits into that longer range perspective presented by the individual team challenge. With Bruyère's C&A team trailing Raleigh by 3:58, it takes only a puff of wind for C&A to knock the yellow caps off TI Raleigh, or for Flandria to deprive Peugeot-Esso of their green caps. That, in effect, was at stake in the escape.

While Knetemann and Bruyère impressively relayed each other — two riders, in effect, keeping at bay a whole pursuing pack — the function of the remaining trio was simply to keep up, since their team interests did not warrant giving aid and comfort to the enemy Bruyère. Still, they had individual interests of their own. Nilsson, whose forte is not his finishing kick, and who moreover knew he had no chance against both Bittinger and the intrinsically swifter Kelly, elected to bolt first on the beginning of the uphill ramp, some 500 yards from the line. Meanwhile, Kelly and Bittinger had divided up Bruyère and Knetemann between them, each taking a wheel. When Bruyère tore after and caught Nilsson at the 350-yard mark, Kelly found himself suddenly projected into the lead, further out than he might have desired. Relatively fresh as he was, Kelly weakened in the last yards of the incline, and when the line finally came up, Sean was only a spoke ahead of the new yellow jersey, Gerrie Knetemann, while Bittinger took third ahead of Bruyère.

The sprint-in of the remaining 100-man pack was more than the usual rugged going. On the last curve, as the approach right-angled between barricades and bales of straw, Maertens found himself deliberately sandwiched between two riders for just long enough to make him lose his sense of direction and crash, taking Bertin, Fussien and Alain Patritti with him. Revenge for his push off on Kelly the day before? While the fall tore great holes in his lovely chlorophyll jersey, no one rode over him and Maertens, more dazed than hurt, managed to cross the finish line with the help of pushes from Tinazzi and Muselet, his chain having jumped off in the crash.

With Maertens *hors de combat*, the sprint for sixth place was easily won by Jacques Esclassan, who picked up 12 points, now to trail Maertens by only 20 points (the margin of a stage victory) in the green jersey competition.

By his day's labors, Kelly picked up 30 green jersey points, which may give him ideas. What could be more fitting than to have a man from the Emerald Isle as our future green jersey? Meanwhile, there is a certain satisfaction in the panoply of nationalities present at the finish: Dutch, Swedish, Irish, French and Belgian — a sign that cycling's frontiers may at last be opening up.

STAGE 7

Poitiers to Bordeaux

At the end of one of the more uncertain weeks in Tour history, today's 150-mile trek to Bordeaux must seem a let-down. Jacques Goddet devoted most of next day's editorial to a defense of the rider-maligned transfers, indicating where future Tours may be headed. Wasn't yesterday's brisk 100-mile leg to be infinitely preferred to this sort of dragging somnolence? Why not then use each team's allotted car to start 50 miles further on, saving two and a half hours of race time, and 90 minutes of rider sleep? For their part, the riders were holding themselves in reserve for tomorrow's dreaded test of truth, the 37.5-mile St. Emilion to Ste. Foy-la-Grande time trial. Even for a specialist of the art like Pollentier, the distance is still six miles longer than he has ever attempted. The only ones facing it with equanimity are Hinault, Bruyère and Knetemann, all veterans of the still longer Grand Prix des Nations.

The feeling of gloom, if not outright fear, has been bolstered by the miserable weather. Even in a year intent on shattering all records for inclemency, six out of seven wet days seems exaggerated. Among the spectators morosely cowering behind their umbrellas, one detected a solemn accusation. In a world where weather is time, these clouds could well seem something the Tour had brought with it all the way from Leiden, tugged along by that guardian helicopter! Never had TV spectators, accustomed to the tar-colored skins of past runnings, seen such pale riders. And the men of the north let it be understood that, had they thought conditions would be so wintry, they would never have abandoned their hearths. It is hardly surprising that the main news as the Tour wound slowly south through the Charente grape country concerned what is becoming known as the *Grand Prix de la Chute*. Perhaps it was the heady fumes of cognac and pineau rising from the pretty vineyards that so bemused the concentration. When the tally of falls was finally counted, it was discovered that out of the 110 riders setting out from Leiden, only two had reached Bordeaux unscathed.

The first fall, at the halfway point, saw Thévenet as always taking part in it (as others take part in the escapes). His role is clearly to be the great *éprouvé* of this Tour — a fact underlined when he punctured in circumstances identical to yesterday, at the last hot-points sprint. Can it be that unlike Hinault and Merckx he keeps other things besides a seven-year stock of tires aging in his cellar? But Hinault too had his come-uppance, succumbing with Jacques Martin to the eccentricities of Fussien. Hinault hurt his knee in the fall. But he could just as easily have ruptured his kneecap and been put out of the race. A third crash, five miles later, floored another four, among them Joseph Bruyère, who as a direct consequence wore pads over his knees for the remainder of the Tour.

Other than these falls, the main notes concern the stage's two regionals, Bernard Bourreau, whose riding style makes him the French Pollentier, and Pierre Bazzo. What better place to shine than before the home folks, and Bourreau obliges his own Cycling Club of Civray by taking its hot-points sprint. At the 80-mile mark, just before the fourth-category Montée hill, Bazzo makes another bid, only to be caught on the climb and passed by Antonio Menendez, the lone Spaniard as yet to show himself. Forty-four miles later, Bazzo again goes into action; by St. Savin-de-Blaye, he has almost a minute's lead when he suddenly stops, hops off his bike and embraces his wife and family and the reigning local dignitary, Michel Hidalgo, the coach of the French national soccer team.

These amiable breakaways used to be part of a time-honored Tour tradition. Then Merckx came along, and immediately started clamping down on each and every permission to leave: "You'll never get away from me." Such family kissing might seem innocuous enough. But one knows how one thing soon leads to another, and rather than have a wholesale insurrection on his hands Merckx preferred to personally accompany every supposed kisser. And where Merckx marched the rest of the platoon marched too, if only to pick up what crumbs he would toss them.

Since Merckx's retirement, there has been an *interregnum* of government by committee. But this has not led to the chaos that some feared. Far from it, and the heavy hand wielded by the committee of elders — Hinault, Kuiper, Pollentier, Zoetemelk and Maertens — has caused a good deal of whimpering among the Tour novices. All this marching in close formation, step by step, straight to the Pyrenees without a chance to kick up your heels, one can see how it might grate on tender spirits. Weren't these elders willing to remember that they, too, were young once, with dreams, ambitions of their own?

But appeals to the charitable instincts have never held much water with the powers that be. The only law they have shown signs of respecting is that incarnated by Bruyère. In a pair of forays, the Walloon has cut an almost four-minute breach in the united wall. The longer Bruyère persists in the lead, the greater the likelihood that others may be tempted to follow Knetemann's example and make common cause.

The Tour's young malcontents have found a leader in the person of Jean-Jacques Fussien. But it is to be feared that, despite this doomed glowworm's daily bravery, he will go down only as the clown prince of the Tour. In that case, the attack on Hinault's knee may represent the high-water mark of their rebellion.

But the leaders were well armed for this sort of skirmish, particularly the arch-conservative Flandria. Kelly's place at the fore was assumed by the veteran Agostinho, who bestirred himself to the extent of taking an unexpected second behind the leader Jacques Bossis at the last hot-points sprint, and then a few miles later joining in an abortive seven-man breakaway — enough to earn him laurels as teammate of the day. Then, with the Tour only three miles from the Bordeaux velodrome and its famous rose concrete track, the Portuguese was duly relieved by his fellow sergeant, Pollentier. Showing no signs of the headaches and constant pain that had kept him from sleeping earlier in the week, Pollentier kept the pack in good order behind him all the way across the Aquitaine bridge. But while De Meyer was able to harness his strength for the final backstretch (he is much faster than Pollentier, but lacks his stamina), Esclassan lost on the bridge the services of his own lead-out man, Guy Sibille, the victim of the day's last fall (bad enough to cost him six minutes).

At the end of the bridge, it was the turn of Bernard Hinault and Michel Laurent to try out their new light time-trial bikes as each sprinted to take a few yards lead ahead of the pack. Then at the entry to the stadium, with a double circuit still to go, the yellow jersey Knetemann streaked forth with Régis Delepine on his heels to steal himself an extra malicious second, times being taken at the beginning of the first lap. Raas came up behind, and had there been a hole behind his fellow Raleigh, Knetemann would have lit out. Unfortunately, what was there was Fussien waving his arms to call his little flock together, and in that very instant puncturing.

On the first circuit, I looked for Barry Hoban, whose eight Tour stage victories include two on this rose track. Instead, it was Karstens who made the first serious move at the beginning of the second lap, pursued by Danguillaume.

As soon as the Peugeot rider had caught Karstens, De Meyer steamed into the lead with Maertens and also Esclassan in his wake. Maertens stayed abreast of De Meyer in order to keep his eyes on Jan Raas, who was preparing to duplicate his St. Willebrord maneuver before the sprint was fully launched. Then at the end of the backstretch, with 250 yards to go, Planckaert bolted. Maertens caught him and then, once in the lead, held out against an Esclassan weakened by the wind-buffeting he had taken on the two laps in Sibille's absence. But as Esclassan said, "A second place is never very good. But behind Maertens it's not so dishonorable."

For his part, Maertens is looking forward to tomorrow's time trial, which he won in its comparative stage in 1976. Much as he would like to repeat that triumph, he feels that the hilly nature of the terrain will be more to Pollentier's taste. The other main duel will be between Bruyère and Knetemann. But in four time trials Knetemann has never been beaten by briary Joseph, and with a 40-second lead he sees no need to relinquish his yellow jersey.

Overall classification after Stage 7 (Yellow jersey)

1	GERRIE KNETEMANN *(Raleigh)*	29:34:35
2	Thaler *(Raleigh)*	at 0:21
3	Bruyère *(C&A)*	0:40
4	Bossis *(Gitane)*	1:21
5	Bittinger *(Flandria)*	1:40
6	Le Guilloux *(Mercier)*	1:44
7	Ovion *(Peugeot)*	2:27
8	Danguillaume *(Peugeot)*	2:37
9	Wesemael *(Raleigh)*	3:26
10	Lubberding *(Raleigh)*	3:26
11	Kuiper *(Raleigh)*	3:26
12	De Cauwer *(Raleigh)*	3:26

St. Emilion to Ste. Foy-la-Grande time trial

For the Tour's prerace favorites, most of whom have been keeping themselves discreetly behind the scenes during the past week, today's 37.5-mile wine-country time trial represents the opening of hostilities. Coalitions are useful; they keep the rabble from interfering in gentlemen's concerns. But with the mountains looming now two days away, the time has come for the leading contenders to wheel their mounts into the lists. Any failure of theirs will be gratefully exploited by the specialist climbers, Van Impe, Galdos, Martinez, *et al.*

Time trials have been traditionally regarded as tests of truth. They represent what is purest in the sport: the knight alone, mounted on the lightest, shiniest of steeds, waging hand-to-hand combat with man's principal enemy — time. Everything up to this, those seven days of skirmishing on the road with its need of constant vigilance, its attacks and counterattacks, have been merely preparatory tests of a knight's captaincy, his ability to marshal and lead his forces. But there comes a moment when the right to rule must itself be tested. For this Tour, convention decrees that every would-be Hercules must present himself alone, without his trusty guard; to be then sent forth into those 80 minutes of solitary terror; a battle both with the elements — the road surfaces, the wind, the screaming fans — and against the ticking clock.

In vino veritas. After all this time cooped up in the vacuum-sealed pack, today's test of truth sees all these youthful spirits jubilantly pouring themselves forth before such ancient château names as Cheval Blanc, Pétrus, Tour Puyblanquer. This partiality of wine for time trials seems more than a coincidence. Was it not in Burgundy last year that Thévenet triumphed and won himself the Tour? And will not this year's Tour be decided, if all else fails, on the banks of the Moselle during the Metz to Nancy trial?

Not that one expects the whole truth and nothing but to come bubbling forth all at once. Riders, like fine wines, don't all travel well; Pollentier, for one, may be below par from the considerable jingling he has taken. In his case, we may have to defer judgment until the Puy-de-Dôme, by when the mountains should have replenished his store of B vitamins. The odds-on favorite is Hinault, who, after all, rhymes with *vino*. But there is also our Dutch cooper, Hennie, who would seem particularly prepared for this joust. Equally determined with his two glasses (alas, not white and red) astride his nose, is his compatriot Gerrie Knetemann. Among the Tour's question marks, will Thévenet find claret as much to his liking as his native burgundy?

In a world where nearly every day brings new destruction, St. Emilion is a lesson in successful survival. When threatened by the Vikings — who had sailed up the Gironde — the good vintners of St. Emilion had only to uncork their casks. Received with friendship, the Vikings spared the town in what must be one of the first successful dopings in history.

After a week of naked French stone, St. Emilion seems Mediterranean with its bright, bougainvillea-covered, yellow stucco. But before I have a chance to do any real savoring, or sampling, I run into Reynaud Vincent, who asks if I would like a lift in the *France Soir* car. They are doing a feature on Hervé Inaudi, next to last on the Tour totem pole, and since time trials are run in inverse order that means he is the second rider to leave. But a lift is a lift, and glad to see something of Vincent, a good fiction writer, I accept.

Vincent tells me that his favorite American writer is Faulkner. He wonders what the author of "Pylon" would have done with a subject like the Tour de France, one in which the yellow jersey not only has to triumph over others, but also frequently over an unfavorable destiny, spills, punctures, cramps, saddle boils, bad drugs, plots and weather. On this score, legend says that the first winner of the Tour was not Garin, but Hercules. On certain backs the yellow jersey can become Hercules's shirt of Nessus that sets its wearer on fire.

This ambiguous aspect of the Tour, where the rider who suffers is as much a hero as the winner, strongly appeals to the French imagination; witness the recent opus, "*Grandeurs et misères du Tour de France.*" It also explains the prestige even now enjoyed by Raymond Poulidor, who never wore the yellow jersey in 15 years of trying, and whose autobiography, "*Ma Vie sans le Maillot Jaune,*" is still leading the charts.

STAGE 8: SAINT-ÉMILION TO SAINTE-FOY-LA-GRANDE

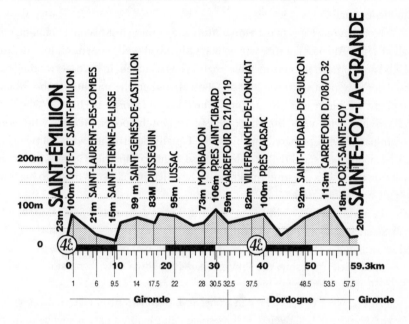

Gironde ─────────── Dordogne ──────── Gironde

This human side of the Tour draws Vincent. He would have dearly loved, were it still allowed, to have spent a day in the sag wagon. Even so, he has written pieces on the motorcyclists of the Tour caravan, one of whom fell the other day and smashed his face; on Jean-Jacques Fussien; on the downfall of a yellow jersey. A dangerous line, and one, he says, that is making his subjects a bit leery, as if he were the Tour albatross.

One can see how Inaudi and the Jobos might stimulate a Faulknerian pen. Since placing fifth in the 1976 world amateur championship, Inaudi has been plagued by injuries: a smashed hip in Paris-Roubaix; a skull concussion in the Tour du Limousin; a triple fracture in the ankle area during the riders' ski championship, which as a native Savoyard he was out to win. There was still another fall earlier this year in the Dauphiné-Libéré. But that wasn't all. On July 2, during the St. Amand to St. Germain leg, as Inaudi was helping escort back Mariano Martinez, who had punctured during Bruyère's breakaway, he collided at full speed with a Spanish rider, falling over him and landing heavily on his right shoulder. The impact was such that his front wheel shattered in eight pieces. By the time he arrived in St. Germain he was covered in blood and had lost 25 minutes.

That evening, the Jobo's voluntary doctor Sauger wrote out for Inaudi his first medical prescription — painkillers. The next morning, he asked his team if he could withdraw: "You don't want me around, I'll just slow you down." But the team was not to be persuaded. "We've started all together, and we're going to finish together," they told him, and all along the way from Evreux to Caen they did all they could to encourage him and make him forget his pain. "Still," Inaudi told Vincent, "ninety-six miles on one hand is no easy matter." Recently things have gone better, and on yesterday's entry to the Bordeaux track Inaudi came close to breaking away, earning Chany's plaudits. Now his hopes are involved with surviving until July 18's mammoth eight-pass stint when the Tour passes within three miles of his village.

After Suarez-Cuevas, it is Inaudi's turn three minutes later to mount the 10-foot-high yellow ramp in the middle of all the café awnings. Then comes the countdown and eagerly, like the sprinter he is, Inaudi catapults himself off in an effort to pick up all the momentum he can for the very steep cobblestone ascent out of St. Emilion. With his shoulder in plaster, Inaudi is obliged to take this fourth-category climb sitting down, rather than standing up *en danseuse* and pulling from side to side on his arms to gain thrust.

At the top of the hill, we enter what looks like any winding country road with here and there pretty hilltop farmhouses stuck out among the famous vineyards. The three-quarter tail wind helps Inaudi, but the course with its pitted road surface and constant barrage of hills is distinctly unfavorable to a rider who can't stand up on his pedals and power his way without having to change gears. At this hour, there are only a few nonchalant spectators: "Of course that's not Hinault, it's only Inaudi."

Inaudi seems certain to finish 15 minutes down and be disqualified when at the 18-mile mark he is passed by José Pesarrodona, a victim of the same first day motorcycle crash that dispatched Andiano. Inaudi recognizes the Spaniard for the potential rabbit that he is and spurs off after him, encouraged, it seems, by Pesarrodona.

Time-trial regulations stipulate that when one rider is caught by another, he must stay on the opposite side of the road so as not to take the other's wheel. Still Inaudi has an advantage in that he no longer has to concern himself with pace, gear changes, breathing (two inhalations for every three pedal revolutions), and all the other solitary concerns. Around a pond, past a swamp of five-pronged cat-tails, Inaudi wheels along in the Spaniard's cross-road shadow, and I'm thinking Inaudi is going to beat him on the final sprint, when Pesarrodona leaves him on the last hill. The rest of the way is mainly downhill, and the chunkier-bodied Inaudi manages to reach Ste.-Foy in almost a dead heat with Pesarrodona to post a time of 1:35:07, good for next-to-last place. But it's enough to keep him from being eliminated and Inaudi is jubilant on the phone: "No, Dad, I'm feeling all right ... I'll see you Tuesday week."

In posting his time, Inaudi may have been somewhat disadvantaged by his equipment. The titanium-framed bicycles that only the best can afford are some two pounds lighter. They can be so light because the rider has less call for brakes, since he is not biking in a group. Also, he does not need a rigid frame for the descents for the same reason. Spokes and wheels are lighter, with 3/10 tubing for wheels and 8-ounce tires — the point is winning and you take your chances on a puncture. Saddles are also pushed forward so that the rider is more over the pedals and thus able to push directly down instead of reaching out. Handlebars are also set lower, so that the back curves to accommodate wind resistance. Needless to say, the lightness gives the rider a psychological boost.

For most riders, the course itself remains an unknown. They have not reconnoitered it unless by car, which does not necessarily allow them to pick the right *derailleur* combination. No matter what you pick, you still have to be ox enough to keep the chain taut throughout the race, even though your leg muscles are permanently on the edge of the pain barrier. For Hinault and Zoetemelk, this means progressing 31.25 feet (9.5 meters) for each turn of the pedals on the flat, or 22 feet (6.7 meters) uphill. Some, like Laurent, favor a 54x12 top, which progresses him a giant 32 feet (9.75 meters) for each revolution. This problem of self-mastery, of not burning yourself out, is particularly acute in a course that begins with a direct uphill fourth-category climb over cobblestones. If you put too much into it, you are apt to have nothing left for the rest of the grind.

While riders like Pollentier and Maertens take the time to bike around the course and warm themselves up so their muscles are ready for that brutal first ascent, there are others like Hinault who, after an early-morning meal, prefer to catch an hour's sleep. He has a local teammate, Pierre-Raymond Villemiane, who has presented to him a verbal movie of the course. After two days of rather petulant behavior, this dozing-off augurs well for Hinault's confidence.

Then, 20 minutes before race time, Guimard wakes him at the Villemiane farm and drives him to the St. Emilion start. Bernard presents himself at the start with his bike of wafer-thin 3/10 tubing weighing slightly under 19 pounds and equipped with super-light 6-ounce tires. With the bad weather pulling the grit to the road surface, there is a risk of punctures. Talking about the tire choice afterward, Hinault said, "With tires like that you pass or you get a flat, and me, I passed." Others were not so fortunate, and Hinault's main rival, Pollentier, punctured at the midpoint while climbing a hill; to be delayed even longer by the new rule requiring the spare bike to be tied to the roof rather than held out of the door by the mechanic. By the time he had tightened his toe straps, he had lost at the very least a minute. Yet unluckier was Yves Hézard, who punctured twice within a few miles. Once more and he would have been out of the Tour. But then Pollentier and Hézard may not have been using three-year-old tires that they have aged themselves in their own cellars. At various points later in the race, Hinault might well have punctured in mountain situations where it could have cost him dearly. That he didn't speaks well for the qualities of his cellar.

Cycling briskly from one great *cru* to another, Hinault posted a time of 1:22:01, enough to catapult him into fourth place in the overall standings, 3:32 behind the new yellow jersey, Joseph Bruyère. Where Hinault won was in the last third of the race. At the 14th- and 23rd-mile marks, he had only the third best time behind Freddy Maertens; a second behind Pollentier at the first checkpoint — where he trailed Maertens by 19 seconds; and 7 seconds behind Bruyère, who had regained 19 seconds in those nine miles. But Hinault's forces are those of the black-haired badger that he ever-so-slightly resembles. In the last 14 miles, enormously stimulated, as he said, by the enthusiasm of the fans, Hinault put on an extraordinary performance, taking back 41 seconds from Bruyère, 55 seconds from a Zoetemelk who seems entirely recovered, and 1:22 from Maertens, whose final fade-out shows that he has some way still to go to recover his 1976 staying power. With this one stroke, Hinault has become in everybody's eyes the man to beat. Flandria's Fred De Bruyne said, "I wouldn't be surprised if Hinault reaches Paris a quarter of an hour ahead of the next man."

Not only did Bruyère's performance have the merit of keeping the issue in doubt until the very end, it was also, as the graph shows, a model of regularity. Bruyère's final weakening (in respect to Hinault) might have been less had he heeded Merckx and not opted for a gear ratio of 54x12 like Laurent. At this distance, it was taking a risk. But as Bruyère said, "When you're going well, you feel like putting on the biggest gear and seeing what you can do. Obviously the Tour has taken more out of me than I'd reckoned on. But I wanted to win the time trial. Last night, I called my wife in St. Rémy, nine miles outside Liège, and told her I'd be coming home if I won today, feeling I'd have left my mark on the race. With the yellow jersey, that's all changed. But I can't believe I'd have beaten Knetemann by well over three minutes. Something must be very fishy there."

For Knetemann, it must have seemed a case of the poisoned jersey. Did he wake up in the middle of the night and realize that this tunic, which he was not destined to hang on to anyway for more than a day or two longer, did not suit him? That he was Gerrie the winner of individual stages, and not Gerrie the yel-

Distance and time in Stage 8

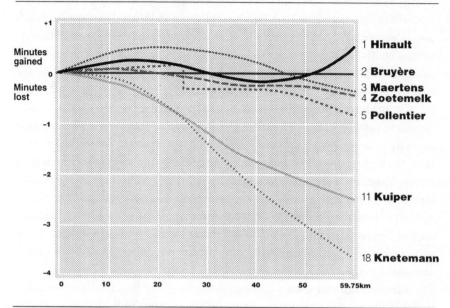

low jersey? The future world champion's race was one of physical horror: cramps, a throbbing head, and at one point actual vomiting. When he broke the finish line he was 4:11 behind Hinault.

John Wilcockson's accompanying graph throws an interesting light on Pollentier's performance *vis-à-vis* Hinault and Zoetemelk. Pollentier's is not really the meteoric miscalculation of Maertens. He does not even start as fast as Hinault. But one notices him bit by bit building up the pressure on Bruyère, and it's this momentum that his puncture clearly costs him. Thereafter he manages only to stay even with Bruyère for nine miles before tailing off decisively. Trailing Hinault now by almost 2 minutes, Pollentier has no choice but to go all out and keep attacking, probing each chink in Hinault's armor. It should make for a highly charged race.

Of those still in contention, the gravest doubts now concern Kuiper. Not a time trialist by build, he should still have been able to do as well as Zoetemelk, if not Pollentier. Instead, as the graph shows, he was never in the race, and were it not for the two-minute bonus from the team time trial he would be in serious trouble. But he knows the course better than anyone, and if the sun — his friend, we must remember — deigns to appear, he may be able to pick up where others falter.

For Thévenet, 4:37 behind Hinault, and for Van Impe 6:17 back, the race was the last cracking of the box. Admittedly, the course layout with its changes in direction and gradient, was not suited to the momentumless progress of the lightly built Lucien; but to speak, as his teammate Bruyère did, of a Tour full of rebounds, is begging the issue. The truth is that the Tour has come too soon for him.

As for Thévenet, the message is clear: One man's bordeaux is not another's burgundy. Unlike Van Impe, he has some title to being a specialist of the art, and if in anything resembling his 1977 form he would have finished near Hinault. To judge by his finish-line exhaustion Thévenet's health is fundamentally impaired, and it will not surprise many observers if he were to abandon the Tour after the first couple of days in the mountains.

On the virtual threshold of the mountains, a quick look at the overall table shows the good turn Hinault has done himself. Not only has he recouped in a single day all that he yielded in the team time trial, he now leads Zoetemelk by 37 seconds, Kuiper by 1:39, Pollentier by 1:42, Laurent by 2:13, Agostinho by 3:20, Galdos by 4:09, Wellens by 4:15, Thévenet by 5:07, Van Impe by 8:54 and Mariano Martinez by 9:06. In fact, of 106 starters, only 15 managed to finish within four minutes of Hinault. Any test of truth that eliminates so many is living up to its name.

Except for the last three, these are not very big margins in view of the mountains where spreads of 10 to 15 minutes in a day are common. It also discounts the special case of Bruyère who, after all, leads the Breton by 3:32. How long Bruyère will be able to keep himself in climbing fettle remains unclear — even to Bruyère, who has been parrying questions of this sort with a prudence not unworthy of a diplomat of the old school. But should there be one of those sudden storms that have always felled Bruyère in the past, Hinault will be there to pick up the falling fruit. But, after watching Knetemann, Hinault is probably sincere in hoping that his turn in the yellow jersey comes as late as possible.

Stage 8: St. Emilion to Ste.-Foy-la-Grande time trial

1	BERNARD HINAULT *(Gitane)*	1:22:01
2	Bruyère *(C&A)*	at 0:34
3	Maertens *(Flandria)*	0:56
4	Zoetemelk *(Mercier)*	0:59
5	Pollentier *(Flandria)*	1:22
6	Laurent *(Peugeot)*	1:33
7	Bossis *(Gitane)*	2:00
8	Vandenbroucke *(Peugeot)*	2:29
9	Agostinho *(Flandria)*	2:40
10	Wellens *(Raleigh)*	2:56
11	Kuiper *(Raleigh)*	2:59
12	Janssens *(C&A)*	3:01
13	Galdos *(Kas)*	3:12
14	Danguillaume *(Peugeot)*	3:35
15	Rouxel *(Mercier)*	3:51
16	Lubberding *(Raleigh)*	4:04
17	Le Guilloux *(Mercier)*	4:06
18	Knetemann *(Raleigh)*	4:11
19	Den Hertog *(Lejeune)*	4:18
20	Villemiane *(Gitane)*	4:18

Overall classification after Stage 8 (Yellow Jersey)

1	JOSEPH BRUYÈRE *(C&A)*)	37:58:58
2	Bossis *(Gitane)*	2:07
3	Knetemann *(Raleigh)*	2:56
4	Hinault *(Gitane)*	3:32
5	Zoetemelk *(Mercier)*	4:11
6	Le Guilloux *(Mercier)*	4:36
7	Maertens *(Flandria)*	4:48
8	Danguillaume *(Peugeot)*	4:58
9	Thaler *(Raleigh)*	5:05
10	Kuiper *(Raleigh)*	5:11

STAGE 9

Bordeaux to Biarritz

After this keg of truth, Saturday's 140-mile run across the pine barrens of the Landes and then down through the Basque country to Biarritz had one sovereign purpose: to ease us on to our appointed rest day before the Tour tackled the decisive sheep-and-goats phase of the program. That this first stopover occurred on a Sunday may have had less to do with piety, than with the fact that *L'Équipe* does not go to press then — what is an "Iliad" without its Homers? Despite its aristocratic past, Biarritz has always nourished a spot in its heart for this proletarian sport, as Hemingway observed long ago in some of the more mordant pages of *The Sun Also Rises*.

The sun may have risen, but the Bordeaux morning was fog-shrouded as we convened on the far side of the Gironde. However, Thillet had thought to provide us with a bit of Basque warmth in the person of a second car-mate, Johnny Ruau. He had also consulted some of our more experienced Tour colleagues. As I jumped with my three bags into the car the first question was, "Would you like some *confit de canard* and *lou magret*."

The Landes is sometimes thought of as the French Texas, for its oil refineries. Flat it is but with flowering heather, shoulder-high ferns and tall pines, not unattractive. Down distant driveways loom castles built in the low mission style, sign of the Spanish influence. Now and then one comes upon a black mysterious pool. It's the first truly villageless region we have encountered. The local industry, other than the refineries and forest products, is the raising of ducks for paté. This single-minded fattening leaves for local appetites a certain excess of highly perishable matter. Thillet assured me that the two-star restaurant he had in mind, on the sands of Paderenc, could well prove the gastronomic high point of the Tour.

Indeed it was: fish soup, skewered duck hearts, a *confit* baked in its own fat and served in a tureen; all plentifully washed down with a delicate, dry, clayey Paderenc, a wine that doesn't ship even as far as Paris. But as is often the case on these occasions, the Rabelaisan wit took precedence over even the food, from the moment our eyes lit on the waitress (of a brave, sprightly skinniness) to that last moment when a wife of one of the Tour directors, who had come in innocuously to reserve an evening table, found herself blushed out of the premises.

By the time we had got back from Paderenc, the sun had emerged and the Tour of the Crash became the Tour of the Cleavage, a suitable foretaste of those mountain gorges in the offing. Had any of us ever seen so many mostly bare breasts threatening a highway? In heels and straw hats, well-endowed women disputed priorities with bathing-trunked men as evidently proud of their own hanging bellies.

The effect of all this fleshly abundance on our traveling phallocracy may be imagined. Soon we were all shirtless, propped on the outside of our car windows (here and there a vigorous smashing of glass) driving straight at a bevy of beauties, or soliciting entries into the rear seat for our Radio Sud beauty contest. Who was to say that the improbable could not become something else than the impossible?

It was a setting made to order for Fussien. Earlier in the day, disturbed by a pace that a postman would have had no difficulty following, he had sprinted ahead to make a photograph of the dawdling pack. That would shame them! Now borrowing a pillow from some campers, he decided to align himself under a cypress, feigning a deep sleep. Despite the organizers' stated intention not to countenance such antics, Fussien was not cautioned, perhaps because on this first truly summery day Messrs Goddet and Lévitan had donned their dark glasses.

We miscalculated ever so slightly our re-entry, and when we got back to the highway there was the whole brightly jerseyed pack pedaling by, policemen's whistles blaring. We had to slip into the rear — annoying for Thillet, but for me a pleasant novelty, since it was like being on some coral reef among these larger-than-life, oh-so-visible rider-fish as they biked in and out among our two files. Johnny Ruau decided to palliate his friend's annoyance by finding us some armagnac, the obvious ingredient missing from our superb lunch. So we pulled up alongside Fussien's manager, Raphaël Geminiani, to see if that man of the region (dubbed the "Rifle," as much, one suspects, because of his nose — pure *commedia dell'arte* Pulcinello — as for the flamboyant way he shoots his wit) had any in his car. Gem had armagnac. He also had a very good bottle of Burgundian Mercurey. Thanking him quite properly, the gullet car moved up to Peugeot's Maurice De Muer; the sight of the riders with their water bottles was clearly encouraging us. De Muer understood the universality of thirst in such sunlight. He gave us a bottle of Johnny Walker Red Label with which to amuse ourselves. When we came back later, he had some coffee sympathetically ready. There was also salami, should we feel inclined to start again — what Tour belt can't be stretched a little further? Soon we were running a distribution service, ferrying and taking orders, with an immunity all the more pleasurable for all the police witnessing our progress.

Frolicking along here in the wake of the race gave me a way of sensing the power of the herd instinct; the utter panic when, with slightly less than an hour to go, back there behind their trees, word came to the defecating riders that the *peloton* had sailed without them. In and out of the cars, all along this beautifully tree-shaded road, we saw Gisiger, Guttierez, Dante Coccolo, and Wesemael scurrying, heads down, shoulders hunched over the handlebars, trying to limit the 5-minute loss that a slight inattention was about to cost them.

Meanwhile at the front a battle royal was being launched, all the more potent in that the previous five hours had been so lethargic. In the front ranks attempting breakaways were Legeay, Raas, Mathis, Vandenbroucke, Lubberding, Didier, Laurent, Teirlinck … and Elorriaga, Fernandez-Ovies, and Menendez — three Spaniards from the bottom of the general standings whose combative spirits had been revived by the nearby frontier. Arrayed against them were the Peugeot and Flandria troops, intent on keeping the door bolted long enough to assure a sprint finish. The Raleighs joined in as the occasion warranted, speeding up or trying to slow down the pursuit according to whether one of their own men was involved.

As usual, Raleigh's Jan Raas was the man to watch. Despite the surveillance, his attack with six miles to go looked unstoppable as he took a half-mile lead on to the highway leading to the Biarritz horse racing track. Then, as he started to climb the final ramp, a mysterious paralysis seized him; his legs were no longer churning, and he wouldn't have been able to stick to the pack if his teammates had not given him a hand. A sign of the same devil that had struck down Knetemann the day before?

As a result of his team's labors, Maertens was where he wanted to be — fifth behind Esclassan — when at the entry to the stadium Karstens pulled one of his patented death-dealing maneuvers, shoving a wheel between Maertens and the rider on Maertens's left. This time, it was Karstens who went down as Maertens somehow kept his balance, only to be upended when Karstens's bike rebounded into his path. Two of Maertens's cohorts, Tinazzi and Muselet, fell behind him along with Beyssens and Pescheux. Had the pack not been strung out by the hill approach there might have been more serious consequences.

The smell of his native soil had revived the courage of the veteran Basque (and only incidentally Spanish, as he made very clear) sprinter, Miguel-Maria Lasa. At the entry to the oval, with two turns still to go, Lasa and a somehow revived Raas scooted away, tailed by Esclassan's bodyguard, Danguillaume. Marc De Meyer had noticed Maertens's eclipse, and to save the family honor — and the green jersey points — threw himself into the chase. After bridging the gap in spectacular fashion, he appeared to have the victory in hand, when on the last curve Lasa's familiarity with these loose dirt surfaces, common in Spanish cycling, paid off as he slipped by Raas and De Meyer.

One might think Biarritz more inclined to Gilded Youth than to the followers of the Golden Fleece. But no sooner had Lasa triumphed than here we were being greeted by a troupe of Basque dancers, holding up skirts and wiggling petticoated knees.

All of this was a prelude to that night and the next day's rest stop. Most of it was to be passed on a narrow strip of sand flanked, on one side, by the Casino and, on the other, by Louis Napoleon's imperial palace; all those smiles circulating as if the sun had never before existed, except on them. Coming from the Viking north we felt this all rather keenly: sun, waves, bared flesh, jeweled earrings. It was our right and we pursued it in typical reporter fashion — Scotch, cognac, beer, Pernod — long into the honkytonk and blazing discothèque night. Next day, in honor of the sequence of yellow jerseys, Raleigh gave a sumptuous buffet around the swimming pool of the Victoria Hotel (a warm-up for their final bash at a Belle Époque garden restaurant on the Champs-Elysées). But I know of it by hearsay, unable to rise for the event. The traditional 5.30 p.m. soccer match between the French and foreign press seemed more within my time frame. In new red-and-white striped uniforms and cleats (ours to keep, naturally), two fierce sides took the field of the D'Aguilera stadium, intent on settling a score or two. A dirtier, more foul-mouthed game among more insistent *prima donnas* would be hard to imagine. There was not a decision of referee Reynaud Vincent's that was not subjected to the most acrimonious debate. Historical record shows that the foreigners triumphed 1-0, a score that might have been more but for some agile goalkeeping by substitute goalie Cyrille Guimard. While kicks flew and knees popped and paunches writhed in their various contorted positions, the central issue of any match's last half-hour — who is to win the brawl — remained in doubt up to the last whistle.

Biarritz to Pau

Now after Biarritz come the infamous and man-killing mountain passes where Tours, and sometimes even lives, are traditionally won and lost. With sufficient preparation, some of us might be able to pedal 150 miles a day over hill and dale. But mountains are another matter, and not even the loosest of gear ratios will keep us from clambering down from our bikes and walking. One is reminded that when educated gentlemen on the Grand Tour first penetrated the Alps, they deliberately veiled their eyes against this evidence of the earth's horrid irregularity.

In a competition, all this is further exacerbated. You have to be able to finish within a certain time of the winner, or be eliminated as half of the pack was last year at L'Alpe d'Huez. Racing here, with the body hunched so any sucking of air into the lungs becomes problematical, the suffering approaches the last rounds of a boxing match. For the Tour follower, there is nothing to do but shut up humbly. The silence is awesome, you want to weep, and the only way not to is to distract yourself by yelling encouragement and, if you are a spectator, running along and pouring water over their gasping heads.

The long march down from Leiden with its war of nerves had ended with the wine-country time trial. Now in a single week, moving always eastwards, the Tour would confront one by one the three principal mountain ranges of France: the Pyrenees, the Massif Central, and the Alps, ending Sunday at L'Alpe d'Huez near Grenoble. Then, after a second rest day, there would be next Tuesday's long eight-pass jolt across the Alps to the ski station of Morzine. None of these ranges are the same, and there are riders who do well in the Pyrenees only to fall apart in the Alps, and vice-versa (Kuiper notably).

To see it and enjoy the Bastille week national holiday fans will come from all over Europe and the furthest corners of the French hexagon. One will see them on Tuesday with their bicycles and camping gear picnicking among the snows of the

Tourmalet, at almost 7000 feet the highest of the Tour's passes. On Friday, Bastille day, there would be something like a million ranged along the volcanic track of the Puy-de-Dôme time trial. A certain portion would still be at the various passes of the next two days, waving pennants, hoses, and water bottles, or bucolically engaged spelling a hero's name with flowers in the snow.

The morning of our departure the news concerns the spectacular resignation of the Peugeot team doctor. His professional feelings have been ruffled by the addition to the entourage of a chiropractor — evidently a last-gasp effort by Thévenet to find some other solution for his cortisone-poisoned system. We, not to be outdone, have taken on just the man we need for the coming hostilities (including the L'Alpe d'Huez football match), the ex-European middleweight champion and the greatest French boxer since Marcel Cerdan, Jean-Claude Bouttier. Before becoming a fighter and becoming known for his little striped cap, his comparatively unmarked mug, his courage and his honesty, Jean-Claude had done some bike racing. A Tour that is one of the most open in years has him very excited. It also means that this time, in spite of Thillet's professional obligations, we may be able to see some actual pedaling.

On the Tour menu, this 120-mile toboggan run through the foothills of the Pyrenees to Pau was meant as a warm-up before hostilities truly commenced with Tuesday's ascension of the Tourmalet and Aspin passes, ending with a first-category 11-percent climb to the Pla d'Adet ski station above St. Lary-Soulan.

But warm-up it wasn't. After two days of sunny enchantment, here we were back in our more familiar gloom. Doubtless, this reassured the traditional minded: "It's been a great Tour up to now, let's keep it that way!" On the notion that the best defense is a good offense, Bruyère ordered his chief lieutenant, De Schoenmaecker, to set a good rattling pace. De Schoenmaecker obliged to such effect that by the end of the day such stalwarts as Knetemann, Thévenet, Sherwen and Hoban had taken a 13-minute drubbing.

Happily, the landscape was up to the rigors of the occasion: deep plunging ravines; bathing suits replaced, alas, with parkas; charming, red-on-white hilltop houses to stir the possessing eye; each of the two major passes shrouded in a white Purgatorial mist down which in five-foot visibility riders skidded, trembling and furious. Through all this, in a role that Bruyère himself had fulfilled for Merckx in other days, the broad-shouldered De Schoenmaecker pumped away at the head of an unnaturally elongated pack.

It was fearful. And it was enlightening. One saw extraordinary examples of courage. Joël Gallopin grimacing with pain from his plaster-set shoulder as he tried to climb his way one handed, his useless left hand hanging limp in front of the handlebars. At the Pagolle hill, a very steep, albeit third-category climb, we came upon Gallopin once more, the wrist no longer flopping across the handlebar, but held in against his chest, like a conventional broken arm. Finally on the seven-mile climb to the Marie-Blanque pass he gave in and abandoned the race. Already in the sag wagon were José Pesarrodona, the runner-up to Hinault in this year's Vuelta, and the Spanish national champion, Martinez-Heredia. That's almost as many abandons as in the previous nine legs.

It is to be feared, though, that it represents but the tip of the iceberg. On the first hairpin bends of the Pagolle pass, Thévenet was already in trouble, unable to hold the pace, his swollen face hunched, plainly asphyxiated over the handlebars. "It's just like the Luitel," he called out, "I can't seem to breathe."

For Thévenet, things might have been dire but for the drop down into the valley of Odiarp which allowed a momentary respite before the Tour tackled the Marie-Blanque. Very quickly, a group of 20 riders found themselves shed. Then it was once more Thévenet's turn. It was like watching a great tree being axed. At each hairpin stroke of the road — all mountains, mist, sunshine, flowers — the agony patently increased. Hands gripping the brake levers, seated on the little beak of his one-inch higher, mountain-elevated saddle, his chest up in order to breathe, and his lips grimacing, he pedaled on, inexorably losing ground. By the time he reached the sum-

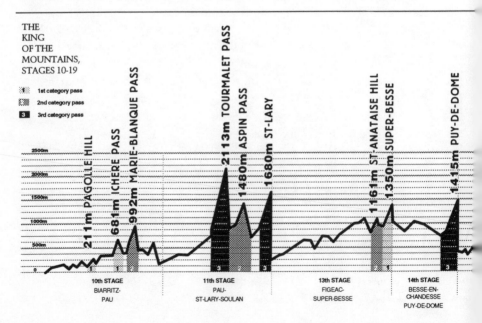

mit with its white mist and spectral crowd shouting out at him, "Nanard," he had lost 3:31. Shortly before on the upper reaches, his team car driver had made him stop, as much to calm his distress as to change the rear wheel. Meanwhile two team-mates, Guy Sibille and Régis Delepine, were waiting to escort him into Pau. But the man who finally rallied the Gascon capital, 12:54 behind the winner Henk Lubberding, was only a ghost of the real Thévenet who had long since departed the race, swallowed up in the mists of the Marie-Blanque.

Meanwhile, ahead of Thévenet on the Marie-Blanque, a battle of enormous interest was being waged among the leaders. In the fore were Pollentier, Hinault and Zoetemelk. The differences with which they breasted the summit line — Pollentier 6 seconds ahead of Hinault, with Zoetemelk trailing by another 4 seconds — are no real reflection of their comparative merit. Pollentier's lead came only because he was willing to sprint for the top to cop the 15 mountain prize points, an issue that did not immediately concern his two rivals. Just behind, separated at 10-second intervals like the points of an accordion were Martinez, Kuiper and Agostinho.

Martinez found the thinner air of the top more to his liking than the first switchbacks, where he seemed to be struggling. Then 50 seconds back came Bruyère and Galdos, followed at 1:05 by Van Impe and Laurent, and at 1:15 by the balding Villemiane.

With Bruyère so far back, we were, in effect, witnessing an attempted seizure

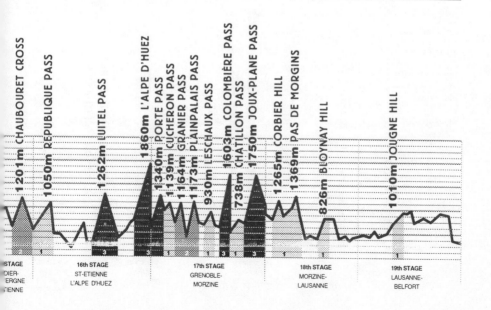

STAGE 10: BIARRITZ TO PAU

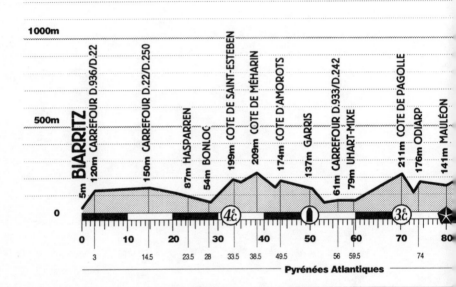

of power by the advance trio. The hold-up might well have carried the day, even to the extent of divesting Bruyère of his yellow jersey, but for the 20-second bonus provision. Neither Zoetemelk nor Pollentier is a speed merchant, and while neither is Hinault, the two of them were sufficiently suspicious not to want to help pad Hinault's lead. But it shows the measure of their ultimate self-confidence that they did not feel the need to risk whatever had to be risked to steal a march on Bruyère & Co. As Pollentier and Zoetemelk let up warily, Hinault had the choice of giving up, or going on alone with 12 miles in which to wrest the 20-second bonus. A Merckx might well have been tempted to play a lone hand. Hinault, who had too much to risk, decided not to.

Zoetemelk's and Pollentier's prudence was confirmed when Hinault copped the Esquillot Hill's hot-points sprint. But, led by Maertens, the best descender in the pack, a group of 22 had by now collected — a number just sufficient to deprive Hinault of his bonus.

On the way in, there was a moment of panic when Bruyère punctured. But

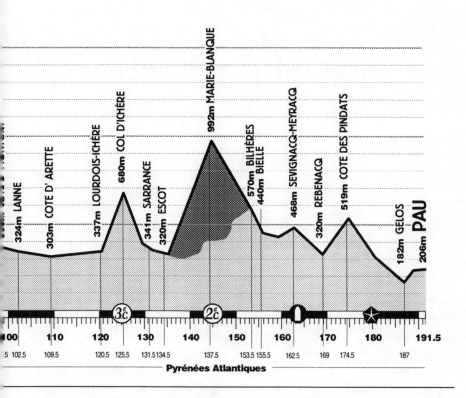

Pyrénées Atlantiques

abetted by Van Impe and Ludo Loos, and with the help of a down grade, he quickly caught up. Soon thereafter, Loos took a horrid fall, finishing in the company of De Schoenmaecker and a dozen others, 3:03 back. For Bruyère it had been a hard day, and odds are that the yellow jersey will feel even heavier about his shoulders by the time he reaches Pla d'Adet tomorrow.

Maertens was denied a third sprint victory through some astute Raleigh maneuvering. This time it was Raas who distracted the Flandria sentries with an attempted bolt four miles from Pau. When Agostinho and Pollentier finally caught up with him after a two-mile pursuit, there was no one left to bar the door as Lubberding attacked in turn. The white jersey, who gets a cow after each important victory, spurred off to cross the finish line 30 seconds ahead of the pack. Behind him, Jobo's Patritti nosed out Raas for second place, as Maertens got caught in the box and had to settle for fifth between Villemiane and Bossis.

STAGE 11

Pau to St. Lary-Soulan

As an introduction to the art of climbing, Monday's Biarritz to Pau stage had more than lived up to its billing. Tuesday, the Tour was to affront the ring of fire, beginning with the Tourmalet, going on to the Aspin pass, and ending with a high mountain finish at the Pla d'Adet ski station.

Going over the Tourmalet pass is a bit like holding a bicycle race on Mount Rainier. This year, the snow has been such that troops have had to be called in to clear the road for the Tour. With the access roads closed to traffic from 10 a.m., many fans are obliged to camp out on the mountain — along with a German television crew filming this strange pilgrimage.

These difficulties are minor compared to what the Tour encountered when it first entered this wilderness in 1910. During the first six years of its existence, the Tour had been obliged to follow the railway linking Toulouse to Bayonne or Bordeaux. By 1910, however, the advance in car design offered a new flexibility. Instead of circling up from Marseille and around the Pyrenees via Toulouse, the car made it possible to go due west from Perpignan to Bayonne with an overnight stop at Luchon. When this idea was first presented by Alphonse Steines, a cycling enthusiast and topography expert, Desgrange's reaction was as usual negative. But, after thinking it over, he decided it was the publicity gimmick the Tour needed and he announced that the four giants of the Pyrenees (Peyresourde, Aspin, Tourmalet, Aubisque) would be scaled in the course of a "colossal" 203-mile Luchon to Bayonne stage.

One can imagine the amazement with which the public learned that the Tour was going into a range of mountains that even as late as 1947 Jean Robic, the eventual Tour winner, called "the circle of death." The announcement provoked an immediate outcry from people of the region who thought fit to inform the organizer that the supposed roads were only mule-tracks used for carting timber down to the sawmills. With a month to go before the race, Desgrange sent Steines to reconnoiter the two mountain passes and see whether the cyclists could get through.

At Bagnères-de-Bigorre on the east side of the Tourmalet, Steines hired an old chauffeur-driven rattletrap. Somehow or other they got it past Ste. Marie-de-Campan and within two miles of the summit when they had to stop because of the snow. Here, Steines sent back the car, instructing the driver to go by way of Lourdes and meet him on the other side. With a shepherd boy to accompany him, he set out in the twilight. Then after an hour came a moment when the boy refused to go further for fear of the Spanish bears known to inhabit the summit. With nothing on his feet but ordinary shoes, Steines trudged on and on into the night, sinking in further and further as he went, but somehow missing the precipices. The descent was, of course, harder still, but Steines groped his way down until he came to the bed of a stream, which he guessed to be the Bastan. Following it by ear as it ran under the snow he reached the village of Barèges at 3 a.m., guided the last part of the way by the lights that the villagers, warned by the chauffeur, had turned on to welcome the mad stranger.

Here accounts differ. One tradition insists that after being fêted by the villagers and inquiring about the summit road, Steines sent Desgrange a telegram, "Crossed Tourmalet stop road usable." In his published version, Steines says he did not get in touch with Desgrange until after he had seen the Aubisque, which was free of snow (it is 1300 feet lower than the 6936-foot Tourmalet). He then telephoned him from the local road engineer's office with the bad news that the Aubisque road would have to be patched if the Tourmen were to cycle over it in a month. After some haggling between the engineer's office, Desgrange, and the local authorities, who thought the Tour crazy to be spending money on a road no one was ever going to use again, the Aubisque was given a face lift costing 600 old francs.

Fortunately, when the Tour came by a month later, it was dry weather. Still, Desgrange and the officials waiting at the Aubisque pass had reason to fear the worst when, after some time, the riders had failed to show up. Finally, one begrimed figure, walking beside his bicycle, trudged into sight. But he was in no state to respond to the officials' questions for news of the pack. A quarter of an hour later, a second man arrived, the eventual Tour winner Octave Lapize. Asked for his comments, he simply shook his fist at the Tour officials and yelled, "Assassins!" Any other man than Desgrange might have felt taken aback. But *L'Auto's* 1910 circulation had already risen by more than three million, and a legend sprang up of a new race of *Supermensch*, the Giants of the Road. As any child knows, they live in the mountains.

There is no hard and fast rule to distinguish a Tour giant. Watching them as they checked into the parking lot of the Pau Nautical Stadium, one might even have thought the term something of a misnomer. Mountain men come in all sizes from flea to condor, a bestiary that does not necessarily exclude the odd archangel, color of snows, wheeling effortlessly away into purest solitude. Among today's climbers, the chamois — *genre* Pollentier, Zoetemelk, Martinez — is at the moment in most plentiful supply. Seen at close range with that bony face, half-bald head and vari-cose-veined legs, he is not the prettiest of creatures. Even his climbing is jerky, all short, aggressive, forward hops, rather than the winged soaring aloft of the true eagle. This may be why at a distance it may be possible to confuse him with the swarthy, generally Spanish, flea, who, it will be remembered, also hops. Nonetheless, the climber is, as far as cycling goes, a rare and very much prized animal, and commands a salary commensurate with this status.

The trouble with mountains is that once you climb them you still have to come

STAGE 11: PAU TO SAINT-LARY-SOULAN (Pla-d'Adet)

down, and there things tend to even out. The Eagle of Toledo, Federico Bahamontes — how much there is in a name! — a rider capable of soaring through the Tourmalet, Aspin and Pla d'Adet in a single 100-mile swoop, was also known, having left everyone else in the dirt, to ask for an ice cream cone when he reached his summit. There, he would sit staring off into the distance and moodily licking it until the first of the goats came into view. There was bravura in this posturing obviously. But mingled with it was his wish to postpone the matter of the descent.

All the qualities that help in climbing — lightness of build, long leg muscles — are apt to turn against a rider trying to corner on a wet, pebble-lined switchback at 50 mph. In these circumstances, a rider needs a low center of gravity, a sprinter's bike-handling abilities, and a lot of courage to take advantage of the laws of aerodynamics. Merckx could in his younger days climb appreciably, but many of his great escapes came on the descents, where he would dare what no one else could.

The Pyrenees stage could be expected to bring both mountain aspects to the

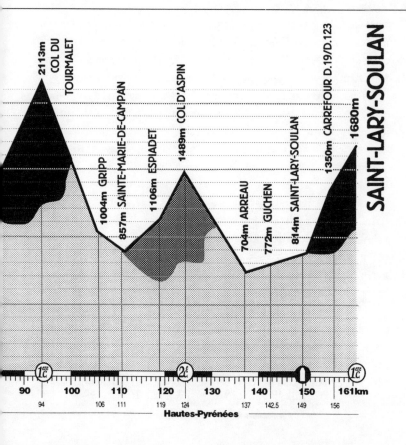

fore: a 20-mile climb to the Tourmalet pass, the last eight being very steep; a *schuss* down on Ste. Marie-de-Campan, followed by a second climb on the shorter side of the Aspin pass. But the very long, steep descent on the east side, along with a short eight-mile traverse, would favor a regrouping of the better elements before the extremely steep, 7.5-mile climb from St. Lary-Soulan to Pla d'Adet.

For the Tour's giants, today's run, conducted under a pea-soup fog, promised another infernal ghost battle of the summits. First, to tax the systems, a very long false-flat in the direction of the miracle town of Lourdes, where, it was to be hoped, something of the Virgin's powers would rub off on Bernadette Hinault and Bernadette Thévenet. For a rider, a 40-mile false-flat can be as wearing as a climb. Climbers work on springiness. They set a loose gear ratio and make their legs churn, whereas on a false-flat the rider has to power his way along on a big chainring as if it were not an uphill grade. Eventually, all that begins to tell on the stomach muscles and on the breathing.

For us, though, the road is something other than agony as, past Lourdes, it enters the picturesque valley of the Gave de Pau, a green river with bubbling rapids set in wild beautiful forest land. Charming, black-capped shepherds, women in colorful scarves, wave out at us. For the first time, we are joined by touring buses bearing the faithful aloft, grim things to scoot around since it is our intention to get ourselves a picnic of local cheese and mountain sausages. Past Argelès-Gazost, where later Barry Hoban takes the hot-points sprint, we begin to run into the true fanatics — the self-pedaling breed — armed with radios, camping gear, picnic material. Hard to imagine them in the inclement weather of the upper slopes, squatting like miners in their teepee capes.

Between Argelès and Alphonse Steines's Barèges, the road rises 2600 feet in a little less than 13 miles. At Barèges the first loops appear as it gets down to the serious business of hoisting itself 2800 feet in seven miles. Here, Thévenet decides to loosen his toe clips and abandon the Tour: a victim of the terrible rhythm at which the pack has taken the foothills.

A little higher, in the van of the first climbing group, while everybody else is hanging face down over his handlebars, a fascinating conversation is going on between Mariano Martinez and Michel Pollentier. Martinez, who is churning at only 70-percent capacity due to his untreatable bronchitis, is proposing to help Pollentier in his quest for the yellow jersey, if his former teammate will relinquish the mountain prize. It is the sort of conversation Martinez has been dreaming of all his career — between equals, cards fully on the table — though how he can imagine that his Jobos can be of service to anyone boggles the mind.

Pollentier rejected the offer of collusion, not out of any overweening sense of principle, but because he was himself almost as poor as Martinez and needed the Grand Prix for the post-Tour *criterium* doors that it automatically unlocked. The man who had dashed all over the place between Leiden and Biarritz to help Maertens secure his sprint victories now saw the mountain prize as a perfect focus for his excess energy. Also, a stepping stone to the ultimate conquest, since the quest of the crimson jersey with the white holes gave him the option of converting each summit sprint into a Merckx-type downhill breakaway. As William James long ago taught, progress is a matter of establishing routines that become second nature; the handle on a door that you turn to enter a room; after a while you no longer have to think about it, you just walk in. It was precisely this freedom of action that Pollentier was not about to negotiate.

But a repetition of the Marie-Blanque's spectral battle in the mist was not to be. Rather paradise, when a third of the way from the summit the sealing layer of mist blew away to reveal a grand treeless vista on the order of some Western national park, all snow and jagged crests and glacier lilies and black brooks, up through which the road worked in one, then another large, white-banded loop. The publicity caravan had long since been by, and the spectators were all in visored caps, gray-and-rainbow-striped C&A, orange-and-carmine Raleigh, blue-and-gold Gitane. They had also probably stocked up on free samples of cigarettes, soap, ballpoint pens, along with their *L'Équipes*. On the grass margin, between sheer cliff and road, their vehicles were parked. A few more inches one way and they would have jutted on to the Sacred Road and been ordered out by the gendarmes. Six inches the other, and the car, or a part of it, would be over the brink.

Most of the spectators were on the meadows between the loops, jousting with their sausages, or culling another wine bottle from a favored stream. A burst of excitement, "Les voilà," sends us all scurrying to the edge of the road. But they are still a 15-minute gulp below, and all we can clearly make out are Alain De Carvalho and Christian Seznec, who have separately struck out. With three hours of the race still to go, these are not necessarily full-scale breakaways.

To honor the dead, the organizers have strewn quite a bit of gold on the far side of the Tourmalet pass in the form of two sprint primes: the first at St. Marie-de-Campan in memory of the Tour founder, Henri Desgrange; the second, five miles later, at Espiadet, commemorating the 1907-8 Tour winner, Lucien Petit-Breton, who learned his *métier* in the Argentine and was killed in a fighter plane crash in World War I. Seznec's breakaway may also give a clue to Zoetemelk's battle plan. With three good climbers as bodyguards, he can well afford to delegate Seznec ahead to pick up the booty and serve as a potential escort, should he be able to break away from his surveillance.

Loping fluently, the giraffe-like Breton soon catches De Carvalho. Working together, their lead grows from 24 seconds to 35 seconds, at which point Seznec abandons De Carvalho to strike out on his own. Further down the slope, De Carvalho's teammate, the young Parisian Van Vlaslaer, last the day before at Pau, decides to unclip his shoes. Bruyère has already dropped off the lead group, and is in considerable difficulty at the head of a second group two minutes back of Hinault & Co., who are inexorably closing in on Seznec. Then Van Impe punctures. But Merckx in the team car has to stay with Bruyère, and by the time Van Impe's wheel is changed he is below even Bruyère's group. He catches that, takes a few deep gulps of the rare air, and is off on his own — a judgment, one might think, of Bruyère's chances of ever hooking on to that disappearing wagon.

Meanwhile, just under the summit, a jilted Martinez hurtles forward, only to be picked up after a short chase by Pollentier, Zoetemelk and Kuiper. Watching the battle a turn below me, among the shrillings of the police motorcycles, anxious that we will be overtaken on the descent, I am struck by the difference in speed between these first people and those in the behind groups. After almost 20 miles of climbing they still look as if they were on an ordinary road.

Pollentier emphasizes his determination by copping the summit laurels by eight seconds over Martinez and Hinault, 11 seconds over Zoetemelk, 31 seconds over Kuiper and Seznec. Bruyère is in 20th position, three minutes back, while another nine-man group with De Schoenmaecker, Villemiane and Van Impe, is a further half-minute behind. (On the *schuss*, Seznec overtakes Pollentier at Ste. Marie-de Campan to win the $700 Desgrange prime.)

In Ste. Marie, Thillet points out to me a historic monument of the Tour, an old blacksmith's forge once patronized by Eugéne Christophe, the first man ever to be awarded the yellow jersey. At that time, you not only had to finish the Tour on the mount you had started with, you also had to repair it yourself, even if it meant jogging, bike over the shoulder, five miles down the Tourmalet to Ste. Marie and welding it back together yourself. At the time of his accident. "Cri-Cri" was leading the Tour by a seemingly invincible 20-minute margin. By the time he had shaped the piece of metal and welded it on (under the watchful eyes of the *commissaires*, and with the illegal help of a 7-year-old boy who worked the bellows), he had lost two hours. But Christophe, who was to ride in 11 Tours between 1906 and 1925, a record time span, was not a man to admit defeat. His mount repaired, he hopped on and, in the spirit of the Tour, pedaled off, only to be docked an extra 10 minutes by the *commissaires* for having allowed the bellows to be worked by another.

Below the blacksmith's forge, just as a large chasing party — singlehandedly towed by Bruyère — is about to make its junction, Michel Laurent decides to break away. But here in the mountains, riders are rarely allowed to go away all by themselves, and Wellens and Nilsson tag along just to see how the new Peugeot leader is pedaling. Despite the unwanted attention, Laurent manages to cop the $700 Petit-Breton prime. Leading all the way, with now only Wellens on his wheel, Laurent is first at the Aspin summit, and by the end of the descent they hold a 1:30 lead over a 30-rider chasing group.

The 10-mile drop into the far valley is a squealing nightmare, riders like forest monkeys shooting under the trees all around us. Even with a head start, there is no way for a car to hurtle its way clear of them. And a skid on a single oil-slick can put them into a ravine, as has so often happened in past Tours. One thinks of Roger Rivière, a week from a probable victory, who plummeted off, never to race again. Here, what's amazing is the way they can pass, three or four together, between the cars. There is one sky-and-mountain shirted Teka, Andres Oliva, whom we keep catching only to see him *schuss* off again. It's what boat hands must feel among a party of dolphins.

By now Laurent, under the advice of Maurice De Muer, has seen the folly of his single effort and dropped back. Then, outside St. Lary, both he and Zoetemelk make the serious mistake of overestimating themselves as they change bicycles, Zoetemelk switching from a 42-tooth chainring to a more powerful, but harder to pedal 44. With the 30 strongest riders preparing to attack the ramp, it's immensely exciting: we know, everybody knows, it's all about to be decided, clots of time, like snowflakes, falling all around them.

Determined not to put up with the ridiculous fear of the Aspin climb, Mariano Martinez launches the assault. But the bluff, if such it is, encourages Zoetemelk. The Dutchman's attack, with only Pollentier at his side, dynamites the pack. Already 30 yards back is Hinault, with Martinez on his rear wheel, unwilling to stick his nose any further than he has to out of that particular window. The rest of the pack behind them is splintered into fragments, falling into each other's shadow, trying to find a rider to pace them. Wiser is Bruyère, determined to follow Merckx's advice and mount at his own clip; slowly for the first part, then, as his body adjusts to the very harsh demands, gradually stepping up the pace; a practice in which his time-trialist's training serves him in good stead.

We, too, try not to panic, content to inch our own way up in their wake. In a few miles, it will be possible to honk our way by them, inspecting each colored blot in turn before passing on to the next. Or perhaps escorting a favored rider, as he does on his own wheels the very same beautiful pull-back.

Meanwhile for four miles, Pollentier lets Zoetemelk carry the attack, turning around from time to time to see how Hinault is hanging on. The French champion represents for both of them an unknown. There is no strategy in this, just a brutal flinging-down of the gauntlet: "Can you follow me?"

At this point, with Hinault using his lower sprocket to generate power and slowly, inevitably, gain back his lost ground, Pollentier decides to attack on his own. Leaving Zoetemelk, who may well have overestimated his forces in making the change of sprocket, Polio (as the Breton calls Pollentier) sprints off. Elbows flailing, legs pumping furiously, balding head visible now without the hurled-away cap, he looks as completely askew as it is possible to look on a bicycle without falling. Whereas Hinault, climbing behind him, his breathing rhythm perfectly synchronized to each regular turn of the pedals, is a model of composed determination, a fox running a hare into the ground. Two miles from the summit, Pollentier wisely lets up, to join the queue behind a Hinault determined now to put as much distance as possible between himself and Bruyère.

But Tours are not won only with legs and head. Sometimes money enters in. Behind Hinault, Martinez is having another of his famous conversations, only this time it is with Hinault's manager, Cyrille Guimard. Guimard, who has earlier turned down Martinez's bid for a job with Renault-Gitane, is asking Martinez what he wants in return for letting Hinault win. A quick calculation, and Martinez spits back $1200 a month — or triple his present salary with Jobo. *Impasse,* presumably. Now, with slightly less than a mile to go, Martinez decides that the time for seven years' revenge has come. Unlike Hinault, he has climbed here in the 1976 Tour and knows the layout: 350 yards down, 200 flat, and a very hard 350 uphill (Hinault must think it's *all* uphill). With Hinault plugging along on sheer determination, and with Pollentier and Zoetemelk in no state to do anything, Martinez thinks, "Why not me?" Despite his lack of speed, he spurts off, surviving a near-collision with an official car on the last curve, to finish 20 yards ahead of Hinault and Pollentier, with Zoetemelk a distant fourth, 200 yards back.

If the stage has another winner it's Bruyère, an example if there ever is one of the yellow jersey's ability to transform its wearer. In 1976, he lost 17 minutes on the climb to Pla d'Adet; this time, he knocks it down to a mere 2:32, enough to conserve the precious tunic by 1:05 over Hinault. Never in his whole life has Bruyère been in such agony — both on the Tourmalet and again on the final climb. Yet he knows that his survival here is simply a stay of execution. "Anyone who weighs as much as me," he tells us, "is going to have trouble on the big hills. A pass like the Aspin I can manage, but when you know what's coming in the Alps and the Puy-de-Dôme, right away you don't kid yourself. This is a really hard Tour, and I'm just trying to honor my calling as best I can. But don't ask any more of me."

The merit of Bruyère's gutty achievement is made more understandable if one realizes that his time makes him a virtual eighth alongside Galdos and Raymond Martin, with Kuiper and Agostinho a minute ahead of him, and Seznec a slightly superior 10 seconds. It's as if all of a sudden on some high peak one were to discover a big horned antelope among a herd of chamois. No matter how unnatural the vision, it still can be, for a spectator, rather gratifying.

Almost rivaling the heroic battle of the tenors are the spectators of the Pla d'Adet. Like people at a zoo they must participate, hysterically running back and forth with their caps, their replenished water bottles and various other dunking equipment. They had their favorites, and burly De Schoenmaecker, whose legs were fiercely, beautifully churning like a small climber, let it be known that even Belgians could appreciate some of these ministrations. But I remember one pot-bellied marvel of energy who, with wonderful impartiality, insisted on sprinting the same 100 feet with whoever came into view.

Among the riders I'm impressed by: white-jerseyed Henk Lubberding, grimacing and biting his lip as he pedals all alone with the most harmonious of styles. And Villemiane, bald-headed, grinning, his legs churning faster and faster the higher we get, until it looks like one of those scenes in a movie where everyone else is going backwards. There are real disappointments, too, like Laurent, obviously fagged by his solo exertions, who finishes four minutes back. At the other end of the scale the little bull, Agostinho, red-shirted, black-haired, forging ahead like Hinault on sheer power to jump into a surprising sixth place in the overall standings.

For the riders, a second three-hour race down to Tarbes still lay in the offing. The first stretch of it went smoothly enough: on the ski lift with their bike and a satchel containing their personal effects, down to St. Lary; the one way of getting off the mountain at that hour. After a quick shower by the town swimming pool, they were hustled into one of the buses the Tour had set aside for them.

A 55-mile journey remained on a road full of heavy traffic where there was no possibility of making good time. Despite the drivers' efforts, it was not exactly a pleasure party. The bus radio got on Raas's nerves to the point that he asked for it to be turned off. Elsewhere, Kuiper and Hinault were making efforts to sleep, Kuiper in spite of his down-beaten air actually succeeding. But the prize for *sans-*

gêne went to the clown, Karstens, sacked out right in the aisle, and after the first few miles fast asleep.

At a window, Charly Rouxel sat, indulging himself in one of those fisherman's reveries, all possible in two years' time when he retires. Right next to him and across from us was his fellow Norman, Jacky Hardy, who had just come in last, 26:09 behind Martinez. "What a stage!" Hardy was saying, "I wouldn't have begged off for anything in the world. Can you imagine dying there, arms out in a cross over the bicycle?"

Those not asleep were poring over their Tour schedules, which showed a 7:35 a.m. start tomorrow. "We're going to have to get up at 4:30," Rouxel said, "and there are those like me who won't be through their massage before 11 p.m. That does not make for much sleep on the eve of a race consisting of two half-stages. But we wanted to come on the Tour, and here we are...."

We of the press did not have it all that much easier. After plunking me in a village 20 miles outside of Pau the night before (from where I had to hitch-hike back on my own), the press service decided to put me and John Wilcockson in a village even further away. With no one to take me from Tarbes, should I be able to get there, I had no choice but to accompany Thillet to Auch, where he had a 10 p.m. interview to record. At 100 mph in the dusk, it was the most frightening journey I've ever made. But with the Tour not due to pass Auch until 9:45 next morning, we were able to get more of a normal sleep.

Stage 11: Pau to St. Lary-Soulan

1	MARIANO MARTINEZ *(Jobo)*	5:47:26
2	Hinault *(Gitane)*	at 0:05
3	Pollentier *(Flandria)*	0:19
4	Zoetemelk *(Mercier)*	1:28
5	Agostinho *(Flandria)*	1:28
6	Kuiper *(Raleigh)*	1:29
7	Seznec *(Mercier)*	2:21
8	Galdos *(Kas)*	2:30
9	Martin *(Mercier)*	2:31
10	Bruyère *(C&A)*	2:32

Overall classification after Stage 11 (Yellow Jersey)

1	JOSEPH BRUYÈRE *(C&A)*	56:19:30
2	Hinault *(Gitane)*	at 1:05
3	Zoetemelk *(Mercier)*	1:58
4	Pollentier *(Flandria)*	2:47
5	Kuiper *(Raleigh)*	4:08
6	Agostinho *(Flandria)*	6:48
7	Maertens *(Flandria)*	6:25
8	Martinez *(Jobo)*	6:34
9	Laurent *(Peugeot)*	7:15
10	Galdos *(Kas)*	7:39

Tarbes to Valence d'Agen
Valence d'Agen to Toulouse

After the triumph of the summits, the descent back to everyday earth had us all geared up for disappointment. All that elation translated into another morning's aching limbs, that unwillingness to rise we all know. But rise the riders must in a three-hour-distant Tarbes for an insanely scheduled 7:30 a.m. start, so that a market town by the name of Valence d'Agen may have the honor of hosting a half-day stage. In the offing a day later is a second early-morning transfer of two hours by train from Toulouse to Figeac. Against this state of affairs the riders staged the first strike in Tour history. A race that was impossibly getting better, day by day, had climbed another summit.

It has been argued that these transfers help intensify a race by eliminating dead spots. But the riders' sleep invariably suffers, and dead legs don't make for an animated race. For their part, the organizers seem to have been aware of a possible letdown. To stimulate the pack, they had announced a special $2000 prime to go to the most combative rider of the day.

The Tourmen were not striking against the physical hardships of the race. Long stages and mountains make giants, and that creation is the Tour's peculiar gift — one that makes arriving on the Champs-Elysées a proud achievement. Rather, they were objecting to the senseless exploitation of a course that has more the aspect of a giant automobile rally than a bike race; one in which the "sweat gang" of an earlier inhumanity has been degraded into the status of freaks in a traveling road show.

A number of signs indicate that Tourmen are approximately where tennis players were 10 years ago — on the verge of a major breakthrough. But the touring tennis player of that era had no professional pretensions. He was frankly a bum, playing for expense money and whatever silver trophies he could melt down.

Today's riders, instead, have let themselves be conned into the notion that they are pros, ready and willing to sprint after every two-bit prime. When a rider retires after a five- to six-year pro career, he will have injuries to cope with for the rest of his life, and he may well die far ahead of the national average. Meanwhile, as an average pro, he draws a nine-month salary of perhaps $600 a month. On the Tour, he has only to turn his head to see 20 of us parasites for each rider, all better paid. One can talk about professional obligations; but only when the wage slave has been minimally certified as such.

There *was* a strike and, except for one early moment of confusion when Guy Sibille felt obliged to go after a fleeing Andres Oliva and wrestle him to the ground, the riders conducted themselves with *brio:* the yellow jersey and the national champions in the front line of a slowly pedaling phalanx that was to arrive in Valence an hour and three-quarters late. There were brief snoozes under trees, simulated crashes by Fussien, Knetemann and Bertin in the forbidden manner, and at the first hotpoints sprint at Fleurance (the starting point of the 1979 Tour), the riders unanimously descended from their mounts and dragged the poor beasts by the horns across the line. The organizers replied by suspending the prize money for *"manque de combativité totale."* Not at all deterred, the riders repeated the gesture at Valence d'Agen before the mayor and the TV cameras.

For the most part, the sight of these terraced centaurs provoked a sympathy in the crowd, delighted at history being made before it. But the strike incensed Monsieur Baylet, the Valence d'Agen deputy mayor. He wanted his sprint-finish blood and his moment of TV glory, and no offer to return to the town its prize money was going to mollify him. As far as he was concerned, it was six months' work down the drain.

Equally scandalized were the Tour media. To virtually a man, we took the strike as a breach of our mutual support contract — a sideshow getting in the way of our own main event. It was perfectly clear why the good people of Valence had invited the Tour to their fair city: so that we might give our gourmet seal of approval to the local wares. What Tour waistline can't let itself out further under free persuasion? The *buffet campagnard* of sausages, pizza, chicken, apple trifle and the celebrated prunes might not have met half-star standards; but bread and butter is bread and butter, and who were the riders to say that Valence d'Agen wasn't worth the detour! It was ridiculous to maintain that neither the riders nor their managers had ever been consulted about the course. They had their contract, and if they did not feel like living up to it, they should not have left Leiden. As for the loss of sleep caused by transfers, what rider is not willing to drive all night to reach another of his precious criteriums?

Before today's strike, people were asking if the Tour riders had a boss. Today, that was answered in a way many would prefer to ignore. His name is Hinault, and there are things he is plainly out to rectify, the insanities of split stages and an over-crowded schedule among them. Doubtless, there will be local apologies claiming, despite Hinault's earlier pronouncements, that he was not one of the ringleaders. But for a future star, who wants to be all things to all people, it shows what has been deemed a want of taste. A young man who can let himself be maneuvered so is hardly mature enough to win the Tour de France. For my own part, I find it highly amusing to see both the French and the foreign Tour press equally determined to give Hinault the verbal lambasting he so deserves. After all, there are things that come before mere pride of country, such as a free lunch!

The afternoon start did not obviously get under way at its appointed 2:30 p.m. as the organizers originally threatened. But a half-hour later was deemed not unreasonable, and the riders went at their 60 miles with a briskness that suggested they had a certain confusion to clear up. An honest strike against unhealthy work conditions was one thing; shirkers they were not.

The first at the helm was, naturally, Bernard Hinault, who was allowed to indulge himself for a few miles in the fantasy of an escape. But with the pack pedaling at a determined 26 mph, we had to wait for the entry by the Toulouse stadium to get the usual last-minute pyrotechnics. Legeay, Gauthier, Mathis, Kelly, Wesemael and Lubberding all flashed onto the TV screen only to have their sortie digested by the pursuing mob. It was like watching a brilliant dessert, baked alaska, *crêpes flambées*, being lit for just that instant of color, of flaming speed, before being followed by those well-worn names, *cognac* Jacques Esclassan, *marc* Maertens, *champagne* Raas.

Here at Toulouse in almost a foregone conclusion, local rider Esclassan triumphed before a clearly intimidated Maertens. A sprinter may have to put up with a certain amount of humiliation in the course of a Tour de France. But it does not do well to brook him in his own lair. Esclassan had the advantage of knowing the course. He also had Sibille to guide him to within 170 yards of the finish line, where Esclassan took Maertens's wheel. On the last curve, Esclassan let go, bolting past Maertens who took a look at him and hesitated, as Esclassan said, making no bones of it, "probably out of fear, remembering his two spills at Mazé and Biarritz." By the time Maertens recovered, he had to settle for third place behind Raas.

Esclassan revealed that during the last 600 yards he used for only the second time a 53-tooth chainring matched with a 12-tooth sprocket (Maertens's favorite sprinting ratio). He had tried it out first in Bordeaux, where it had proved, on the double circuit, unsatisfactory. Here it had not tired him. It is nice to think that for all these years he has been underestimating his strength.

With my people I have insisted, for once, on being among the favored: those allowed to spend a night in Toulouse. The city may not be what it was before the 13th-century Albigensian "Crusade" — the capital of love. But in its modern way it exudes a hot southern vibrancy of red-brick buildings and shadow, which stirs the sensational appetite. The squares are full of people sitting around their café tables, and even after midnight the streets are still relatively animated as they would not be anywhere north of the Massif Central. In one of the squares, I sit for a long time listening to a camp Dixieland band, 20 strong, mostly trombones oompahing out into a tolerant night.

STAGE 13

Figeac
to Super-Besse

Thursday's 8:30 a.m. train transfer to a two-hour distant Figeac proved more to the rider's taste. The time was not totally wasted since they could have breakfast and a massage on board. That left it up to us scribes to notice what the passengers missed: the most superb of tree-canopied roads held in that quick dance of early morning, wide, shimmering wheat fields to one side, and on the other, distant orchards and hilltop vineyards. In haste, we cross river after river with tall, ancient, reflecting stone bridges, a fisherman's rod making a single silvery line against bush and water. As we reached the valley of the Tarn, a new almost orange-colored stone made its appearance. While alone in the blue-gray light of a hillside, rippling into an indefinite aerial serenity, were 13th-century towns with names to whisper like Cordes as we roared by.

Between 960 and 1228, Toulouse was the capital of a civilization based on the poetry of the wandering troubadours and their loves. This poetry so permeated the civilization that it finally lost its bearings. Out went the Christian God as represented in his son Jesus and in came Woman seen in her spiritual-erotic aspect as a pair of eyes radiating light. Dante's Beatrice was the last aspect of this conception before the romantic revival of the last century. Only now the lady was called Death, and she was there only for the adventurous few, those willing to risk being maimed in her pursuit. Finally, with all the madness and the syphilis, things reached a point where something had to be done about the Old Lady. She could go on, but not in human form. What incarnation would she choose for her last appearance? She thought about it a moment and said, "The bicycle — two wheels and a bar — everything is there." And that's how M. de Sivrac's invention came to be called *la petite reine*, the Little Queen.

Today's 133-mile stage in her honor through the lower Auvergne has long defied my notion as to how a bicycle race can be run through it. There is not a flat 100 yards in the whole trajectory, and most of it is upwards along the chain of *puys*, or sundial-shaped volcanoes, that will culminate in tomorrow's mammoth Puy-de-Dôme. The country is as poor as any in France, perhaps because it is lost in the middle and one can't so easily emigrate. With even hay precious, women can still be seen, as they would be on today's route, laced to a tree trunk as they scythed on a steep hill. In a region where people have been ever since the time of the Lascaux cave paintings, these rustic survivals are highly instructive. Add the bathing suits that a sunny day has brought back, golden "Bruyère" pennants flying between obviously Belgian camp-poles, pines and scotch broom and long-horned Salers cattle, and one might almost have a certain reason for elation.

In a landscape calling for attacks, they were not long in coming. First into the field, picking up where he had left off on the lower Tourmalet, was the local De Carvalho, author of three separate escape attempts in the first 60 miles. The last of these, coming right after Pollentier had taken the Nozière Hill's three climbing points, was the signal for the beginning of an all-out skirmish. For the next 70 miles, attacks came from all directions, until capped by Paul Wellens's personal crescendo as the winner of the recent Tour de Suisse brought off a 31-mile solo breakaway.

Stimulating the hostilities was the very close team battle in the overall time classification. At the outset of the day, all that separated the Raleigh team from C&A and Mercier were four and seven minutes respectively. In the other team battle, the points race, based on the hot points and finishing sprint positions, the Peugeots had a clearer lead, with 369 to 392 for Renault and 396 for Raleigh. With times based on the first five men of each team there is a considerable latitude to maneuver.

The actual break was set off by two Lejeunes, Patrick Friou and Michel Le Denmat, attacking one after another. Le Denmat's took away Raymond Martin, Zoetemelk's lieutenant and a fine climber, Thévenet's former caddy Bourreau, and De Schoenmaecker. They were joined in turn by Yves Hézard, another good second-line climber working for Peugeot, and the strike-breaker Oliva, the first Spaniard to come out of his shell. Bourreau failed to survive the Mauriac ramp, but with Martin and Hézard loyally relaying each other, and occasional assistance from Oliva, the quartet's lead grew to 3:20 in 14 miles. That's on a par with the Bruyère-led nine-man escape on the St Amand to St Germain leg.

Normally in these circumstances, the chasing work falls to the yellow jersey's team. But Bruyère felt himself absolved by the presence of teammate De Schoenmaecker, hanging like a dead fish behind the relaying trio. This put it up to the Renault-Gitanes to reestablish order. The blue-and-gold jerseys took over the front line, and with their general Hinault overseeing them from a protected position, the gap began to close. After 35 miles of chase it had fallen to 1:43 when

STAGE 13:
FIGEAC
TO SUPER-BESSE

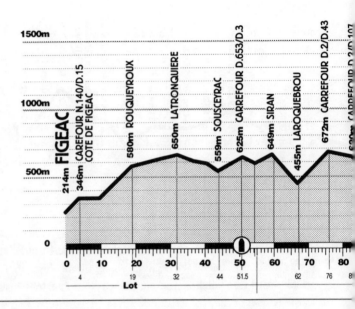

Wellens, who was lying right behind, decided to spring an ambush. The site he picked, the feeding point of Condat, was perfect: the Gitanes would be too busy picking up their lunch bags to sprint after him. In 10 miles he had caught the quartet. But they were no longer pedaling fast enough for him and, after catching his second wind, Wellens decided to push on. There remained the short, but very steep second-category hill of St. Anastaise, followed immediately by a third-category climb to the finish at Super-Besse.

On the last climb, Wellens lost a half-minute. But with the help of the 20-second bonus, he still finished 1:30 ahead, enough to jump him from 12th place to seventh in the standings. But the consolidation of the team position that he sought was not to be, as C&A with Bruyère, Van Impe, Janssens, Loos and De Schoenmaecker placed high enough to take over first place by 53 seconds, with the Merciers in third place, only 43 seconds back.

Behind Wellens on the Super-Besse climb, a real battle had broken out, touched off by Laurent and Agostinho. Their 37-second advance over Hinault, Bruyère, Zoetemelk, Kuiper and Van Impe might have been more had not Agostinho hesitated for a moment about pitching in. But when he turned around in his saddle, plainly questioning, Pollentier flashed him the high sign, and Agostinho took off. For his pains, Laurent took the stage's second place, while Agostinho finished an admirably planned third — excusing him from the drug control. I can even see him coming in third all the way to the Champs-Elysées. For a rider in the twilight of his

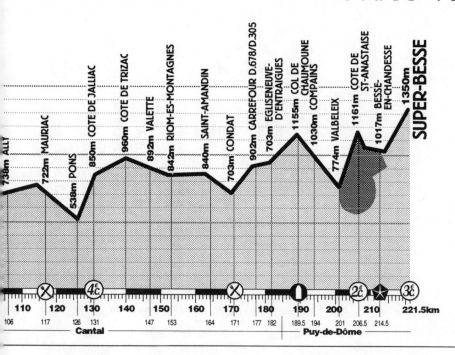

career it would be a sweet revenge for so many dope-disallowed Tour victories.

Others who tried their luck on the last four-mile ramp did not come off as well. Lelay had opened a 100-yard gap when Kuiper decided to test Hinault. The second of his sprint attacks catapulted him 40 yards in front, with Pollentier and Zoetemelk in his immediate wake. Hinault parried the attack exactly as he had done at Pla d'Adet, not attempting to keep pace, but climbing within his own gradually accelerating rhythm until with a last few luminous thrusts of the pedals he had drawn even. Right behind him, Bruyère maneuvered so as to take the six-man sprint, rewarding De Schoenmaecker & Co. with the fourth-place points.

Stage 13: Figeac to Super-Besse

1	PAUL WELLENS *(Raleigh)*	6:43:49
2	Laurent *(Peugeot)*	at 1:30
3	Agostinho *(Flandria)*	1:31
4	Hinault *(Gitane)*	2:07
5	Pollentier *(Flandria)*	2:07
6	Zoetemelk *(Mercier)*	2:07
7	Bruyère *(C&A)*	2:07
8	Kuiper *(Raleigh)*	2:07
9	Van Impe *(C&A)*	2:07
10	Seznec *(Mercier)*	2:19

Besse-en-Chandesse
to Puy-de-Dôme time trial

I t is Bastille day, the 14th of July, the start of a national holiday weekend, and the 14th stage of the 1978 Tour de France. But even at this season not every revolutionary castle is of sand, and a colorful human switchboard, variously estimated as between 400,000 and a million, has erupted onto the flanks of the Puy-de-Dôme for Friday's 33-mile time trial. With the roads closed since 8 a.m., most of the fans have been up on the extinct volcano with their gas lamps since the pre-dawn, drawn by the legend of the Puy-de-Dôme and the promise of a Tour more open than any in recent memory.

As mountains go, the 4641-foot Puy-de-Dôme is not all that high. What makes this sugarloaf so unique is the abrupt way in which it rises 2400 vertical feet in less than five miles out of the Auvergne plateau. A mountain for Mohammad, you don't come to it, it comes to you. When the first Tourists churned their bicycles up its final 3.75 miles of impossibly steep slopes, they felt as if their hands were going to strike the road.

A sacred mountain to the Gauls — *puy* in old French means sundial — the Puy-de-Dôme has, near its summit, the ruins of a temple of Mercury, the god of thieves. At its feet lie the twin towns of Chamalières, the banking capital of France and the former legislative bailiwick of President Giscard d'Estaing, and Michelin's Clermont-Ferrand. One might think that a mountain with its own private tollgate road (fans would be charged a whopping $4 a head), near such a sizeable metropolis, would have been annexed by the Tour earlier than 1952.

In the years since, this thumb in the sky has become famous for the film clips of its agonized shoulder-to-shoulder stage finishes: Anquetil and Poulidor in 1964 with the Tour at stake; Van Impe and Zoetemelk in 1976. Federico Bahamontes won a 10-mile time trial here in 1959; his winning yellow jersey of that year is now a relic in the Toledo cathedral (the other was ripped into pieces and thrown to the mob).

This year's innovation was to change the Puy-de-Dôme from the end of a road race into the end of an hour-and-a-half-long time trial; that is, from a historic moment that flashes by into a continuous four-hour spectacle where, at three-minute intervals, some 96 riders surge into view in their various climbing profiles, to be ticked off and compared against some private time-table of previous and forthcoming.

Basically, there are two ways of running a time trial: to go all out from the beginning and trust to whatever second wind from whatever source one might be able to catch (Pollentier's usual tactics — hoping to stampede his adversaries into a similar stupidity?); or, like Hinault at the Bordeaux wine trial, to get a pace going and gradually accelerate, turning it on where one has to. In a course divided into two distinct sections — 27.5 miles of normal then 5.5 miles of mountain, all but the first at a steady 13.5-percent grade — a rider has to take advantage of the terrain that best suits him.

Being the site and holiday it is, most prognostics favor Hinault planting his tri-colored jersey atop the Puy-de-Dôme to take over the race leadership from Bruyère, his inferior in both aspects of the discipline. His qualities as a time-trialist, and the convincing fashion in which he parried Pollentier's and Zoetemelk's attacks on the Pla d'Adet, support this view. Against it are the imponderables, including the after-effects of the strike as it may have told on Hinault's ability to sleep, and the extra efforts demanded by yesterday's 60-mile pursuit, the elbow-to-elbow jousting with intruders trying to break into the Gitane ranks to undermine the pursuit. A law of the Tour is that each extra effort has to be paid for, one day or another. If Hinault does take over the yellow jersey today, the odds are he will keep it all the way to Paris. Otherwise the sole certainty is for the time gaps to grow. Bad for the race, but in a mountain time trial of such length what else can one expect?

Friday morning, under skies heavy with the threat of rain, I find myself with Patrick gloomily driving past Chamalières and its parading military band and up the single-lane road toward the sacred mountain. But with radiators overflowing and fans in exasperation parking their cars we can't make any headway, and Patrick takes me back to the press headquarters with its TV screen. But the motorcycle-held camera, great as it is on sprint finishes, has no way of rendering steepness, glare, crowd, rocks, all that makes a climb different from a steady pedaling effort. Fortunately, I find a car heading out to the start at Besse-en-Chandesse.

When we arrive at Besse it is past noon, and some 50 riders have already set out. Near the starting point, a dispute has broken out between young Bernaudeau's parents, who have driven halfway across France to cheer him on, and the Tour officials, unwilling to relax the ban on women in cars. At 22, with his body still growing, Bernaudeau did not originally want to risk his health in this year's Tour. He

STAGE 14: BESSE-EN-CHANDESSE TO PUY-DE-DÔME TIME TRIAL

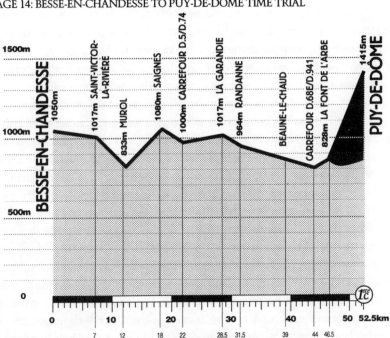

was flown in only as a last-minute replacement. Still, he has done well, trailing Lubberding by a half-minute in the battle for the white jersey. The Tour officials *will* permit Bernaudeau's father to follow, but he is reluctant to abandon his wife for a whole afternoon.

Meanwhile, I have secured a back seat in the car following the tall flaxen-haired Norman, Charly Rouxel, who is in 44th place, 28 minutes behind Bruyère.

In our car are a father and two sons from the Clermont-Ferrand cycling club promoting the race. Since it's up to us to replace the tires, we ask Charly what happens if he punctures more than twice. "In that case," he says, laughing simply, "I'm out of the race." He tells us that when he retires in a year he would like to go into coaching. Meanwhile, it behooves him to do well today, as he is in the last year of his contract. His trophy chest is not particularly full, the main item being a victory in the Circuit de l'Indre in 1974, his readiness to keep himself in the van, and his courage, have earned him a considerable following. When half the peloton was eliminated last year at L'Alpe d'Huez, it was Rouxel, struggling on despite multiple injuries, who was regarded as the most unjustified victim.

Physically, Rouxel is in the mold of Bruyère: too big to climb easily. But he descends as well as anyone, and the first part of this time trial is more descent than rise through large-vistaed, serene orchard country. With his height and pink-shouldered Miko-Mercier jersey, Rouxel is easily recognizable and the spectators, stopwatches and pads in hand, make it plain that he is negotiating it very well.

We have gone 20 miles when, at a turn in the road, the driver signals to me the Puy-de-Dôme. I can hardly believe it and my first response is to burst out laughing at the idea that anyone could be expected to cycle up such a tall green tower-of-Babel.

We have been rising through a *faux plat* for eight miles when all of a sudden we hit the "wall" at the tollgate. Crowds thicken. The path through, in spite of cops every 20 yards, is as thin as a church aisle. This is not sheer obstinacy; there is not that much room for so many people on this barely two-car-wide tarmac spiral, which is why it is closed to bicycles except two days a year. The heat, the glare off the reflecting surface right in the eyes, the impossibility of breathing among such a claustrophobic crowd, would in themselves be major obstacles, did we not have to keep worrying that at any moment some idiot might stick his face in front of Rouxel's bike with something more than just his camera. In such intensity, anything can happen and once in a while it does — in 1975, a chauvinist spectator rabbit-punched Merckx as he was cycling up. Merckx received a bad bruise, contributing to his Tour defeat, and his assailant landed in jail. For Rouxel the danger lies in the toll on his concentration, the inability to maneuver, to see ahead, and in the danger of the pushes, each of which, if seen by the stewards, will cost him 5 seconds in penalty and an accompanying fine. Here it is a bicycle-wise crowd, but even so we are shaking our fists and honking every yard of the way.

Rouxel has been alternating styles, sitting and thrusting himself forward *en danseuse* over the handlebars, when, some 200 yards from the summit, he fails to anticipate a sudden steepening of the gradient. Forced to shift, his wheels spin, and Rouxel saves himself from falling only by grabbing on to the inner rock face. Two spectators rush out to steady him and push him off, but the momentum against the gear he has chosen still isn't enough, and he requires — and gets — a second push further up when he again weaves into the wall. Even so, his time, 1:33:29, is the best so far.

Flashing my green press card, I do my best to walk down, aiming for that bit of 14.5-percent grade where Rouxel ran into trouble. For a while I can use the footpath, a foot above the road where most of the spectators are squatting like gulls at a beach.

Around us, riders who have finished are coming down, stopping to exchange remarks with fans from their home regions. But most are in a hurry, wanting to get their sweating bodies out of the coldness and watch the race on television.

Vendors are offering ice cream cones at over a dollar a scoop; understandable in a steepness that has me pausing every 50 yards or so just to draw breath and right myself from the dizziness. Rider names are everywhere: an "Agostinho" pennant suspended between pine and rock face over the road; "Hézard" scrawled in chalk across the road by what seems the best viewing spot. The scrawler, a young woman with a large pink face and curly ash-blonde hair, tells me that she has been rooting for Yves ever since she presented him with a victory bouquet in her hometown three years ago. Since then, like his Peugeot teammate Michel Laurent, he has been struggling back from the ravages of hepatitis. But, she says, even when Hézard was not going very well, she always knew he'd make it. Nonetheless, each time a rider pops into view, one of our male neighbors insists on identifying him as Hézard.

Every three minutes or so, a rider comes around the boulder below and into applauded view, the sun smack in his face. I watch Lelay, the best young climber, arrive looking absolutely green; then Nazabal, sweat spitting from his longer, black-haired head; then the overtaken Villemiane of the melodious name, bald-headed and smiling and obviously in nothing like his stride of the Pla d'Adet, 1:30 slower than Rouxel. After him, putting an end to the suspense, the suspicions, appears this so-long-awaited Hézard, pedaling briskly, a full three minutes up on Rouxel. Next comes the last of the great race of winged angels, the once-effortless climber, Van Impe, coughing horribly: mouth open, asphyxiated plainly, and so annoyed at one would-be pusher he takes his empty water bottle and hurls it in the man's face. But his time, 1:29:40 is the fastest yet, good enough for sixth place in the eventual reckoning. I watch young Bernaudeau, very handsome — and fast too, having done the four miles from the tollgate in 17:12, the fourth best of the day.

Next of note is Mariano Martinez, who was spitting blood in the back seat of Guy Faubert's car two hours earlier. Exposure to the cool Pla d'Adet air after his victory has fired the bronchitis he has been carrying into a serious lung infection, and one difficult to treat because the drug control laws ban such products as ephedrine. Haggard as he looks, Martinez is only a minute behind Van Impe.

The next shock is seeing the little red-jerseyed bull, Agostinho, arrive ahead of both Wellens and Laurent. He chose to shoot his bolt on the first part of the course, and trust in his stamina to somehow or other stagger up the mountain. At the foot of Puy-de-Dôme, he was in second place 28 seconds back of Pollentier. From there, he faded considerably (as the accompanying graph shows), but his time of 1:27:53 is the fifth fastest of the day, enough to catapult him into fifth place in the overall standings.

Distance and time in Stage 14

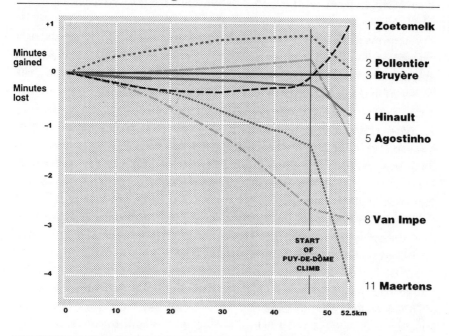

After him comes Kuiper, as always fresh as a daisy, but the legs not pedaling fast as he suffers the humiliation of being overtaken by an exhausted, wide-eyed and ashen-faced Pollentier, who looks like he could have a stroke right then and there. Weaving horribly, he makes it to the finish line and, once across, raises an arm motioning people out of the way, only to crash against the hood of a parked truck that he has failed to register. As his probable winning time, 1:26:37, is announced, Pollentier says, "Never in my life have I felt so exhausted."

But no, a fast, powerful, pedal-risen, red-haired Zoetemelk flashes by on his 22-toothed sprocket, a full 46 seconds up on Pollentier. He is followed quite an interval later by the people's choice, Hinault, seated and grimacing.

At the tollgate, only seven seconds down on Zoetemelk, he had experienced a minor *contretemps* when his lighter climbing bike struck a spectator as it was being held out of the car, losing its front wheel. But Hinault did not lose any appreciable time as he kept pedaling while a new wheel was being readied. To some observers it seemed odd that this specially stripped machine with its longer crank arms, should have a full water bottle strapped on. Precaution or not, it's something most would have jettisoned.

The real surprise on this afternoon of surprises is the last starter, the man we've all forgotten about, Bruyère, yellow jersey, gold-capped teeth, blond hair, who arrives at the finish line collapsed on his bike, demanding, "Air, air!" What that augurs is unclear. But his time, the result of a remarkably consistent performance (see graph) is only 11 seconds slower than Pollentier — enough to preserve his yellow jersey for the sixth successive stage by 1:03 over Zoetemelk, who now precedes Hinault by 47 seconds and Pollentier by 1:35.

Of all these results, Hinault's augurs best for the race. Where before the Breton was in a position of strength with Zoetemelk and Pollentier obliged to come at him, or be beaten on his chosen ground — the Metz to Nancy time trial — he now finds himself in a more vulnerable position; one not helped by Bruyère's astonishing performance. For Hinault, his off-day may be a matter of fatigue and loss of confidence induced by the shellacking he has taken at the hands of the press. The power of Tour de France scribes may not be what it once was, but for Hinault to be battered off his course says something for the maligned pen.

After scrambling down the mountain and walking into Clermont-Ferrand, I remember seeing Pollentier and Maertens hanging out of their third-floor hotel window, smiling like a pair of idiots at all that was going on below. When I came out of dinner an hour and a half later they were still there in the window. Doubtless, the life in a street of B-girls bars around the corner from the railway station, had its seedy fascination. But you felt they were remaining in the window for us, too; like children who have just pulled off some marvelous trick and wanted everybody to see them.

Stage 14: Besse-en-Chandesse to Puy-de-Dôme time trial

1	JOOP ZOETEMELK *(Mercier)*	1:25:51
2	Pollentier *(Flandria)*	at 0:46
3	Bruyère *(C&A)*	0:55
4	Hinault *(Gitane)*	1:40
5	Agostinho *(Flandria)*	2:02
6	Van Impe *(C&A)*	3:49
7	Kuiper *(Raleigh)*	4:02
8	Martin *(Mercier)*	4:42
9	Martinez *(Jobo)*	4:51
10	Hézard *(Peugeot)*	4:52

St. Dier-d'Auvergne to St. Etienne

To accommodate the riders, the 15th stage was shortened by 27.5 miles, with the departure deferred to St. Dier-d'Auvergne at the foot of the Doubais hill, a five-mile third-category climb. Leaving aside the varied problems in getting there, it seemed one hell of a place to shake oneself awake with the flash of a starter's gun. Bang, crash, and away all the goats go! As we arrived in St. Dier, we saw Joseph Bruyère racing the other way up the hill as if he had forgotten something and was off to retrieve it before the race got underway. More than anything it shows how seriously the yellow jersey is taking his new responsibilities. This jersey that he had worn so casually four years ago is now to him what a lollipop is to a child. No one is going to take it away from him without a battle. He may not survive the Alps with his yellow jersey intact. But if he keeps his losses down he may regain it in the Metz to Nancy individual time trial.

The battlefield again won aesthetic marks, most of it wild rugged forest. Perhaps for that very reason there were some bad accidents, Gauthier and Pescheux colliding on the way down the Lavet hill, forcing Pescheux out with a damaged elbow and a bad concussion. A little later, Ludo Loos took his second crash in three days, fracturing the metacarpal bone at the base of his hand. Loos's retirement from the race was a serious blow to Bruyère and, even more so, to C&A in the team struggle. Loos was always near Bruyère's side, especially in the hills.

With the thermometer hovering around 85 degrees Fahrenheit, and a sun strong enough to melt the tar in certain parts of the road, Hennie Kuiper came into his own. Twice in conjunction with Hinault he tried to break away. The third, at the 85-mile mark, sprung Kuiper free. Though the Dutchman's lead never grew beyond 46 seconds, and for the most part hovered at the 20-second mark, it still could have its taxing effects on Bruyère's and Zoetemelk's troops. They caught Kuiper just below the summit of the Croix-de-Chabouret pass, the western gateway to St

Etienne, the bicycling capital of France. The vehemence of the pursuit demonstrated the general belief that Kuiper is still very much to be feared, especially with the two alpine legs coming up.

The 11-mile descent past the Rochetaillée hydroelectric station and on into St Etienne was sufficiently long to permit a 40-man regrouping, including riders like Freddy Maertens and Sean Kelly who had been left behind on the climb. With De Meyer delayed by the problem of hauling his carcass over the mountain, it fell to Kelly to act as Maertens's pilot fish. In his nervousness, the Irishman made the mistake of launching the sprint too far out for Maertens. Also, unbeknown to him, he had a second shark on his wheel in the form of Hinault. With 70 yards to go, Kelly had a second Tour victory all but wrapped up. But fearing to play his own personal card at the expense of Maertens he let up, and Hinault wheeled to a surprise and no doubt immensely satisfactory second stage victory. While his win did not affect the time standings, it showed that Hinault has other strings to his bow than this prowess as a time-trialist and power climber.

In a generally satisfactory day, the only note of horror concerned poor Inaudi, banished from the race for having suffered too many pushes. In the Tour, riders are fined and given a 5-second penalty for each unsolicited push. When added to a rider's finishing time, it can put him outside the permissible limits. One can see the Tour wanting to stamp out the sort of excesses prevalent in Italy, where riders are often pushed up a mountain pass from hand to hand without ever having had to turn a pedal.

In defense of the law, it is said that it falls only on the weak, people like Inaudi who should be eliminated anyway. But that's not true, it's just that the pushes the better riders benefit from don't get remarked, like the two Rouxel received on the Puy-de-Dôme. Also, the international commissaires have their own national grudges, and fine accordingly. Besides, how is a rider to control his unsportsman-like fans — by clouting them in the face with an empty water bottle, like Van Impe on the Puy-de-Dôme? In a race where there is so much prestige in finishing, it seems unfair to penalize an Inaudi for the Tour's own fault to inform the public and provide sufficient police protection. As it is, Inaudi won't have the joy of pedaling by his parents' village two stages from now.

Overall classification after Stage 15 (Yellow jersey)

1 JOSEPH BRUYÈRE (C&A)   6:51:24
2 Zoetemelk (Mercier)   at 1:03
3 Hinault (Gitane)   1:50
4 Pollentier (Flandria)   2:38
5 Agostinho (Flandria)   6:20
6 Kuiper (Raleigh)   7:15
7 Martinez (Jobo)   10:42
8 Maertens (Flandria)   11:29
9 Galdos (Kas)   12:01
10 Wellens (Raleigh)   12:31

STAGE 16

St. Etienne
to L'Alpe d'Huez

The St. Etienne stage hasn't altered the general standings, which show Bruyère leading Zoetemelk by a minute, trailed in turn at three-quarter-minute intervals by Hinault and Pollentier. But while the standings remain unchanged, the suspense grows. There are only two mountain stages left: today's 150-mile stint with its two afternoon first-category climbs of the Col du Luitel and L'Alpe d'Huez; followed after the rest day by another eight-pass ride to Morzine. If no decision is rendered by Morzine, then the Tour will be decided by next Friday's Metz to Nancy 45-mile time trial. To contend at that distance, Zoetemelk needs at least two minutes in hand on Hinault, Pollentier and Bruyère.

Otherwise, the revelation of the day has been the return to form of Hennie Kuiper, last year's Tour runner-up. To be sure, at 7:15 back, his chances of taking the yellow jersey are slim, given the former Olympic and world champion's relative weakness as a time trialist. But with today promising to be the first truly hot day of the year, and with nine members of his family waiting for him at L'Alpe d'Huez, this self-styled Friend of the Sun may be able to repeat his last year's stage victory.

There is a summery freshness as the race gets under way with the third-category Col de la République. It was here in 1904 that the first pitched battle occurred between the Tour riders and their spectators. There had been advance warning when an open car drew up alongside the two leaders, Garin (the first year's winner) and Pothier. The men in the car, their anonymity protected behind goggles, threatened the two with bodily harm if they didn't let the St. Etienne rider, Faure, win the stage. Garin and Pothier must have refused, for at 3 a.m. (still the time of all night rides) there was a mob armed with clubs and stones awaiting them near the summit. The mob let through Faure, who had taken the precaution of sprinting ahead. Pothier also managed to follow. Then to cries of "Vive Faure!" "Down with Garin!" "Kill

A FIRST
Irishman Sean Kelly (l) won his
first-ever stage of the Tour de France
at Poitiers, where he held off Gerry Knetemann.

AGOSTINHO
(A-GHOS-TIN-YO)

ESCLASSAN
(ES-CLASS-ON)

FUSSIEN
(FOO-SYEN)

TOUR DE CRASH
At the Poitiers finish, green jersey
Freddy Maertens suffered one of his
several crashes in the opening week.

HINAULT
(HEE-NO)

HOBAN

KELLY

CLIMBERS' BATTLE
On the Tourmalet, early attacker Christian Seznec
was hauled in by Pollentier, Hinault and Zoetemelk.

KNETEMANN
(K-NAYT-A-MAN)

KUIPER
(KY-PER)

MAERTENS
(MAYER-TENS)

NO GO
The Valence d'Agen strike was led by Hinault (center), Maertens (r) and Pollentier (l).

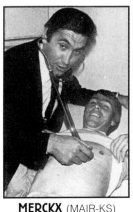

MARTINEZ
(MAR-TEEN-EZ)

MERCKX (MAIR-KS)
VAN IMPE (VAN-IMP)

POLLENTIER
(POLLEN-TEER)

VALIANT
Bruyère (center) climbed better than expected in defense of his yellow jersey, but had to concede in the Alps to Pollentier (l) and Hinault (r).

RAAS
(RARS)

ROUXEL
(ROOK-SEL)

SEZNEC
(SAYS-NECK)

BEFORE AND AFTER
Prior to his disqualification, Pollentier (in polka-dot jersey, top)
was the most aggressive rider, earning the yellow jersey.
Later, with the Belgian out of the race, Zoetemelk (r) took over
the yellow jersey, and was challenged on the Morzine stage
by Hinault (c) and Kuiper (2nd from left).

VALEDICTORY
Hinault finally took over
the race lead at the
Metz-Nancy time trial.

THÉVENET
(TAY-VE-NAY)

WELLENS
(VELLENS)

ZOETEMELK
(ZOI-TE-MELK)

ALL THE WINNERS
In Paris (from right), Lubberding (best young rider), Martinez
(King of the Mountains), Maertens (points), Hinault (yellow jersey)
and Kneteman (time trials) celebrated their success.

them!" the assailants fell on the riders. The two Garin brothers took a drubbing, the older catching a stone in his face. The main object of their attentions, the Italian Gerbi, was thrust from his bike and beaten to a pulp. The mauling might have got worse if Geo Lefèvre hadn't arrived with the official car, firing pistol shots into the gray light to disperse the crowd. In a little while, Faure, who wasn't strong enough to profit from the escape, was hauled in, though the officials waited until Marseille to disqualify him for his complicity.

Fussien, always willing to show his impudence, takes both the Col de la République and Côte de Chambaran climbs, preceding each time Pollentier and Martinez. By now, Pollentier's tactics are becoming clear. These hilltop sprints for a prime and the mountain prize points are preparation for some great final one perhaps days off when he must attack and re-attack until everyone cracks and he can be off undisturbed, only his heart and breath and good legs singing as he draws away into this impossible dream of his, of actually flying, on a bicycle, uphill.

By the same token, it is possible to criticize Pollentier, like Van Impe before him, for foolishly exhausting himself in pursuit of these hilltop primes instead of husbanding his energy for one particular moment when a decision is to be made. But Pollentier's red-and-white polka-dotted mountain jersey (for which he has willingly exchanged his red, black, and gold Belgian champion's jersey) is more than idle braggadocio. By continually padding his lead, he keeps chipping away at his opponents' resolve, so that when the moment to escape finally comes they are already resigned to it, and unable to make the last-ditch effort that might thwart him.

The chance to put this to the test comes soon enough. On the way down from the Chambaran hill, with 90 miles still to go, Kuiper launches his first attack. This sparks off a chain reaction, and 15 are swept off with him, among them Raas, Seznec, and two Renault-Gitanes, Bertin and Villemiane. Of these, only Raas is willing to abet Kuiper. Relaying each other they manage to increase the lead from 18 seconds to 26 seconds. By now, Hinault's manager, Cyrille Guimard, realizes that if Kuiper's attack is going to have any sapping effect it will need support, and he orders Villemiane and Bertin to collaborate. But their lead never gets beyond 37 seconds as the C&A and Miko-Mercier riders take over the pursuit. When they are absorbed after a 20-mile chase, Bertin tries to sprint free. Then it is Villemiane's turn, then Chalmel, then Bernaudeau. The Renault-Gitane strategy seems obvious — to keep the bunch moving rapidly so that Zoetemelk and Bruyère can't save their energy for the two great climbs ahead. The yellow jersey becomes in this sense a curse. Your team is obliged to defend it, which here means taking on the brunt of the chasing work. For Bruyère, who has not had a chance so far this year to accustom him-

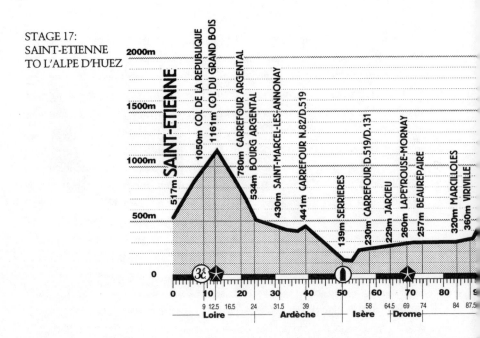

STAGE 17:
SAINT-ETIENNE
TO L'ALPE D'HUEZ

self to any real heat, the pressure is intense. It is possible to surpass yourself once, twice, three times; but how long can you keep on doing it before you crack?

At the 100-mile mark, the road enters the Isère valley, all rushing green and black rapids set off against the sensuous, mist-clad abruptions of the wolf-gray Dent du Loup. Then, the other side of Grenoble, the valley narrows. Suddenly we are in the Alps. A thick, murky light falls across a hydroelectric station's parade of pylons. Here Den Hertog, who made a long successful escape in last year's Tour, plays his card, accompanied by two Belgians, Willy Teirlinck, the ex-national champion, and René Martens. But the pack, having learned its lesson, lets them go, even though their lead is almost a minute approaching the first switchback of the Luitel.

The Luitel is not one of those mountains like the Puy-de-Dôme that loom suddenly out of nowhere. Rather, its style is more sylvan, the sort of alpine paradise where you might want to put up a vacation cabin. But, as with any mountain, there lurks under the seeming bucolic a whole other Sturm und Drang, where golden dreams can turn into nightmares with all of a mountain storm's sudden rage.

In this case, the squiggle of worms on the car map may indicate a truer note. Each hairpin is slightly steeper, and that much more demanding than the last. The surrounding air is heavy. Breath does not come easy. Nor, after five hours of riding, is there much food fuel left in their systems. On top of all this there is the

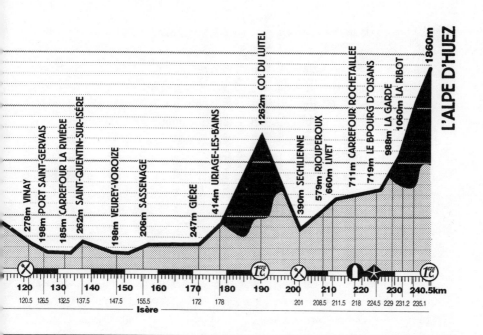

water loss in the heat, 10 to 16 pounds that must somehow be made up for. All around them as they climb is the thick pine forest green, bringing a sense of gloom, of claustrophobia.

Within the first bends, Den Hertog's trio has been absorbed. In the middle of the forest, we see a sign of trouble. Bruyère has changed to the titanium-based climbing bicycle that he had used on the Puy-de-Dôme, and which he will have to change again at the top as it is too flexible for the descent. Now, exactly where Thévenet fell during the Dauphiné-Libéré a month ago, it is Bruyère's turn to experience the same attack of hunger cramps. His face screws up in pain. Three of his team, Ward Janssens, De Schoenmaecker, and Martin, have their arms around him, trying to tug him along. Again, a descent to earth for a change of bicycle from his team car, chauffeured by a shirtless Eddy Merckx in black sunglasses. But these changes of mount, apart from the chance to breathe standing up that they give, are so many straws in the wind. At that moment he already knows that the Golden Fleece has flown.

Left is his honor and the honor of the yellow jersey that is still his to bear, since the Tour de France does not strip the shirt off a man's back out in open country. In the midst of this forest, like some elm stricken by a mysterious fungus, he battles on accompanied by a jackal caravan, out to report the fall of a yellow jersey. Among the bright clusters of spectators hanging several deep on both sides of the steep, winding road, a thousand transistor radios are giving him a live playback of his own struggle. A spectator shouts, "He's cooked!"

Indeed he is, for at the first sign of Bruyère's pain, the 14 left at the front have accelerated. As the battle proceeds through dense, flower-dotted alpine meadows, Hinault attacks, but not sharply enough to get away from Pollentier and Zoetemelk.

Then, 200 yards from the summit, Pollentier counterattacks, sprinting violently to open up a gap of several wheel lengths before being hauled in by a grimly pursuing Martinez, who brings in his own wake Hinault and Zoetemelk. But where there is honey there's the pollen animal, and 100 yards later he renews his effort, pursued mildly by a Martinez seemingly content with his 16 second-place points. At the summit, Pollentier leads Martinez by 13 seconds, and the five-man group of Kuiper, Agostinho, Galdos, Hinault and Zoetemelk by 22 seconds. The yellow jersey, Bruyère, trails at 4:53.

At the top, a tiny, gray-paved, single-car-wide track plunges down and down to the Romanche valley. It is the longest and most vertiginous drop in the whole race, and extremely dangerous with cars and riders rubbing elbows at 50 mph. A month ago, Barry Hoban crashed here, breaking a bone in his arm. For a tall rider like Bruyère, the difficulty is such that he will lose an extra three minutes. Feeling strong, and sensing the others' exhaustion, Pollentier resolves to go for broke, even though the Alpe d'Huez finish is some 35 miles away at the end of a nine-mile, 8-percent climb.

A single rider can plummet down a mountain faster than a group who have to look out for each other. Pollentier negotiates it without taking any chances. Still it's enough to give him a 50-second lead at the Séchilienne feeding-point where he must make his decision: to press on through the 20 miles of riding grade, one man against 14, all relaying one another; or save himself for the bottom of the Alpe d'Huez climb, content with having placed his banderillas. The same decision faced Lucien Van Impe last year when, on the descent of the Glandon, he opted for the same suicidal raid. Had Van Impe waited for the foot of the Alpe d'Huez to attack he might well have won the Tour for the second year in a row.

With 15 more miles to go up the valley than Van Impe, Pollentier might well have suffered the same fate, but for a helping tail wind and a certain dilatoriness on the part of his pursuers in organizing their effort. Hinault's team, which carried the brunt of the policing at Figeac to Super-Besse, are loath to commit themselves again, especially since it is Zoetemelk who will now inherit the yellow jersey. Emissaries from the two approach Kuiper, asking him to collaborate (just as Thévenet had a year ago). But tactics are tactics, and Kuiper, who has designs on a repeat of last year's stage victory, refuses to throw in his forces (Lubberding and Wellens), reminding them that he might have won yesterday except for their efforts. If Zoetemelk and Hinault want to burn themselves out in the chase, that's their affair.

While a compromise is being hammered out — Zoetemelk, who has more and better men, will lead during the first part, Hinault the second — Pollentier's lead keeps increasing, reaching 3:20 in six miles. By then, with the pursuit under way, it starts dwindling, down to 2:35 at the hot-sprint point of Bourg d'Oisans, where he picks up a 20-second breakaway leader bonus, and 1:58 at the first hairpin bend. But Pollentier chinks through the first couple of switchbacks in his own normal style, giving his body time to get itself accustomed to this seven-mile, 22-bend ascent (or one for each stage of the race), climbing through a vertical height of 3810 feet.

Here Kuiper has a dilemma. He can attack early, and as the freshest of Pollentier's pursuers, help cut him down. But only at the price of drawing on Hinault, who would in all likelihood wipe out the two of them. By now, at the 12th hairpin bend Michel's lead has shrunk to 1:13. They can even see Pollentier just two ramps higher up, hunched like a rabbit over his tortured machine. Now is the moment for Zoetemelk to go all out, aware that it's the best chance the Tour is likely to offer him. But his pedaling is uneven, and Hinault behind him, his lips half open, looks more securely harmonious. As Hinault shifts powerfully into a smaller 42x15 *braquet*, Zoetemelk gives up. That leaves Kuiper, spurred on by his fans' "Allez Tonton" pennants (a moniker deriving from his look-alike Tintin), to battle it out with Hinault. Then, just below the church at the top of the ascent, and some 1400 yards from the finish line, Kuiper churns into action, launched by a 50-yard push from a fan. The French champion doesn't try to match him, being more concerned to maintain his rhythm, while conceding as little ground as possible to Pollentier. At the finish Kuiper trails the Belgian by 37 seconds, while on overall time Zoetemelk and Hinault find themselves respectively 4 seconds and 18 seconds behind Pollentier. These are the sort of figures one might encounter in an opening day time trial, not the 16th stage of the Tour de France.

Meanwhile, we have managed to get our Radio Sud car down the Luitel without maiming anyone, only to discover at Séchilienne that we have lost our brakes. As I step out of the car I see this little balding blond whom Hinault calls Polio pedal by, all contorted knees and elbows. Next comes a group of 20 with green-jerseyed Freddy Maertens of all people in the lead, proving once again what sheer bikemanship can be worth on a descent. As Pollentier's teammate, Maertens is actually slowing down the pursuit, while profiting to reach into his pocket and feed himself before the Alpe d'Huez ascent. By now, I've found a spare seat in the Antenne 2 station wagon — provided I don't mind waiting for Bruyère.

Some eight minutes after Pollentier, Bruyère appears at the head of a 12-man group of survivors. Their attitude is not really, 'It's Joseph's yellow jersey, let him defend it!' Rather they are too exhausted themselves to do anything but hang on. Of Bruyère's teammates, only Janssens is able to help with an occasional relay. Most of the time it is just Joseph, tall body slung forward over the machine, rocking it with that beautiful, sexual, shoulder-dipping style.

After Bourg d'Oisans, the road starts to mount more severely, and Joseph, though still leading, is in serious trouble. On the first turn, De Schoenmaecker and Janssens take the high side of the road like some great faithful St. Bernards, coaxing, encouraging him. But the 11-percent grades of these first painful switchbacks are too steep for them to push him. Our driver points out the almost sheer rock wall that we will be ascending for the next 22 turns. In its far upper right corner is the church of Huez, itself 1300 feet below the summit. Above that is a little bit of blue. All around is the chain of snow-clad peaks that make up the Grandes Rousses, with Chamonix and Val d'Isère the best expert-level ski areas in France.

The sky is now very blue and the heat more intense than ever. Along the road, a constant hedge of parti-colored spectators. Crying, shouting, or filling up from stream and waterfall discarded water bottles and running along to pour them over the heads. One man has something even more efficient — an orange hose he has rigged up to the outside spigot of a chalet hotel. As Joseph struggles, legs churning in a kind of dead space, the crowd encourages him; but almost as many "Ahs!" are for Eddy Merckx, black-goggled, imperturbable, in the car behind. Then come us and Reynaud Vincent in the yellow *France Soir* car, sometimes across, sometimes behind. "Eddy, Eddy, it's all up now," Vincent hears a female spectator yelling to Merckx.

Now he is among the first chalets of L'Alpe d'Huez with its chair lift rising to the summer ski glaciers. But Joseph doesn't look at them; just the head down, the shoulders bobbing, his long body rising out of the saddle when he has to. Here the air is perceptibly cooler and Joseph, whose problems stem from the heat, is looking better. Five turns from the end, a radio tells him that Pollentier has already won. Three turns and Pollentier has donned the yellow jersey. But Bruyère is driving now. He passes Roger Legeay. Next come Kelly, Friou, Menendez, so many billiard-ball jerseys to be shot past. At the top, actually sprinting now, he erases first the green of Maertens (who has dropped 10 minutes on this one ascent) then the red of Maertens's teammate, René Bittinger. When he crosses the finish line ahead of some 68 others he is 11:50 behind Pollentier — good enough for sixth place overall.

As I get out of the car, an English correspondent turns to me: "This race sure beats anything I've ever heard of. Except for sailing single-handed around the world, I can't imagine anything so demanding." I myself am in tears, as I have been most of the way up; it's the race and the altitude and the bravery hitting me all at once.

Meanwhile, we watch an exhausted Bruyère slip out of his toe clips. When he looks up, after dousing his face in water, there on the podium above him is the beaming countenance of a little bow-legged compatriot whose huge bouquet of flowers only partly conceals a brilliant yellow jersey.

As Pollentier smiles, Bruyère is weeping. But the whirligigs of fate have not stopped spinning, and by the time the next hour is over Pollentier will be weeping a good deal harder than Bruyère.

Both had, in fact, lost the yellow jersey. One, while fighting to the end. The other, by cheating. So, the celebrated tunic wends through its round, from one shoulder to the next.

Overall classification after Stage 16 (Yellow jersey)

1	JOOP ZOETEMELK *(Mercier)*	80:06:41
2	Hinault *(Gitane)*	at 0:14
3	Kuiper *(Raleigh)*	5:31
4	Agostinho *(Flandria)*	6:10
5	Bruyère *(C&A)*	9:32
6	Galdos *(Kas)*	12:46
7	Lubberding *(Raleigh)*	14:30
8	Wellens *(Raleigh)*	14:30
9	Martinez *(Jobo)*	14:56
10	Van Impe *(C&A)*	16:17

"To pee or not to pee?"

In Pollentier's mind the question, "To pee, or not to pee?" was not merely displaced Shakespeare. He had already, in the violent exertion of the nine-mile 8-percent Alpe d'Huez climb — and for the nonce that precluded further efforts. Across the finish line at 4:10 p.m., we saw him 25 minutes later freewheeling off, his red-and-white polka-dotted mountain jersey flopping out under his new yellow jersey in the direction of the Hotel du Castellan et des Cimes a half-mile away. Doubtless, to change those wet pants before presenting himself within the next hour at the drug control. In the Tour de France, five men are tested each day: the overall leader, the stage winner and runner-up, and two plucked at random from the pack. At L'Alpe d'Huez this meant Bruyère, Pollentier, Kuiper, Antoine Gutierrez and José Nazabal.

One look at the profile of this 150-mile alpine stage with its two first-category climbs at the end of a gruelingly hot day, and one might consider arming oneself for the fray. Glucose pills, chocolate, tea spiked with lemon juice, are among the accepted poisons. But there are others and Pollentier, given his various options, chose a preparation called alupin. Whether he was taking it, as he said, for the first time in the Tour remains unclear. One way or another he must have drugged himself with some stimulant in the Puy-de-Dôme time trial two days earlier, as his vomiting and his crash at the finish line over a parked car would suggest.

An adrenaline-type stimulant, alupin is not a dangerous drug. In France, 12-year-old children take it as Pollentier did to help their breathing in the high mountains, and in Belgium it is sold over the counter. The Flandria masseur, Joseph Dhont, had authorized it for his team in Italy, and Pollentier had taken it there and in the Tour de Suisse without being reprimanded.

Pollentier guessed that this state of affairs might not apply in France, but no one had been caught taking an illicit substance so far, and it was hard to desert a proven luck charm. He himself had been controlled at the Puy-de-Dôme, and knew that the UCI regulations — that shorts should be lowered to the knees, and the jersey raised to the chest — were not being enforced.

That Pollentier panicked seems clear. Had he peed and been found positive, which is not at all certain, he would have exposed himself, at worst, to a 10-minute penalty on the last finisher's race time, plus a fine, while retaining the right to an appeal. There was even some reason to believe that a yellow jersey was, perhaps by reason of its color, immune to a test intended to apply only to lesser hues. Rumor, in fact, insisted that no less a personage than Thévenet had been found "positive" in the 1977 Tour. But with all of France waiting to acclaim its first winner in a decade, and with President Giscard himself set to greet Thévenet on the Champs-Elysées, that cat could not be let out of the bag.

For a Belgian, though, such niceties might not apply, and Pollentier decided to rig himself out in a "pear" contraption, with the rubber bulb concealed in an armpit out of which a length of taped tube ran across and then down the small of the back and under the buttocks to emerge below the penis. This was apparently not a novel idea, for the Frenchman Antoine Gutierrez was found with a similar if less sophisticated gadget, a discovery that led directly to the apprehending of Pollentier. Whether Pollentier intended to appear day after day with the same device remains unclear. Once a substance enters your blood it is apt to stay there, as the American swimmer Dumont found when he lost his Olympic gold medal as the result of having sniffed some ephedrine to relieve a case of acute bronchitis.

UCI rules require three officials to be present at a drug test. At L'Alpe d'Huez, these were the UCI medical inspector, Renato Sacconi, a regional inspector for the Ministry of Youth and Sport, and the man, who actually conducted the test, representing the French national cycling federation. This was a Dr. Le Calvet of the Atlantic-Anjou region, who was conducting the tests for the first time. Also present was the first-year Flandria manager, Fred De Bruyne, a former commentator with Belgian television and a winner of the Milan-San Remo and Paris-Roubaix cycling classics. It was obvious to all that Pollentier could not have rigged himself up in his plastic tube contraption all by himself. If there was collusion among the Flandrians, how far did it extend? Could one not suppose, as Claude Lambert of *France Soir* suggested, that De Bruyne had gone to the medical caravan in order to distract attention from Pollentier?

Since the last thing a trade team wants to suggest is that one might ride over a mountain on something other than their nickel-plated marvel, there was much at stake for De Bruyne and Flandria, if not the good name of professional cycling. With this in mind, De Bruyne called an impromptu press conference in Nancy in order to explain what exactly had happened in the medical trailer. Speaking in Flemish and then in French, De Bruyne explained, "I had followed Pollentier through his long breakaway, five yards back, all the way up to Alpe d'Huez. It was a magnificent athletic exploit and, after parking some 250 yards away, I wept like a child, I was so moved and full of joy. Imagine, there I was on top of the world, a manager on my first Tour with both the green jersey and the yellow jersey."

De Bruyne went on to explain that he stayed talking with a journalist and two friends for half an hour before walking down to the medical control caravan at the finish line. "There I was told that Pollentier had left by bike, something I couldn't fathom. I presumed that in his excitement at winning the yellow jersey he had forgotten about the drug test."

De Bruyne reached the Hotel du Castellan at 5:10 p.m., only to find Pollentier had already left. "On returning to the trailer," said De Bruyne, "I congratulated Michel and then sat down. On my left was Guttierez, trying to provide a specimen for the doctor, while Pollentier was in the other corner. Both were having trouble urinating. I then spoke with Sacconi, who kindly expressed his congratulations on Michel's ride. Suddenly the doctor cried out, 'What are you doing?' to Gutierrez. I looked around and saw there was some urine in the Frenchman's test flask and a small plastic tube in his hand. He was confused and tried to say the tube had been in his pocket. I was overcome with astonishment and I thought I am glad he isn't one of my team.

'But then, about a minute later, panic returned when the doctor pulled down Pollentier's shorts and revealed this plastic tube that you all know about by now. At that moment, the caravan could have exploded. 'Michel,' I cried, 'What are you doing? You have no need to fuck up like that!'"

De Bruyne then went on to say that a little liquid had in the commotion spilled down Pollentier's leg. But the doctor said that as Pollentier had not actually used the plastic tube apparatus he would go on and take the two normal 50cc urine samples. These flasks were then sealed, signed, and countersigned by Pollentier and the official inspectors. Guttierez was also asked to provide a proper specimen. The Frenchman emerged from the trailer at 6:52 p.m. and remarked, as he hopped on his bike, "That sure took a while!"

Looking tired and downcast, Pollentier followed four minutes later, and announced that he too had completed the test requirements. Then, without a word, he got into the team car with De Bruyne, who quickly drove him to their hotel. Pollentier climbed the steps four at a time all the way to the fourth floor where he and Freddy Maertens were lodged in room 32.

There, between friends who had shared everything for 13 years, it was a festive occasion. Freddy, a glass of champagne already in hand, poured one for Michel, who accepted the toast and drank. On Michel's bed, his suitcase was lying open with the yellow jersey out on top — his first ever. At that moment, he had no idea that he would never wear it again. Although clearly tired, for the sake of the interview he was willing to talk about the race and his current expectations, just as if nothing had happened.

In the interview, he made clear that his breakaway on the Luitel pass had not been planned. "On the top, as I was sprinting for the Grand Prix de la Montagne, I saw that the others were tired. That put it into my head to keep going. Still, I didn't take any risks. The drop down the Luitel is quite dangerous, and I took it cautiously. Once down in the valley, I rode on at my usual pace, without trying to stretch my lead. When Fred De Bruyne rolled up to tell me I had a three-minute lead, I couldn't believe him. Fred kept insisting that I slow down; he kept saying, 'Don't force yourself, or you'll pull a Van Impe. Take your time now and start feeding yourself, it's not here but on the Alpe d'Huez that it's all going to be played out.' He was obviously right and I heeded him.

"The first four miles of the Alpe d'Huez marked the hardest going for me. But I had no fear of their catching me even when Fred pulled up alongside to say I had no more than a minute. From now on the Tour is going to be very hard. There are three of us who can win it, but I really feel it will be a duel between me and Hinault. In all likelihood it will all come down to the time trial between Metz and Nancy. Zoetemelk's one chance of winning lies in breaking away on Tuesday's stint. It's up to him to take things in hand and me to repulse him. Anyway, that's my opinion.

"But I was lucky today that I had the wind with me in the valley — a real plus."

When asked then why he had had such a time of it with his drug test, Pollentier answered, "Going up Alpe d'Huez was so hard on me that I pissed down my pant leg and on to the bike. That's why I had so much trouble satisfying the doctor's requirements."

"But, Michel, everything is all right now?"

"Yes, I suppose."

"Do you suppose, or are you sure?"

"Well, the doctor told me that I might not have urinated enough, but that's all. As far as I know it's all going to be okay."

It was now 7:30 p.m. and Pollentier was going on about the future, Zoetemelk, Tuesday's stage, the forthcoming time trial, and this yellow jersey, which he was terribly happy to have just picked up. "You know," he said, "it's every cyclist's dream to wear this jersey, even if it's only once in his life." He then turned to the controversial 20-second bonus to which he owed his yellow jersey. "I'm dead set against it and because I've profited today is no reason to change my mind."

"Heh, Michel, how about a little more fizz?" Freddy asked.

But Michel had only one wish — to slip into a shower and go down to dinner.

At that, he was still late in joining his Flandria mates. One table over, the Renault-Gitanes had already put away their meal.

With no wish to intrude on Pollentier any further, we returned to the press headquarters in the non-denominational church of Notre Dame des Neiges. A handsome concrete-and-wood structure in the form of an ark, it had been erected at the personal expense of its priest, Joop Reuten, out of the profits of a local distributorship of Dutch beer. How fitting after all our previous venues that the Tour, at its spiritual Ararat, should float up on the first church ever built out of beer bottles! That was a proposition we could drink to, and there we all were in our ski parkas and track suits and army surplus gear, glasses raised to the ecumenical principle.

But there is no place the devil likes better to hide himself than in some holy well. At 7:30 p.m., as we were getting down to a sumptuous barbecue, we had been told that Pollentier was experiencing difficulty in urinating for the control. Now at 8 p.m., as we were finishing our grilled chicken, lamb shish-kebab, and cold roast beef, and about to move on to cheesecake and strawberry tarts, Felix Lévitan came before us to solemnly announce that Pollentier had been caught *in flagrante delicto* trying to defraud the controls. The International Jury of Commissaires had decided that, under 1978 UCI rules, Pollentier would receive an immediate two-month suspension and be fined 5000 Swiss francs ($3000). This meant Pollentier was banished from the race.

At the same time, Lévitan announced that seven Tourmen, including three Peugeots, had also been disqualified for having received more than 10 involuntary pushes.

In the circumstances there was nothing to do but return to the Hotel du Castellan. There, in room 32, Maertens was alone with Dhont when we arrived; Pollentier was still downstairs finishing his yogurt. The news couldn't have left them more dumbfounded, Maertens twice repeating, "*Mon dieu, c'est pas possible.*" Dhont then pointed out that it was he who treated the two of them. "But I can assure you," he said, "that if I give them vitamins and some pick-ups, that's where it stops. All that aside, Michel might well have been afraid of being declared positive."

By now, Maertens was black with rage. "There is so much to be said about tests, that it's better not to get started. My own feeling is that they've all been after us for some time because we're a bunch of small-time Belgians who get in the way. Anyway our boss, Paul Claeys, is here, I intend to speak to him, and if so we won't be leaving Tuesday. Michel is my friend, he's not just a teammate, and after what he's been through I don't see how I can be expected to want to race. As far as I'm concerned, the Tour de France is over."

Down below in the dining room, among a swarm of reporters, Pollentier was trying as best he could to get through his dessert. "Michel," we're all saying, "what the hell was going on in there?"

Pollentier, his head sunk, brazened it out, "Search me, as far as I know everything is in order. I've been told nothing, and I've had no official notice."

Then, with no wish to say anything further, he let big Marc De Meyer clear a passage for him through this dining room where, to say the least, the hotel guests were eating in something less than the desired tranquillity.

Looking worn out and forlorn, Pollentier made his way up to room 32. Maertens was there to greet him. But how could we go on pestering a rider who in shooting for the moon had put up such an effort only to find himself banned? Michel slumped down on his bed. Then, thrusting aside his suitcase, he took out the yellow jersey, stared at it, and then tossed it in the corner.

Then with a sigh Pollentier said, "Tell me, why on earth is this happening to me? True, I took a long time pissing, but it's also true that the doctor himself made no remark to me. When I inscribed my 'P3' everything seemed fine. The papers were all signed and countersigned. And why then did they wait for a whole hour before declaring a fraud? That beats me. You should also know that this is my second drug test of the Tour, and I've been through a lot of tests this season. Why today then am I getting all this?"

If Pollentier went on in his evident distress asking all these questions, while not replying, it was certainly understandable. Whatever may have been Pollentier's fault, he was undergoing a lot of pain, and one that for us embarrassed lookers-on verged on the insupportable. "What's left for me to say," he went on in a choking voice, "we've made up our minds and we're going home tomorrow, and I promise you — and I mean what I'm saying — I, for one, am never going to ride another Tour de France. You see that yellow jersey there, why don't you just deliver it to Hinault, it's his and that must be what some of them have been wanting all along."

In the midst of a heavy silence, Freddy turned to Michel Pollentier: "Don't worry, we're all going home, that'll suit me just fine." Pollentier replied that it was the boss's decision, and that the matter was out of his hands. "But why," he went on, "you all know the rule, why didn't I get a suspended sentence? I get a fine, a time penalty, but I can remain active as a racer?"

We answered that, according to the terms of the communiqué, he had drawn an immediate suspension of two months, which meant he was out of the race. Pollentier put his hands over his head before again muttering, "But why, why?"

Three floors down, the hotel lobby was buzzing. There was an announcement that the heads of Flandria were calling a press conference for 10 p.m. to announce that the team was quitting the race.

There was precedence for a withdrawal. In the 1930s, a Belgian team had declared forfeit after spectators had flung pepper in their faces. Then in 1950, the Italians withdrew at the end of the Pyrenees stage, even though they had the yellow jersey in Fiorenzo Magni, and the principal victim, Gino Bartali, a mystic who bicycled with a medal of Pius XII around his neck, had won that day's stage. Earlier in that Tour, between Niort and Bordeaux, there had been a series of incidents provoked by the Italians. Then on the Col d'Aspin an over-enthusiastic crowd had swarmed on to the roadway, causing the fall of Bartali and 1947 Tour winner Jean Robic. Among the fans who rushed over to help them on to their feet were a few who had been drinking, including a man with an open knife that he had been slicing a sausage roll with. This guy shouted to Gino, "Get away from your bike, we're going to get you." While some rabbit-punched Bartali and kicked him in the ribs, others threatened to waylay him further on. In spite of all this Gino crossed the finish line at St. Gaudens as the winner, only to learn that the yellow jersey had fallen on the shoulders of his arch rival, Magni. This was, indeed, rubbing salt into his wounds, and that night on behalf of the *squadra* Bartali announced his team's wholesale abandonment as "they had been victims of aggression." The next day, Magni sadly yielded his yellow jersey to the Swiss Ferdi Kubler — who refused to wear it — and Goddet felt obliged to halt the Riviera stage at Menton, rather than cross the border into Italy and the designated San Remo finish, for fear of stirring up further reprisals.

With a rest day ahead and no need to announce an immediate decision, the Flandria press conference kept being set back — three times that evening. Behind the scenes, though, the team was active, trying to stir up rider support for Pollentier. I know that Bruyère, for one, had been summoned to room 32, for what had all the markings of a united Belgian front. But Bruyère could hardly be counted upon to make common cause with the man whose diabolic pace on the Luitel had destroyed his own chances of preserving his yellow jersey.

This was on the whole, the reaction of the team leaders. Once the initial feelings of dismay — and disbelief — had passed, they each felt in their own way victimized by the presence of a hopped-up Pollentier. Most bitter of all was the new yellow jersey, Zoetemelk. When we told him the news, he was in the process of finishing his trout and about to set in on his roast veal. For a whole long moment, his fork stayed in a suspended gesture, faithfully imitated by his teammates. Then, as the full significance of his new position came over him, he drank a bit of mineral water before pouring out two glasses of wine, one for us and one for his father-in-law, Jacques Duchaussoy, whose naturally pink cheeks had assumed under the emotion a bright red.

"As for the yellow jersey," he said, emphasizing the nature of his, in fact, Pyrrhic victory, "I'm certainly not going to turn it down, though I would have much preferred to have won it on my own. Not only does Pollentier use illicit substances, but, because of them, he forces Hinault and me as well as our teammates to undertake the pursuit. We arrive at the bottom of the climb all exhausted, and from that moment on the race is not what it should have been. Instead of attacking, all we can think about is reducing the lead. While everyone watches everyone else, the teammates who have done all the work in the valley keep dropping off. With both Martin and Nilsson along with me, we could have tried a few things, and I'm sure Hinault would have reacted differently. What a mess, and God knows what the public reaction is going to be!"

In effect, Zoetemelk was running out of time, with only one mountain day left to build up the two-minute advantage that he needed to forestall Hinault's superiority in the forthcoming time trial. With Martin and Nilsson, both top-notch climbers, to attack in turn he could have drawn off Hinault, whose team was undermanned. Instead, the pursuit had forced him to sacrifice both Nilsson's chance in his individual battle with Lubberding for the white jersey, as well as victory in the team challenge, which went to TI Raleigh. Meanwhile, his own 47-second advantage over Hinault, the fruit of his Puy-de-Dome victory, had shrunk to 14 seconds.

Pollentier's attempt to cheat may have been heinous, but the manner of dealing with it left many an eyebrow raised. In the first place, the statute itself was so vague that the expulsion and two-month suspension was determined only after a 7:30 p.m. phone call on Sunday night from Jean Court, the president of the International Jury, to Mr. Jekiel, the UCI secretary-general in Geneva. Again, if Pollentier's fine and dismissal from the race were in the regulations, why had they not applied to Tourman Pedro Vilardebo riding here even though apprehended with the very same device in the Midi-Libre run a week before the Tour started?

Equally rankling was to see Guttierez, whose clumsiness in cheating had led to Pollentier's detection, go scot free. This may have been, as the Tour directors insisted, an oversight, and, as a result of Michel's letter, Guttierez found himself similarly penalized. But while a banned Pollentier moped on the beach at Rimini, there was his fellow culprit blithely pedaling about his French criteriums. Was there one law for French, and another for Belgians?

This suspicion of prejudice on the part of the race organizers, determined to have a Frenchman, Hinault, win the Tour, became all the more exacerbated when Lévitan announced, after he had finished reading Pollentier's poignant letter, that the ban on the Pushed Seven had been rescinded — too late to save Inaudi. Since Peugeot provides all the Tour cars under a favorable long-term contract, Lévitan's announcement was greeted by a huzzah of, "*Vive Peugeot!*" from the Belgian press.

Hinault was similarly dumbfounded. "I can't make any sense of it," he said. "In fact, it's for me utterly dismaying. Here we've had up to now one hell of a race. How can a champion of Michel's class commit such errors? As for the future, it's a whole new ball game, and one that deserves study. But Zoetemelk can't break away as brutally as Pollentier. In the time trial, I should have him in my sights."

While some of us Tourists moped, wits had a field day. One Belgian drew a caricature of Pollentier on the flagstones in front of a tall memorial to World War I dead. In the satirical *Canard Enchainé* a banner headline, punning on the comparative, gloated, "*Tour de France: çà va de mal en pisse'*" Another column of the same paper, under a provocative lead. "Urine regulates the world," compared Pollentier's indignities with the loss of liberty the nation as a whole now faced through the new alcohol test that had become law just two days before. This made it a crime to drive with more than 0.8-percent alcohol in one's bloodstream. As with Pollentier, the narrowness of the sampling process drew their fire. Was it fair to submit only car passengers to breath tests when it was well known that pedestrians are the cause of half the number of road accidents? Shouldn't they also be given breath tests? Why not start by testing each pedestrian as he emerged from his bistro? Moreover, in a great democratic society like France's, it was up to the nation's elected officials to set an example. A queue could be formed at the exit to the Assemblée Nationale bar. Political banquets and garden parties might be similarly promising. That would keep a deputy like Alain Peyrefitte from euphorically sounding off on such topics as reopening Devil's Island and the brothels. A piss test for everyone and let the Belgians be warned!

The next day dawned very clear, mountains sparkling under snow in a bright reflecting glare. There were skiers about, back from early-morning runs. But while much reporter gas and saliva was being spent on pisses and pushes, the Flandria team remained incommunicado. The excuse given was that no press conference would be given until President Claeys, who in the absence of any hotel space, had spent the night curled up in the front seat of his car, had caught up on his sleep. But the longer the conference was postponed, the less was the likelihood there would be a withdrawal. Too much was at stake — both for Maertens and Agostinho, and for Flandria in any future Tour. Finally, in early afternoon, a letter, written in French, and in Pollentier's hand, was delivered to Messrs. Goddet and Lévitan.

Dear Directors,

I am writing to you in order to do what I can to clarify yesterday's dramatic events. But first of all I want to ask you to accept my apologies for that part in the incident for which I am responsible. In this I can only assure you, gentlemen, that, all appearances to the contrary, I have neither the soul, nor the mentality of a cheater. I realize that you can only take into account the facts and decisions effected by the competent personnel of the medical board and the international commissary; all the same, I dare hope that you will open your heart to those other aspects of the question that my friends in Flandria and myself would like to bring to your attention. Without in any way attempting to minimize my alleged culpability, but for the sake of truth, I am asking you to bear in mind the following attenuating circumstances:

1) My career as a racing cyclist is certainly no more sullied with doping infractions than the majority of my Belgian or foreign colleagues;

2) The circumstances in which the urine tests were conducted make me wonder why the rider preceding me, whose instrument was similarly seized, was not accused, like me, of an attempt to fraud?

3) This last point is exactly what I want to underline. I stand accused of an "outright fraud," whereas in fact I have not committed a fraudulent act. The presence of a receptacle has been interpreted as such, whereas my own view is that the most one could talk about is an attempt to fraud. I never went so far as to make a substitution of urine, since under the doctor's eye I filled flask P3 with my own urine, in the most natural way in the world;

4) While I can't claim that I'm innocent, still the harried state in which I found myself after my exertions on the roads up to Alpe d'Huez accounts for quite a bit. You are familiar enough with the cycling milieu to realize that those sanctioned aren't always those most to blame.

I would like to thank both you, M. Goddet, and you M. Lévitan, for your patience and I promise you that I will be exceedingly grateful for any mitigating gestures that you might see fit to make. In this connection, may I ask you to inter-cede on my behalf with those international commissaires who make up the jury? If, thanks to your intercession, I am able to enjoy a measure of clemency I assure you that Michel Pollentier will be grateful to you for the rest of his life.

Believe me when I say that what hurts the most is the accusation of my hav-ing besmirched the Tour. You know and you have seen to what degree I have suf-fered along the roads of the Tour so that this holiday might be the most beautiful day of my career. Alas, I fear that it is going to remain my saddest.

In thanking you for whatever you see fit to do for me, I hope you will accept my feelings of sorrow.

Sincerely yours,

MICHEL POLLENTIER

As Pollentier's letter makes clear, the report the Tour issued that he was caught *in flagrante delicto* is simply not true. Perhaps he could not get his contraption working; but the fact remains that in all that hour of standing around he had not done anything to fill up his capsule. That put him in the situation of a man found with a gun outside a bank — whatever his intentions, the penalty should not be the same as if he had actually pulled the trigger. Rather than being summarily chucked out of the race and banned from riding for the next two months, he should have been docked the usual 10 minutes on race time. This was the penalty later given to José Nazabal, positive at the same Alpe d'Huez control. That would have allowed him to go on pollinating his mountains in quest of his chocolate company's prize. Being Pollentier, the chances are that he might have made up his time deficit in the next day's eight-pass Alpine stage.

In the old sweat-gang days when riders were their own physicians and traveled, like the Pelissier brothers, with a huge pillbox labeled "Dynamite" (containing cocaine for the eyes, chloroform for the gums, and nothing to prevent the toenails from falling out little by little, to an average of six in a 15-stage Tour), officials were content to look the other way. It didn't matter what you climbed your mountain on, so long as you got there and got down it.

Then came the death in the heat of the Rome Olympics of a Danish team time trialist, the first death that could be directly traced to amphetamines. But the real shocker was the death during the Mont Ventoux stage of the 1967 Tour de France of the British 1965 World Champion, Tom Simpson.

More successful than any previous British rider, he had won four single-day classics. When he became the first Englishman to hold the yellow jersey, his personal triumph became that of an entire sport. As a comparative outsider, Simpson brought to cycling a new flamboyance and a willingness to take risks. It has been argued that the bad luck that dogged his career was something he had brought on himself as the result of impatience and greed. But the author of a memoir titled "Cycling Is My Life" may not be able to afford the luxury of a self-perspective. From 12 onwards, when he received his first clunker, all he had wanted to be was a "good racing cyclist." If now and then he went into a ravine, that was the chance a winner took. The only real thing that scared him, he wrote a year before his death, was being "too old to ride." In these circumstances, it is hard to begrudge this 29-year-old rider his death at the hands of the sun on his own chosen terrain. In the palette of cycling, Simpson's place is in the ephemeral hues of his world champion's rainbow jersey.

That Simpson's death came on the Tour de France and where it did was no accident. For economic and professional reasons, it was the one race he needed to win. "If I fail, it will not have been for want of trying!" he wrote on the last page of his autobiography. "But I cannot afford to have any bad luck, such as in past attempts."

Between Simpson and the yellow jersey a singular impediment loomed, the Mont Ventoux that he had earlier called, "The Giant of Provence."

"This is a great mountain stuck out in the middle of nowhere and bleached white by the sun. It is like another world up there among the bare rocks and the glaring sun.

The white rocks reflect the heat, and the dust rises clinging to your arms, legs and face. I rode well up there doing about five miles to the gallon in perspiration. It was almost overwhelmingly hot up there and I think it was the only time I have got off my bike and my pants have nearly fallen down. They were soaked and heavy with sweat, which was running off me in streams and I had to wring out my socks because the sweat was running into my shoes."

In front of an ogre so daunting, one might feel tempted to reach blindfolded, into the pharmaceutical sack.

Overnight, though, the supply of magic substances capable of transporting riders over mountains had become drastically limited. To some observers it seemed more than coincidental that the morning Simpson started out from Marseille on his last ride was that of the Tour's first drug test. Anquetil, writing in *France Dimanche.*, laid the blame squarely on the new restrictions. In the Ventoux's heat, he wrote, "it was absolutely necessary to take something simply to breathe. Some *solucamphre*, for example. But with this new idiotic prohibition of all injections, it is possible that Tommy, that day, used a product less proven, less understood and perhaps more dangerous than solucamphre."

That next morning, the riders left Marseille, where a number of them had been tested, for Carpentras. At 120 miles in torrid heat (a café thermometer registered 131 degrees), the first attack began, set off by Jimenez and Poulidor. Behind them formed a trio made up of the eventual winner, Pingeon, the 1965 Tour winner Gimondi, and Simpson. Then Simpson started losing ground. Some two miles from the summit among the rocks and sand of a suspended lunar desert, he began to weave back and forth. Then he fell. Some spectators rushed out, righted him on his saddle, and pushed him off. Propelled by anonymous hands, he went on for some 300 yards, head hanging down typically over his right shoulder, all color drained from his face. Then he fell again. This time, no one tried to right him; he had lost consciousness. A spectator immediately tried to apply mouth-to-mouth resuscitation. Seconds later, Dr Dumas, the Tour doctor, arrived to give him an injection to steady his heart flow, while radioing for the police helicopter. He continued giving him oxygen until it arrived and Simpson, accompanied by another doctor and a nurse, was put aboard and flown to an Avignon hospital, where he died at 5.30 p.m.

But a couple of capsules had been found in the pockets of Simpson's jersey, and the autopsy revealed traces of amphetamine and methylamphetamine throughout his system. The medical report emphasized that while the dosage was not enough in itself to have killed him — he died of a heart attack brought on by heat prostration — it could have short-circuited the fail-safe mechanism that normally tells an athlete when he has reached the limits of his endurance.

The next day, the police, operating under a year-old Law 65412 — which made it a crime with a year's imprisonment to consume, prescribe, or offer certain listed drugs that artificially improved an athlete's performance — searched the British team's effects. In the baggage van they came upon a box belonging to Simpson. It contained, among other medical supplies, several tubes of Tonedrin and Stenamina, both drugs in the methylamphetamine group.

It seems clear now that Law 65412, which made it necessary for the Tour to come up with a form of drug-control testing, grew out of the state's reaction to the menace of a drug-changed society. The first searches under the new law were so clumsily carried out that they provoked a three-minute rider stoppage on the road to Biarritz. As Blondin wrote, "When four people dressed in trench coats knock on your hotel door to ask for your urine and papers, i.e. to ransack your luggage, we're not on the Tour de France, but in a Pigalle line-up. The stoppage, under the leadership of Anquetil, must have been rather grotesque: 100 champions dismounted and in the cause of their professional dignity chanted 'Merde!' with each pigeon-toed step as they dragged their mounts by the ears."

But the protest, as Blondin observes, fits the mood of the time, "Jockeys at the weigh-in circle, students dancing on some turned-over police car, pilgrims' backs bent on the road to Compostelo, nothing can give any indication of the effect of this painful march under the sun except the 'March of Fear' which, at the same time, saw the American blacks marching from Jackson to Memphis." We weren't there yet, but the riders had made clear the lengths to which they would, if necessary, go — no more testing, or no more Tour.

Like the runner from Marathon, Simpson's death made a deep and, it seems, lasting impression. Even today, hundreds of cycling fans still make an annual pilgrimage to Harworth, England, where Simpson lies buried. But the Tour officials were determined to exploit the circumstances of his death, and the 1968 Tour, which started from the mineral water spa of Vittel, became billed as the Tour of Health. "Doping," wrote Goddet on the eve of the start, "is no longer a mysterious sickness; uncontrollable and uncontrolled. Among the riders there is now, it seems, a common determination to be rid of this scourge. Dear Tom Simpson, you will not have fallen in vain on the stony desert of the Ventoux." The riders' unanimity may have been exaggerated — two were found positive and expelled from the race. "Still," as Geoffrey Nicholson wrote, the 1968 Tour "established certain principles. If a rider took dope he might well be caught. If he was caught he would be punished. And if he was punished he could expect no intervention from his fellow professionals. The days of organized boycotts and mass protests were over."

But in an issue of this sort, battles are never and can never be won. What is one to think of the current law voted in during an all-night session by delegates strung out on maxiton?

The battle shifted from direct confrontation to a duel between the riders and their trainers, on the one hand, and the medical labs on the other. Instead of stamping out a vile practice, the controls merely made it that much more injurious as the riders shifted from amphetamines to the even more harmful cortisones and anabolic steroids, which weren't detectable. One has only to look at the inflated, rugby-ball-size face of Eddy Merckx, forced to stop at only 32, to realize the harm this has done. If a man is determined to become the greatest cyclist of all time, he is not going to let a proscribed list get in his way! That list is, also, much too large, containing over 100 products of which only some three or four are actually dangerous. Since cyclists can't be expected to know their pharmacology, we have been treated to such sights as Agostinho stimulating himself with a laxative thinking it might help him run a time trial!

By the time Pollentier's letter was announced, I had learned that our return French-foreign press soccer match had been canceled because of the mass of business — a wise decision, for the hostilities could well have gotten out of hand. With the afternoon at my disposal, I decided to take in the glassed-in Alpe d'Huez swimming pool. Topless bathing suits, against the snow-clad backdrop, might well offer a consolation.

On the way to the swimming pool, in respect to a long-standing appointment, I stopped off to see British rider Barry Hoban. It was Hoban who, after Simpson's death, was given the honor of being allowed to take the next day's stage at Sète. A few years later, he would marry Simpson's widow, Helen, and adopt their two children.

Hoban with his wide melon mouth has one of the most expressive faces in cycling. A little man with a deep chest, he has won a number of classics, as well as eight Tour stage victories. This year, at 38, Barry was enjoying one of his better seasons when, as he was whizzing down the Luitel in last month's Dauphiné-Libéré, he skidded off the road breaking an arm bone. He is just now beginning to get himself back into shape, enough to give him some hope of pulling off a sprint coup once out of the mountains.

When I called him, Hoban had just finished lunch and was preparing to go up to the room he shared with Zoetemelk to nap. He invited me to have coffee with him on the balcony. "How do you feel?" he said, wanting to put me at my ease.

"Lousy," I found myself answering. For almost a day I have carried around, beside the usual tears, a dry burning sensation at the back of the throat. The only thing like it I have ever felt before is when I had my wallet picked in a Tananarive market.

"But you have to remember," Barry said, "that cyclists are just ordinary people."

Giants of the Road ordinary people? A rarer, more specialized calling would be hard to imagine.

Cycling is, no doubt, one of the great fitness sports. Because the body's weight is taken off the legs, the blood is constantly being recirculated through the system, with a consequent slowing down of the work required of the heart. Cyclist's heart muscles are unusually expanded. They have also one of the slowest heart rates.

But at the competitive level bicycle racing, because it calls on every muscle of the body except the sexual, is very draining. Add the long mountain stages, where difficulties like the Luitel and the Alpe d'Huez climbs come at the end of the race, and one can see why riders require four hours more sleep a day than most people. But it is precisely this sleep that the riders, partly because of the transfers, have not been getting. This is because the course structure is largely determined by commercial considerations — which towns will pay the most for the publicity that the race brings. At L'Alpe d'Huez, many riders complained that they had difficulty sleeping because of the unaccustomed high altitude. But the Raleigh team's petition to spend the second night in Grenoble at lower altitude, which would have meant two hours of extra sleep next day, was turned down for fear of offending the civic authorities. Englishman Paul Sherwen told John Wilcockson, "I never needed anything as an amateur. But I now have injections daily of C and B vitamins."

Others, "more than 50 percent," according to Pollentier, resort to something stronger than vitamins. Jean-Luc Vandenbroucke was found to have traces of anabolic steroids during the August world championships, a drug that he had begun taking during the Tour to survive the long stages. Anabolic steroids are synthesized male hormones that retain the minerals that pass through the body. In that sense they nourish, and one can see bodybuilders with T-shirts proclaiming, "Dianobol, the Breakfast of Champions." They also can have, like birth-control pills, dangerous side-effects: Blood pressure goes up, liver rots, and the testes atrophy. But this is only in a small percentage of cases, and there is a school of sports medicine, in East Germany notably, that believes these can be prevented if intakes are continually monitored as to dosage. Also, changes are not necessarily permanent. Those bloated bodies with the husky voices and veins pushing through thin, tight, colorless skin disappear under a program of down-training. Where most athletes put on weight alarmingly after they retire, we can see a Kornelia Ender 14 pounds lighter and much slimmer only a year after her triple swimming gold medals in the Montreal Olympics. But she comes from a country where athletes are not thrown away like old shoes once they have ceased competition .

In a single-day race it is possible to treat riders like a car that has sprung an oil leak. In the Tour de France, riders have to be treated. They fall off their bicycles, they become sick, and they suffer nutritional breakdown. In the old Tour, there used to be a rest day after each stage. In the modern streamlined Tour, there is one every eight to 10 days. And the bicycling season is itself just as crowded. Restaurants cannot supply enough nutrition to offset what is being consumed in exercise. One result is that the vitamin companies are now sponsoring trade teams. Renault-Gitane is also

Vitagermine. Others provide hand-outs at the start and the feeding-points on a licensed basis. One can be a health nut like Barry Hoban, whose whole family diets with him. At 38, he is living proof that such clean living, and attention to sleep, pays off. But at the same time one might agree with the point Jacques Goddet raised at a press conference later that Monday afternoon. "The problem is whether we are to allow cyclists to prepare themselves as they wish. Are they to be allowed the freedom of their destiny?"

One step toward sanity would be to concentrate on dosage rather than a pro-scribed list of products. It's one thing for an insomniac to take a sleeping pill; it's quite another if he swallows the tube. Hallucinogens are a case in point. In an exper-iment highly significant for human longevity, the curer of Parkinson's disease, George Cotzias, discovered that, whereas most rats live to seven months, those fed on mescaline attained an age of 16 months and were twice as large. Again, mor-phine, a great curative drug, is not addictive if prescribed in very small, but numer-ous, daily amounts.

As it is, a great deal remains to be learned about athletes and their metabolism. Why are certain riders such as Laurent, Bruyère and Pollentier essentially wet-weath-er performers? Why do Kuiper and Agostinho thrive in hot sunlight? If performances depend so on a rider's morphology, we should find out more about the human mus-cle structure and its nutritional needs. Instead, most doctors have only been able to conceive of medicine in negative, curative terms. Because of this, they have tended to put the generalities of their so-called science at the service of state repression.

Beyond all this, the present system of controls encourages cheating. A number of riders, among them Van Impe and Agostinho, went through the whole Tour with-out being tested. If a law is to apply, then everyone should be tested. If this can't be done, then, as Pollentier suggested, controls should apply to the first 10 of a stage.

In a sport as brief and dangerous as cycling, riders very quickly acquire pru-dence. A Tom Simpson may have believed in luck; most riders don't and can't afford to. Blondin sums it up well, "It's neither with medals nor millions that men are lured to their tombs. On the contrary, I would assert that most of the time everything possible is done to arm riders against a misleading view of their own powers. But this is done so that the essential, of knowing what it means to go too far, will never cease to belong to them.

"The temptation to hitch our systems to an outside motor is as old as the human race. The improvements that can be brought to this, in the field of mechan-ics, are such that they can generally excite the technically minded. In our field, one quick look at the stage map and the weather within the perspective of a climb in torrid heat or an endless flat-country haul in the wind and the rain, and it becomes obvious that exceptional measures are required. That a rider shoots up concerns only himself — up to the moment when the surrounding conditions verge on the invidious. Nonetheless, in a rider's life there are moments and places where circumstances require that he transcend himself. Each struggles to face up to that obligation.

"As sports fans we prefer to dream about angels on wheels, Simon Pures somehow immune to the uppers and downers of our own pill-popping society. My own opinion is that there is, all the same, a certain nobility in those who have gone down into lord knows what hell in quest of the best of themselves. We might feel tempted to tell them that they should not have done it. But we can remain, nonetheless, secretly proud of what they have done. Their wan, haggard looks are, for us, an offering."

Grenoble to Morzine

With the king Bruyère unfrocked and his successor, the kamikaze Pollentier banished, our poor plot had considerably thinned. It was as if the wide-open mountain landscape of the earlier race with its constantly fluctuating rivers, lakes, prairies had been suddenly replaced by a long narrow tunnel. That it led all the way to Nancy, five days away, gave the Hinault-Zoetemelk duel a certain perilous eeriness. With only 14 seconds between them, the knives had to be razor sharp; one unattended puncture and Hinault could be off the cliff. But the swordplay, riveting as it might be, hardly consoled for the adventure and majesty taken away.

This feeling was particularly poignant in Pollentier's case. If ever a rider represented the beloved uncertainty principle it was this Belgian gnome. Waging a war with plainly insufficient means — witness the streak of bad luck in the team time trial, the puncture in the wine test of truth, the several serious falls, and the near-death on the Puy-de-Dôme — he nonetheless conducted himself with brio in the spirit of a great guerrilla captain. Wherever there was the slightest chance of an action, even if the action did not concern him personally, there he was, gambling brilliantly and with great courage. He was willing to try anything, anywhere; on the top of a mountain or in some finish-line toilet, it hardly mattered. That his bag of resources was not as unlimited as he made out only added to the drama — when would he run out! When his very versatility with its element of hocus-pocus, of bluff, finally caught up with him, we still felt the way fans do when the referees start playing the game among themselves. Rules are rules, but to dish out a virtual goal for each inconsequential trip or nudge in the penalty area cheapens what should be a rare, decisive act. Entertaining and very brave, the little balding doped-up rider in the clown-like jersey had showed what it was to play with everything you had, and a bit more.

Where Pollentier was the perfect clown, making you laugh and weep within seeming instants of one another, Bruyère was majesty incarnate. Part of the satisfaction, doubtless, was physical. Tall, slope-shouldered, fair spoken, his gold-capped teeth glinting against his yellow jersey, Joseph had looked the regal part. But his charm, and the charm of his reign, came also from the panache with which he seized the yellow jersey in the course of those two bold raids, and then confirmed what he had won in the two time-trial tourneys. His strength came in this sense from his innocence. He had not plotted and schemed to acquire the precious tunic. His willingness to renounce the Picardy breakaway once it had reached four minutes testifies certainly to the purity of his intentions. Nor did he ever regard the yellow jersey as his eternal possession. There were others, he made clear, better entitled to it by build, if not by bearing. Like anything else that is beautiful, it represented a trust to be renewed on a day-to-day basis. Never did he let the badge of high office mislead him into thinking that he was somebody he wasn't. By remaining always a commoner he was able to demonstrate the true magical power of the yellow jersey he represented. Many of us can rise to an occasion. But to go on day after day surpassing your own and everybody else's expectations reveals a very special state of grace.

As eight-day reigns go, Bruyère's was singularly beneficent. Diversity flourished, a great race became all the more open. His defenses were offenses bringing credit to the Tour. Wherever he was, in the high pastures of the Pyrenees, or in a Bordeaux hotel bar on the night of his coronation, amid the ringing phones sitting up until 12:30 a.m. with his two glasses of beer, he brought out a sense of what being a yellow jersey was all about.

For all concerned, today's eight-pass, 117-mile jog from Grenoble across the French Alps to Morzine, represents the last running-out of the tide. After that, the loop back to Paris begins. The kids in the "cigarette" Jeep lifting me in the foggy early morning gloom out of the Alpe d'Huez mountain citadel tell me that for customs reasons they won't be accompanying us to Lausanne, but will instead cut up along the Jura to await the Tour at Belfort. With each further day, the publicity caravan will continue shrinking, as the individual vehicles detach themselves to slink back to their provincial roosts.

For the mountain men, it's the last chance to make a difference before the race gets handed back to the road sprinters. While all eyes are riveted on the yellow jersey duel between Hinault and Zoetemelk, it's possible that other actors may step forth from the wings to take up where Bruyère left off. Had Pollentier remained in the race, we might have been treated to one of Agostinho's patented 100-mile solo escapes. But that possibility is not to be ruled out by other teams playing the same game. All depends, as always, on the speed at which the Alps are to be taken. After 16 days of racing, systems are stretched to the breaking point. The tighter that cord is pulled, the more likely something is going to snap, as Bruyère snapped on the Luitel, and as Zoetemelk almost did on the Alpe d'Huez climb. Today's stage, with its three first-category climbs alone, has been designed as a festival of possible explosions. And there are riders about with nothing to lose, like Kuiper, who are willing to bring on that kind of anarchy. If that happens, we could be in for a whole new race.

If others' organisms have not yet snapped, our poor car's has. The brakes that melted on us in the heat at the bottom of the Luitel are apparently not the sort that can be fixed with a new lining. Fortunately there is no sun overhead to threaten us, and if we can stay far enough ahead so that we don't have to descend in a tight, honking, rubber-squealing file, we may not have to drive on to Morzine by a mountain-skirting route.

The 10-mile climb to the Porte Pass has thus for us, too, its experimental inter-

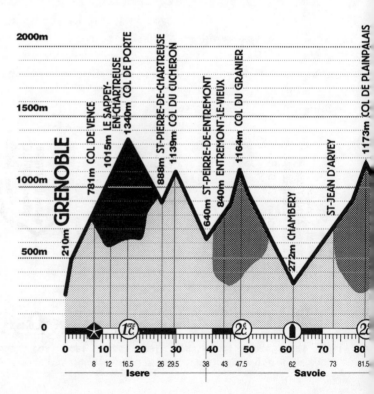

STAGE 17:
GRENOBLE
TO MORZINE

est. Thillet negotiates it in rally-winning style, never once touching the brakes, followed at a distance by Martinez's delegate, André Romero. One would think that, with his new mountain jersey and an extra day to complete his recovery from bronchitis, Martinez's troubles would be over. But for some reason the gods are not inclined to favor this dour individualist. On the rest day, as he was coming out of his hotel — the same where I had, in spite of my people (who had me banished to other valleys), secured a cot by the boiler room — he missed one of the steps and fell, receiving an ugly gash along his left nostril. But X-rays taken at the Grenoble hospital where he was whisked by helicopter showed nothing broken, and he was able to take the start. But knowing himself impaired by the antibiotics he had to take, it made sense to delegate Romero on an early breakaway. Romero takes the hot-points sprint at the Vence Pass and 20 points at the Porte summit, where he has a 1:12 lead.

On the Porte descent, Hinault tries to break away, only to be caught by some 10 riders. Their pace is fast enough to swallow up Romero at the Cucheron Pass.

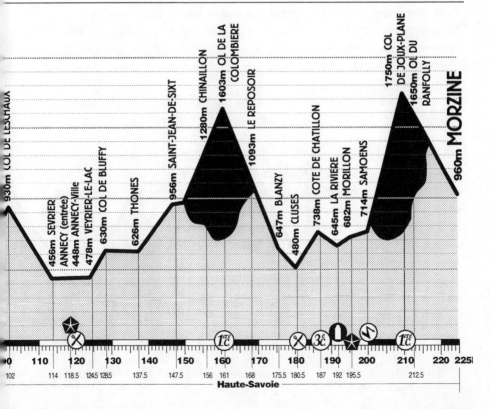

Here Kuiper, pedaling with a power he has been unable to show until now, goes on the attack, taking the pass, followed by what becomes a 26-man chasing group. The battle is really raging now, riders being left behind and catching up on the descents, only to be left behind once more. Kuiper pursues his offensive on the much steeper Granier Pass, taking that too. On the descent Hinault replies, breaking away with Zoetemelk. Pursuing them, Kuiper found his path on a curve barred by a pair of rocks. Kuiper elected stupidly to cut between them, only to miscalculate and have his rear wheel nick. For a moment as Kuiper crashed it looked as if he was going to land on his head. Instead, his left shoulder took the brunt of the impact. With the clavicle fractured and the bone sticking out, there was no choice but to put Kuiper on the helicopter and fly him to Chambéry to be operated on. Aware that he had got off comparatively lightly, Kuiper still felt chagrined at having stupidly fallen at a moment when he was coming into his own, and had his whole family waiting for him at Morzine.

With Kuiper, the last rider able to explode the race, gone, tactics shifted. Where before there were two leading entities — Zoetemelk and Hinault — there was now one Siamese twin, each of its members tied by an umbilical cord of caution. Zoetemelk had certainly the better team. He was also intrinsically the better climber, as his performance on the Puy-de-Dôme amply testified. But climbing in a time trial under your own momentum is different from climbing with a rider like Hinault dogging your wheel.

As the pace abruptly slowed following Kuiper's crash, René Bittinger saw a chance of righting the score a little on Pollentier's behalf, and at the same time furthering Agostinho's chances. That the race still had 82 miles and five major passes to go hardly mattered. By attacking, he was forcing the pack into a pursuit that would have to be led by Hinault and Zoetemelk. In that case, they would be exposing themselves to a challenging counterattack by a fresh Agostinho, with Bittinger well placed ahead to serve as a relay man.

Something of the same logic also occurred to Seznec, Zoetemelk's head lieutenant in this situation, as on the Tourmalet a week earlier. When Bittinger took off, Seznec went after him, partly to neutralize him in the interests of the team challenge, partly to be available as a rallying point should Zoetemelk manage to extricate himself from Hinault's paralyzing grasp.

With Zoetemelk covered, it was up to Hinault to react. Had Hinault anyone like Seznec available, he might have pursued the same tactic. But having just lost his one available climber, Bernaudeau, to appendicitis, he decided to slow the pace down and await reinforcements. Besides, he had nothing too much to fear from Seznec and Bittinger, respectively 18:34 and 39:44 behind on overall time.

Thus developed the most moving of all the escapes we were to witness, one that saw them at one point leading by more than 18 minutes. That was stepping out of the wings with a vengeance! Moreover, most of this lead was attained with Bittinger doing all the work, Seznec stirring himself only to cop the hot-points sprint alongside the lake at Annecy with its 20-second bonus. It was shortly thereafter, past that deepest, most magical of mountain-ringed lakes, that negotiations between the pair were finally, concluded: Bittinger was to take the mountain-pass primes, and Seznec the hot-point sprint; also Bittinger, in reward for his efforts, was to be allowed to claim first place.

With Seznec pitching in with a ready will, the lead grew from 12:30 to 18:00 in 15 miles, enough to make Seznec the virtual yellow jersey. Under pursuit, this dropped to 11:30 at the Colombière summit, only to lengthen again in the valley with the help of a favorable sidewind. By now, Seznec must have begun seeing things: a whole house, maybe someday, of his own; 30 to 35 criterium invitations; a boost in salary, not to mention whatever stakes were to be gleaned on the way. He had just garnered the largest of these, a $2000 prime at Samoëns, when he saw his Alsatian colleague suffering from an attack of hunger cramps. In the circumstances, Seznec might have given Bittinger some of his own food. At the very least, he might have said something to his flight companion, such as "Thank you," or, "I hope we see each other again in Morzine." But doubtless this would have led to some further entreaty, and more time loss. Instead, Seznec decided to drop Bittinger without a word, and mount the Joux-Plane on his own.

The Joux-Plane is a new pass to the Tour riders, opened only in 1976 to tie the Upper Giffre with the valley of the Dranse. Its south side rises 3609 feet in about eight miles at an average 7.3 percent grade, with certain passages of 13 percent. Knetemann, for one, was to call it the single hardest mountain in the Tour. But Seznec, his long legs falling evenly on his pedals, climbed it well, losing only a minute and a half to his much fresher, and equally battling pursuers. In spite of his 6-foot 2-inch, 146-pound. build, he negotiated the acrobatic descent in the mist well enough to win at Morzine by 10 minutes. With the help of 40 seconds in bonus, he shot into fourth place in the overall standing between Agostinho and Bruyère.

Once Seznec left him, Bittinger faded rapidly, and for some moments we had reason to fear that the Flandria rider might not even make the Joux-Plane summit. In his haste, he had neglected to take in a musette bag at the last feeding station, and the result was the first attack of hunger cramps he had ever had. He might well have had to quit but for a spectator who gave him a bottle of beer and some salad leaves. He crossed the summit line in fourth place, but in such a weakened state that 10 riders passed him in the run down to Morzine.

In retrospect, the alpine showdown we had been promised was clearly fudged. For one, the course itself was too long to allow for an all-out battle, even of the sort Kuiper was proposing. In this connection, the Porte pass placed at the outset was clearly wasted. Had it come in the middle, or even better yet, at the two-thirds point, it might, like the Luitel, have provoked another dénouement. And the Joux-Plane for all its rigor lay too far away from Morzine. What was the point of battling elbow-to-elbow to the summit when the defeated rider could so easily catch up again in the long descent? Still, the reality of Seznec's achievement throws a backward light on what Kuiper was well on his way to accomplishing. Had he broken away, would Zoetemelk and Hinault have been able to overcome their difference, and the disparity between their two teams, in order to undertake a common pursuit?

Instead of an all-out battle, we witnessed in the wake of our fleeing tandem a series of *pas de deux* between the mated couples. Thus all the way up to the Joux-Plane, preceding the yellow jersey pair and in a sense announcing them, came the white jersey duo of Nilsson and Lubberding. Lubberding's ability to grit his teeth and keep pace with a specialist who soundly trounced him in the 1976 Tour de l'Avenir shows future promise. And for elegance of pedal thrust the Dutchman is already in a class beyond Bruyère and Hinault. But to precede a pair that had beaten them both by five minutes on the Pla d'Adet shows the temporizing nature of the yellow-jersey duel.

It is not exactly fair to second-guess a rider of Zoetemelk's veteran stature. Riders know to a precise shade their limits, and had Zoetemelk tried to accomplish more, no doubt sooner or later he would have had to pay for it. We had seen him attack when he was able to on the Pla d'Adet. But his astounding victory on the Puy-de-Dôme was his high-water mark. His performance at L'Alpe d'Huez, where he was distanced by Kuiper and Hinault, revealed a new fragility. Nor was this helped when at one of the day's passes a spectator dumped a bucket of water over his sweating self. In the cold of the long descent, that turned to bronchitis, and Joop only barely made Paris.

A clue to the peculiar nature of the duel between Zoetemelk and Hinault occurred in mid-race when Hinault punctured as he was leading the descent down the Colombière. In last year's Tour, Zoetemelk had been a victim of just such opportunism when he had got tangled up in a crash, only to see his main rivals, Van Impe excepted, spurt off. But for neither Zoetemelk nor Wellens to take advantage of the proffered opportunity could show the limited nature of their goals. Second place may, after a while, breed its own familiarity, and after three such what is wrong with a fourth, especially if cushioned by a few days in the yellow jersey?

This capacity to underestimate himself, shared by Wellens, Bruyère and so many other Tour riders, was one that Hinault had the confidence to exploit. With Hinault, as with his manager Guimard, everything seems the result of the most precise and full preparation. A more lucid, more French, temperament would be hard to imagine. To this, Hinault is capable of adding his own earthy, pugnacious Celtic twist. The combination is not exactly foolproof, and we had seen it go awry on the Puy-de-Dôme as the result of a strike for which he knew himself in a large way responsible. That knowledge, and the guilt he had to bear, interfered for two days with that most precious of all things to a rider — his sleep. Here though, perfectly recuperated after a rest day spent loafing with his wife and family friends on an alpine meadow above L'Alpe d'Huez, Hinault was able to put his rivals to the test. Accelerating on each of the passes, leading the descents to avoid getting caught in a spill, and above all pulling his enormous sprocket, Hinault left Zoetemelk, Wellens and Agostinho without the resources to generate a counter-offensive of their own. In circumstances that called plainly for an attack if he were to wrest his needed two-minute advantage before Metz, Zoetemelk found himself struggling to hang on in the hope of an eventual remission. When a mile from Morzine Hinault made a last effort, Zoetemelk was only barely able to keep touch and save his yellow jersey. Now, his main chance gone, he is obliged to pin his hopes on the unlikelihood of his own time-trial victory. He reminds us that he had, both on the long flat before the Puy-de-Dôme and in the first part of the wine-country time trial, kept more or less pace with the French champion. In other words, he is not going to go out there, three days from now, already beaten.

Other than the continued confirmation of Zoet's Merciers in the team challenge, and Martinez's loss of his one-day-old mountain jersey to Hinault, the main news concerned the eight who found the going too hard for them, among them three Peugeots, Sibille, Danguillaume and Ovion. This time, given a second chance, they disappeared quietly on their own. They didn't need to be pushed. Meanwhile Karstens, who did, found himself chucked out of the Tour. It is perhaps worth noting that our not-so-lovable clown was wearing No. 13 in this his ninth Tour.

Morzine to Lausanne

After a week of bouncing about from mountain to mountain, a stop in Switzerland seemed de rigueur before the Tour moved northward to tackle the more ancient chain of the Jura. In the spirit of Switzerland the 86-mile Morzine to Lausanne stage had all the attractions of a miniature: three mountain passes of third-category scale; with two at the outset and one in the foothills of the Bernese Alps above Montreux, separated by a run around the Lake of Geneva, and a final three-lap circuit of Lausanne-Ouchy. With the scale rider-sized, rather than giant-sized, everybody had a chance, and the result was a real race with a lot constantly going on from start to finish.

The Corbier pass at the outset was a bit more than the usual third-category endeavor. One of those hurdles that, if you're a Martinez obliged to make a last ditch effort, it perhaps behooved you to take at a flying leap. That he did, streaking out at the start, with Van Impe on his jersey tail. Despite the impediment, he still managed to reach the Corbier summit 3 seconds to the good, and 40 seconds ahead of Hinault, Zoetemelk and Agostinho. On the descent to La Solitude, in a steeply winding smugglers' countryside already more suggestive of Switzerland than the Savoy, Van Impe tried to sneak away, only to be countered by Maertens leading on Martinez and the Siamese pair. One hundred-fifty yards behind them, and struggling in the rain that would endure for the whole race, was Agostinho. But Maertens, the moment he saw that Agostinho was in difficulty, let up in order to act as the Portuguese's squire, another novel role for him. But such was the respect of the breakaway quartet for Maertens that the moment he stopped, they renounced, realizing they were not going to outrun the two of them.

From La Solitude, the road ran, by one of those sleights-of-hand well known to linguists, past Abondance before crossing the Swiss border as we climbed the last of the Alps, the 4500-foot Pas de Morgins. Watched by natives sheltering pleasantly under giant rhubarb leaves, Martinez beat out Menendez to draw virtually even with Hinault in the Grand Prix de la Montagne. Here on the descent, such is the power of the Swiss franc to enthuse the heart, Pierre Bazzo and Ward Janssens decided to launch themselves out. Down against the distinct, finely vacillating line of crests (patched with fog in its lower reaches), the two of them shot, to be overtaken and passed in turn by a quartet of Nilsson, Maertens, Oliva and Laurent — the Frenchman who is always at his best in rainy going.

Behind them the pursuers split into two chasing groups, with a moment of panic as Zoetemelk found himself in the second of these, 12 seconds back. After a chase along the lake road, a junction was finally made at the Porte du Sex as the Tour crossed the valley of the Rhône. Some idea of the speed of these proceedings may be gleaned if one realizes that at this point, the 42-mile mark, the 26-man lead group held a five-minute advantage over the main 45-man pack. It was also touchy for Hinault. As the lone Renault in the lead group, he was opposed to a concerted attack. Much further back was Jacques Esclassan, pedaling bravely despite a horrid fall on the Corbier pass.

With the Canton of Vaud not willing to turn over to the Tour more than half of the road, there was understandable caution as we climbed the Blonay hill above the hotels of Montreux. Nabokov used to say that up here he had the wonderful sense of having once again come upon his childhood Russia; not the landscape, but the butterflies that still were to him that lost landscape. Here, after a long elbow-to-elbow battle among the vineyards, Hinault saw Martinez pull ahead of him in the last yards to retake the mountain jersey.

With the pack obliged by the slippery conditions to proceed gingerly down through the terraced vineyards towards Ouchy, the port of Lausanne, it was the turn of the Teka riders to try to redeem themselves. First it was the victor of Biarritz, Miguel Maria Lasa, countered by Knetemann, who went on the offensive; then

STAGE 18: MORZINE TO LAUSANNE

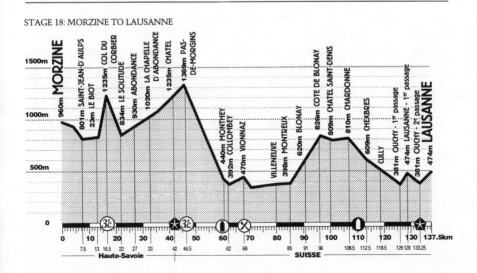

Oliva and Menendez together. The third and real break was launched by Michel Laurent, working here in a congenial sniper's role. Freddy Maertens bounded on his wheel, only to attack in turn. Bazzo, who has come out of eclipse in the course of these last two days, countered him just long enough to permit Oliva and Knetemann to shoot forward to dispute the hot-points sprint at Ouchy on the first turn of the three-lap circuit.

Oliva remained up there just long enough to serve as a magnet for Wellens, Janssens, Bruyère, and Agostinho in that order, the Portuguese mainly concerned not to let the former yellow jersey sneak ahead of him. At this point, seven miles of the race remained, enough time to light a few fires in the overall race standings. With Hinault and Zoetemelk locked in their own negative game in the midst of the 18-man pursuing pack, Bruyère decided to go all out. With Agostinho, Wellens, and Bruyère's C&A teammate, Janssens, of a like mind, a most interesting flame developed. By the time it was finally extinguished, they had all improved their positions by two minutes, Bruyère taking back from Seznec his rightful fourth place, while Agostinho now trailed Hinault and Zoetemelk by only four minutes. Meanwhile, eyes most open of all, was Gerrie Knetemann. Making use of a series of very difficult attacks by Wellens, he barreled by from his last place position to win the stage by 13 seconds. As a victory it pleased him far more than his two-day charade in the yellow jersey; after all that was what riding was about; all of this said with a vehemence that made us suspect that there might be more in the offing between Lausanne and Paris.

Knetemann has long since finished giving his views when Esclassan straggles in, 24:36 back, but 15 minutes ahead of Jacky Hardy, the first Tourman to be disqualified on time. Esclassan's condition is such that he can barely walk. The doctors decide that he must go to the hospital to have any traces of gravel properly washed out of his sores. Since Thillet has an interview with him, we go off to the Peugeot team hotel to try out the local *fendant* (if ever wine came out of a mountain river it would be fendant).

When Esclassan comes in, he tells us that he almost climbed into the sag wagon, "After all, I was entitled to, after a fall like that. But with so many teammates begging off, I felt obliged to try to go on. I have no hope of winning another stage, just getting to Paris will be enough. You know every day is painful, and if a rider can't stand the suffering, he doesn't stick around long."

Next morning at 9, a heavily sedated Esclassan was at the starting line. At the finish in Belfort, as he wheeled in five hours later, he was told that he had won for the second day running the bank prize. Only this time it was for his courage.

STAGE 19

Lausanne to Belfort

The main point of next day's 113-mile trek from Lausanne to Belfort was to get the Tour somewhat in the neighborhood of Metz, the starting point of Friday's time trial that would decide the ultimate issue of the yellow jersey. I emphasize "somewhat" since Belfort, its wonderful lion aside (by Frédéric Auguste Bartholdi who sculpted the Statue of Liberty), is still a good hop, skip and a jump from Metz, as is in turn Nancy from Épernay. It was as if this beautiful loop that we had been patiently drawing, spoke by spoke, around the puzzle map of France had suddenly at the three-quarter mark broken down, necessitating a pair of ungainly leaps over the missing pieces.

The course, albeit of a real beauty up the escarpment of the Jura and then along the headwaters of the Doubs, had the disadvantage of having its major obstacles all located in the first part of the race. As Seznec proved, a solo rider can mount a hill just about as fast as his pursuers. But 70 miles in the flat is a long way to go against a pack intent on preserving positions.

For the Big People of the pack, the day was an occasion to relax before tomorrow's time trial. Only at the Franco-Swiss border did Hinault bestir himself from Zoetemelk's side long enough to glean a few mountain points and make Martinez squirm that much more fitfully on his king-of-the-mountain hot seat. Then he was back where he wanted to be, talking to his new friend.

Neither Zoetemelk nor Hinault are what one might think of as talkative, the Dutchman to a degree that imperils his standing as a team leader. Yet even after they had arrived in Lausanne, they were for hours talking on and on, as if unable to believe all that they have in common. In some sense, theirs is a confrontation of two different generations — Zoetemelk being a survivor of the Merckx era and almost 10 years older than the French champion. But they have both gone to the bottom and tested each other, and the experience has left them with the most obvious respect. Even biking side by side, under the closest of guards, they are constantly smiling. Since Zoetemelk has the better team and Hinault has been, on the whole, rather isolated, the Frenchman's tactic has been to try to intimidate him. So, we have seen him spurt off, or lead a descent, or suddenly in the middle of nowhere accelerate only to turn around and see if the Dutchman is still there. Why not enjoy once again some of the privileges of childhood?

While spent organisms were trying to repair themselves in view of tomorrow's time trial, the Tour's Little People — the sprinters — found themselves given an unaccustomed leave with which to settle their own personal accounts. At Beaulieu, with 16 miles to go, just as we were resigning ourselves to another Freddy Maertens mass sprint victory, and after escape bids by Plet, Fussien and Coccolo had all been suppressed, an 11-man breakaway developed: De Meyer, Raas and Wesemael (Raleigh), Lasa and Vilardebo (Teka), Hoban, Beucherie, Vandenbroucke, Teirlinck, Dillen, Gauthier. As a conflict in styles, in personalities, it was everything one could wish, complicated by the team factor, since two men have an advantage over one.

As a front bodyguard for Maertens, De Meyer's role was to restrain, but with

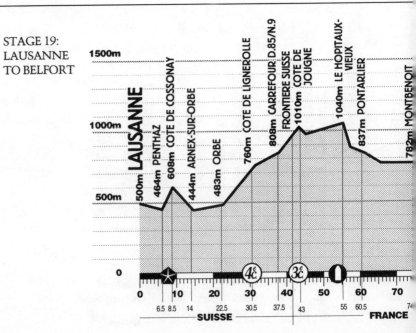

STAGE 19:
LAUSANNE
TO BELFORT

10 wild horses doing the pulling ahead of him there was not much that even a man of his threatening capacity could accomplish. In less than six miles they had built up a two-minute lead, one that would decline only 10 seconds in the next six miles. With nine teams represented in the breakaway, one can understand the pack's lack of interest. Then, with only four miles to go at the hot-points sprint at Trévenans — won by Teirlinck— the Merciers finally reacted to protect their yellow team caps from the Raleighs. With Mathis, Perret, Le Guilloux and Mollet leading the chase, the advance soon declined to a respectable half-minute.

With two miles to go, Vandenbroucke, whose strength lies more in his stamina than his sprinter's spurt, tried to launch himself on his huge 55x13 gear. When De Meyer countered him, it became Wesemael's turn to try the same tactic, in effect preparing the way for Jan Raas. Then Dillen tried to catapult himself free, only to give way to De Meyer, who at the last-kilometer red flag realized the time had come to assume command. Our eyes, meanwhile, are on Barry Hoban, who has a chance for once of wresting a ninth career Tour stage victory. Where a De Meyer relies on his strength to burn every one else out, a sprinter of smaller build such as Hoban must rely on suppleness. His asset is the little man's quickness of acceleration, sustained by a smaller gear ratio than the huge sprockets that allow the power sprinters to launch themselves from further out, using momentum to

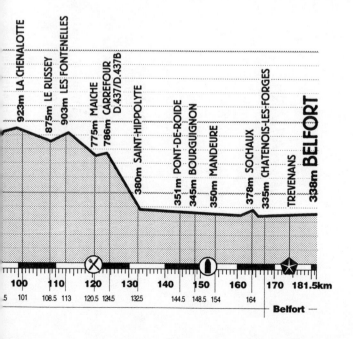

make up for lack of acceleration. A small man, Hoban's weight is in his upper body. In the mountains, this disadvantages him, but here his relatively deep chest allows him to gulp in air and quickly convert it to his own particular rocket fuel.

Hoban had taken a position just to the right of De Meyer so as to be on the inside as the final curve straightens out: a coveted position, and one Raas had his eyes on as well. Hoban did not seem to have anticipated Raas's surge, or for that matter the full extent of Wesemael's accompanying harassment, shunting him to the right at the 250-yard mark just as the track itself curved in that direction. With Hoban eliminated, since you can't sprint on a curving track, Raas sailed through and had the victory seemingly within his grasp when De Meyer staged one of his patented comebacks, standing up and smashing down on his pedals in his great 1976 Paris-Roubaix manner to win by a tube length. Furious at having every trick in the book perpetrated on him, Hoban found a measure of comfort in De Meyer's revenge, the Belgian's first Tour victory: "De Meyer, at least, is a real rider, and I couldn't be happier for him."

STAGE 20

Metz to Nancy time trial

The Tour was now down to the wire: the very long individual time trial between Nancy and Metz, two great and still culturally preserved Lorraine cities. Whoever at the day's end possessed the yellow jersey would probably hold it all the way to Paris.

The 14-second advantage that Zoetemelk brought in may not in itself have been much — about 180 yards in this 46-mile time trial. But the psychological advantage it gave was not unappreciable. On the one hand, being the yellow jersey is always an asset, especially in a time trial where the responsibility, the sense of what he represents, can allow a rider to transcend himself. On the other, by starting last, Zoetemelk had the advantage of being able to pace his own effort so as to make the most use of his own reserves.

Hinault, too, had his advantages, not the least being that he had beaten the Dutchman by three minutes over a similar distance in last year's Grand Prix des Nations. He was further helped by the relatively flat profile of a course with its two slight hills: the first, a 265-foot vertical rise between Solgne and Secourt at the 22-mile mark; the second, of 600 feet at the Morey hill five miles later. On a flat stretch, with both making it clear that they would go with their most powerful harness, power and the ability to churn it counted. Here, Hinault with his youth, build and better health possessed a clear-cut advantage.

Pre-race prognostics varied. Some like Poulidor saw Zoetemelk winning by a parcel of seconds, whereas Bruyère favored Hinault by slightly under a minute. Yet Zoetemelk himself, at the start of the Tour, saw himself losing to Hinault by three minutes. Even now he probably would not have shortened that by more than a minute. His best chance lay in Hinault's having an off day of the kind he had experienced on the Puy-de-Dôme.

Instead, it was Zoetemelk who had the off-day, due to the bronchitis that had begun to take hold of his system. For a moment, there was a suggestion advanced that he avail himself of ephedrine, a drug that had the double advantage of being both a stimulant and the only medical means of curing bronchitis. But Zoetemelk categorically refused. He had been badly scarred by last year's positive control after his Morzine to Avoriaz time-trial victory, the first such in his career, and one that may well have been inadvertent on his part, as he claimed.

Beginning near St. Stephen's cathedral, with its tall, luminous stained glass, the course followed the valley of the Moselle, albeit on a fairly straight false-flat. As the first starter of the two, it behooved Hinault to go all out in the beginning in order to put his rival under a maximum psychological pressure. After this first thrust, he would change to a more steady pace, saving himself for the two hills. Whereas for Zoetemelk, it was the two hills themselves that would be his primary focus. Here he hoped to catch up any ground he might have lost earlier, after which he would do his best to keep pace with the Breton.

So no one in the Dutchman's camp was unduly alarmed as Joop yielded 11 seconds in the first four miles, and 30 seconds at the 13-mile mark. In the next six-mile stretch, this narrowed to a mere four seconds more — perhaps Hinault was beginning to pay the price for having bolted off at too fast a clip.

But at a moment when the sidewind was beginning to pick up in force over the exposed gravelly road, one look at a TV screen would have shown two utterly dif-

STAGE 20: METZ TO NANCY TIME TRIAL

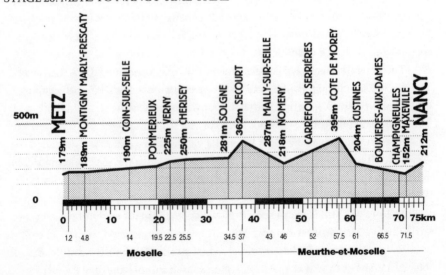

Distance and time in Stage 20

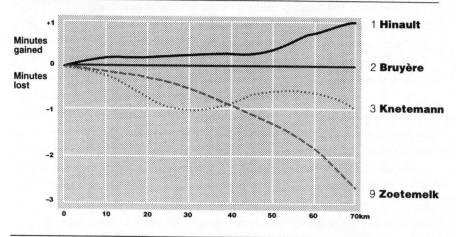

ferent profiles. Hinault's might not have been the crouched cat, aerodynamic profile of a Merckx, but the regularity of his pedaling even as it now and then lifted him free of the saddle, the meeting of the arched curves of his body, always aligned over the bike, was not without its harmony. Once more, he proved himself the master of the detail: fussing with the length of his shorts (couldn't their design be improved?); or reaching down with a practiced gesture to pick a flea from his tires, so thin that a bite would be enough for a puncture. Whereas Zoetemelk seemed a trifle stiff, and his jerky chest action as he lifted his head at the bottom of each incline to adjust his breathing, his moments of hesitation, all betrayed the pain he was undergoing in keeping to his chosen cadence.

The two hills, instead of favoring Zoetemelk, only confirmed the French champion's physical superiority, as his lead grew by a full minute. For Zoetemelk, although he was able to finish sprinting, the next hour was torture, as he finished ninth, 4:10 behind Hinault, and only 9 seconds ahead of Van Impe.

By then, Hinault knew he had won the yellow jersey and in all likelihood the Tour. Not having been able, for tactical reasons, to stage the long solo mountain breakaway that he had originally intended, he did not want to muff this last occasion to show his class. With Bruyère only 16 seconds behind, and 20 miles still to go, the issue was still far from settled. Now, dipping into his superior reserves on a ground of an almost utter flatness, Hinault began turning it on to such an extent that he was able to overtake Agostinho, who had the fifth best time of the day, in Nancy. Hinault's time was 1:39:28, an almost exact minute ahead of Bruyère. For a

Tour winner, a more complete demonstration would be hard to imagine.

If the anticipated duel between Hinault and Zoetemelk failed to materialize, the time trial still settled a number of accounts. One concerned Knetemann's return to form. If for the second straight time he had to yield to Bruyère, he still managed to come in third, a creditable 1:58 behind Hinault. Fourth was his teammate Paul Wellens, almost another full minute back. For a rider not tough enough to withstand the suffering of the Evreux to Caen team time trial, these last stages have brought a whole new confidence. If anything like this progression continues, one can imagine him a candidate for the yellow jersey in a couple of years. Something of the same promise may some day hold for a third Raleigh, Lubberding, dueling here with Nilsson for the white jersey. Lubberding's time, 4:29 behind Hinault, may not have been particularly impressive, but with Nilsson a further two minutes behind he may have had some reason to lift his feet from the pedals. Nilsson's performance cost him a place in the first 10 overall, as Martinez edged him out by two seconds. Better still was Van Impe, who vaulted over them into ninth place, proving that for him too the Tour had been a couple of weeks too early in getting started.

Stage 20: Metz to Nancy time trial

1	BERNARD HINAULT *(Gitane)*	1:39:29
2	Bruyère *(C&A)*	at 1:01
3	Knetemann *(Raleigh)*	1:58
4	Wellens *(Raleigh)*	2:47
5	Agostinho *(Flandria)*	3:01
6	De Meyer *(Flandria)*	3:36
7	Vandenbroucke *(Peugeot)*	3:46
8	Galdos *(Kas)*	3:58
9	Zoetemelk *(Mercier)*	4:10
10	Wesemael *(Raleigh)*	4:14

Overall classification after Stage 20 (Yellow jersey)

1 BERNARD HINAULT (Gitane) 97:55:08
2 Zoetemelk (Mercier) at 3:56
3 Agostinho (Flandria) 5:54
4 Bruyère (C&A) 9:04
5 Seznec (Mercier) 12:50
6 Wellens (Raleigh) 14:38
7 Galdos (Kas) 17:08
8 Lubberding (Raleigh) 18:48
9 Van Impe (C&A) 21:01
10 Martinez (Jobo) 22:58

Épernay to Soissons
to Compiègne to Senlis

Tours are literally "turns" as well as "towers," and now after all the swirling monuments of Nancy the Tour de France transferred by train to Épernay to begin the closing of the final northward arc. The Big Loop — La Grande Boucle — as the Tour is known, was about to be buckled. What better place to punch in a last hole before the final procession on to the Champs-Elysées than in the town of champagne's Dom Pérignon?

In the race, the remaining question concerned the mountain jersey. That Hinault had no love lost on Martinez had been evident ever since their epic battle of words, of pocketbooks, and finally of sprinting skills on the Pla d'Adet. Martinez may for the moment have copped that round; all the more reason then to teach this upstart a lesson in the art of respecting one's betters. A reign, and Hinault's promises to be a fairly long one, should start with a certain firmness. One may suppose that arguments of this kind were not lacking, buttressed by the thought of all that additional booty to be parceled out among his deserving retainers — can a cyclist's coffers ever be too full? One might even think that a Knetemann, a Pollentier, a Seznec, would have hardly given the issue a thought before stepping in.

But there was, also, another side of the scale, involving what has become a Tour tradition. When he of the insatiable jaw, the terrible Merckx, grabbed all three jerseys for the first time ever in 1969, the public let it be known that this was going a bit too far. There may have been charity candidates before, worthy of a yellow jersey's generosity, but this year Martinez and his fleabag Jobos have managed to present themselves as the purest waifs going, living day-to-day, hand-to-mouth. When the waif, after years of neglect, the public dole, and all that, manages to catch bronchitis and is actually spitting blood in his boss's car before the start of a race that in other circumstances he might have won, the public may well take him into their hearts.

While Hinault and Guimard kept up a circumspect silence as to their intentions, interest shifted to poor Zoetemelk. In the middle of the night his chest pains were such that a doctor had to be summoned, giving him a light sedative and a pill for inflammation of the lungs. Married to a French woman, and living at Germigny l'Eveque, only 25 miles from Senlis, Zoetemelk was, along with Fussien, one of the locals of the course. That made it all the more important to stick it out, though there was a reason to fear he might have to give up a fourth second place that he had amply merited.

The 129-mile race involved a novel experiment. Instead of half-legs as at St. Willebrord and Valence d'Agen, we were going to have third-legs at Soissons and Compiègne, with a finish on the banked velodrome at Senlis. With the riders staying on their bikes, the course amounted to a kind of bicycling leapfrog, times being taken at each measuring point and added to the overall classification. But after the humiliation of the mountains, it gave the sprinters a penultimate chance to display their muscles before Sunday's rendezvous on the Champs-Elysées.

With Hinault in the yellow jersey, the task of maintaining order fell to the Renault-Gitanes. In rolling thickly forested country, set with occasional open fields of tall white opium poppies and glinting yellow colza, their mission was very much facilitated by a strong head wind that kept the pack of 78 survivors tightly bunched.

Five miles into the day on the steep climb past the Taitinger vineyard to Hautvilliers, our most important question was answered, although Martinez had to yield first place to the Britisher Sherwen, who had ridden it the year before in the Paris-Reims amateur race. The same pattern was apparent on the two remaining smaller hill climbs, with Sherwen's teammate, Dominique Sanders, preceding Martinez, while Hinault stayed discreetly within the bunch.

The first bunched sprint at Soissons (49 miles) was won by the reigning master, Freddy Maertens, ahead of a surprisingly recovered Esclassan. To forestall a repetition, a small six-rider breakaway got underway on the outskirts of Compiègne. In the ensuing sprint, Wesemael beat Fussien. But no one wanted to make anything further of the 11-second advance, and once the sprint line was passed everything returned to the status quo.

This could hardly have been satisfactory for Fussien; to return from one more thwarted breakaway and have to hear, "Why don't you take off again? If you don't the speed per hour will fall!" Perhaps they had forgotten his exploit earlier this year in Paris-Nice, when our clown had gone off at the start of a leg to wheel 120 solo miles at an average 26 mph.

His occasion came at the hot-points sprint at Liancourt, with 20 miles of the race still to go. With a chance to pick up a few more shekels for his denuded coffers he took off, so successfully, that he had a 1:18 lead as he passed his home at Verneuil-en-Halatte. At the second hot-points sprint at Creil, 10 miles from Senlis, his lead was still about a minute. Now with all the cameras focused on this one fleeing form, there began a very exciting pursuit. Had Fussien survived to Senlis there is reason to believe he would be alive today. Contracts would have come in, and instead of being run down at an intersection while training near his home, he would have been racing at a criterium. Instead, cycling all alone into a strong head wind, Fussien ran out of strength five miles outside the cathedral town of Senlis, and Chalmel caught up with him at the head of a seven-man posse that included Jan Raas.

Meanwhile, moving at its usual end-of-race clip, the pack was thundering down on them. Three miles from Senlis, the junction was made. But in the ensuing confusion, and just as we were prepared to see De Meyer taking over in another Maertens sprint operation, Raas pulled a virtual replica of his St. Willebrord triumph, extracting himself to win by a vigorous 14 seconds. Behind him, true to form, Maertens regulated Bertin, Esclassan, and a very creditable Barry Hoban. For Raas, it was a fine way of bringing the Tour full circle. That the symmetrical regularity also included, besides the aborted triumph in the Leiden prologue, three second places and a share in the team victory at Caen, must be a hopeful portent to a rider who had no idea beforehand if he could even get over the mountains.

Forgotten in the symmetrical perfection of Raas's achievement were the examples of courage: Esclassan risking another fall on the velodrome; Zoetemelk hanging on in the Reims mountain climb and in the Oise valley to arrive despite a 102-degree temperature.

St. Germain-en-Laye to Paris, Champs-Elysées

Sunday July 22 has been proclaimed National Bicycle Day. In honor of the two-wheeler, the famed Champs-Elysées cobbles have undergone a complete scouring: gallons of detergent, followed in turn by an army of hoses and brooms. If rain could cancel a prologue, might not dust do the same for the epilogue? Meanwhile, a vast rectangle, extending from the Place Charles de Gaulle and the Trocadero Square down to the City Hall, has been cordoned off to traffic. To entertain the expected million spectators come to witness "Bernard Hinault's Apotheosis," as a banner front-page headline has already titled the event, there will be two preliminary races: a Prix Henri Desgrange-Victor Goddet for the male amateurs, and a Prix Geo Lefèvre for the women. Then, at about 2:40 p.m., the Tour riders will burst on to the flag-draped Champs-Elysées for a six-lap circuit at the end of a 100-mile race.

The Tour de France has always ended in Paris, but the Champs-Elysées never figured in the ceremonial pomp until 1975. When a sixth of the city turned out for the event, a number exceeded only by the Liberation, it became an annual fixture, a triumphal parade that was also a sports event drawing spectators from all over the globe. For an apotheosis, there could hardly be a more fitting site than the Elysian Fields, that happy hunting-ground of Greek mythology and modern pocketbooks.

Meanwhile, I have been whisked out to the St. Germain start by an Antenne 2 television crew, the same bunch I had got a lift with when they were filming Bruyère's loss of his yellow jersey. On what is certainly the most radiant day of the past month, if not the year, I have an image of what another year's Tour might be — jerseys and faces reflecting in the sharp, unpolluted, sabbath light; a beautiful sport becomes even more so. We are early, and while waiting for a crowd to assemble one of the TV technicians and I go down to the swimming pool to fetch some coffee.

STAGE 22:
SAINT-GERMAIN-EN-LAYE
TO PARIS

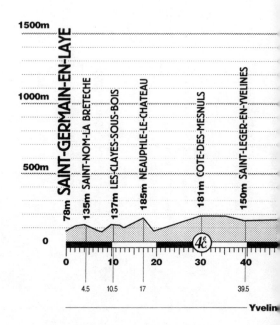

There, by our former press headquarters where people are now once again swimming, he tells me how much he envies me as an American. Everything in France, he says, is so small, and closed-in, and finally bourgeois. Whereas in America things are open, and there is adventure. People are willing to experiment, one is not so bound by family and social structures. A visitor's view, and one valid for those who don't have to take in the accompanying mayhem, that daily discothèque that, say, California is. But I ask him how can he say that Europe lacks adventure when we have just seen in the Tour de France an adventure to rival any ever created? How could people be poorer, more unprotected, and braver than these cyclists? So often one feels one lives in a dwindled time, and here are these Tourmen, appearing from the bottom of the social echelon, to prove that grandeur still wonderfully exists, and doing it with a camaraderie, a respect for one another, that goes straight to the heart. I think of Mariano Martinez spitting blood at the Besse-en-Chandesse start; of Pollentier and Maertens smiling silently in that hotel window in Clermont-Ferrand; of Bruyère fighting off his cramps at the head of a band on the Alpe d'Huez;

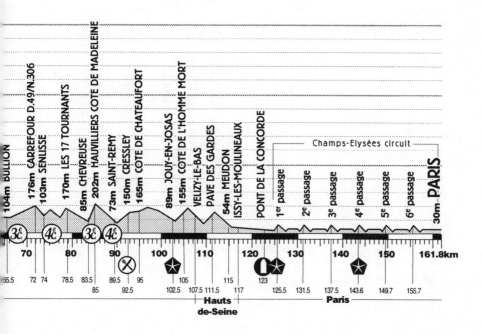

104m BULLION
176m CARREFOUR D.49/N.306
103m SENLISSE
170m LES 17 TOURNANTS
85m CHEVREUSE
202m HAUVILLIERS COTE DE MADELEINE
73m SAINT-REMY
150m CRESSLEY
165m COTE DE CHATEAUFORT
89m JOUY-EN-JOSAS
155m COTE DE L'HOMME MORT
VELIZY-LE-BAS
PAVE DES GARDES
54m MEUDON
ISSY-LES-MOULINEAUX
PONT DE LA CONCORDE
1er passage
2e passage
3e passage
4e passage
5e passage
6e passage
30m PARIS

Champs-Elysées circuit

70   80   90   100   110   120   130   140   150   161.8km

65.5   72 74   78.5 83.5   89.5   95   105   115   123   125.5 131.5   137.5 143.6   149.7   155.7

85   92.5   102.5 107.5 111.5   117

⊢ Hauts ⊣
de-Seine

⊢ Paris ⊣

of Fussien pedaling alone into the wind at Senlis; of Geminiani, bottle and jokes in hand, leaning out of a car window anywhere.

There, side by side with them, is the countryside, these 2.500 miles of routes that remain even for the riders a privilege to pedal through. If certain of them, the Tourmalet or the Puy-de-Dôme, are marvels of nature, most of it is a countryside that people have helped shape and preserve. All along the roadway we meet their successors, smiling, encouraging, with a joy I have never encountered this side of Nepal.

All of this is, like the bicycle itself, highly positive, and a tribute to the Tour organization. Similarly, any race that goes down to its next-to-last stage waiting to be decided is a good race. Of those left in the Tour, Hinault is clearly the best rider. One might wish that Pollentier and Kuiper were still around to put Hinault and his team to a final test. In their absence, a shadow of a doubt remains, and one that will not be fully resolved until after the 1979 Tour.

In the history of the Tour, there have been only two last-day surprises — in

Route of Stage 22

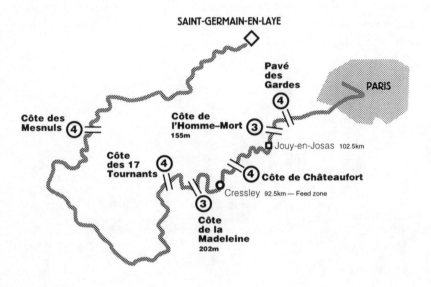

SAINT-GERMAIN-EN-LAYE

Pavé
des
Gardes

④

PARIS

Côte des
Mesnuls ④

Côte de
l'Homme–Mort ③
155m

☐ Jouy-en-Josas 102.5km

Côte
des 17 ④
Tournants

④ Côte de Châteaufort

Cressley 92.5km — Feed zone

③

Côte
de la
Madeleine
202m

1947, when Jean Robic escaped with Fachleitner to win the yellow jersey; and 1968, when Jan Janssen overtook Herman Van Springel in the final time trial. And forewarned is forearmed. Not that sufficient obstacles have not been provided, the organizers having scoured the Parisian region to come up with no less than six hills; but with the last 35 miles from the finish, there is not too much chance of a successful breakaway. At the 60-mile mark Maria-Miguel Lasa attacks to take a 22-second lead at the top of Dead Man's hill, but the Renault-Gitanes led by Chalmel succeed in restoring order, as they do after Paul Sherwen's escape bid on the descent from the Pavé des Gardes toward Meudon.

So it is that the Tour arrives on the Champs-Elysées in almost martial formation — as the tradition warrants. Here at the outset, Lubberding attacks to take a 16-second lead, followed after a regroupment by Legeay. But as so often on these occasions, it is the Foreign Legion that provides much of the color. Profiting from a moment of inattention on the part of the Gitanes, three Dutchman, Knetemann, Lubberding and Fedor den Hertog, and a lone Belgian, René Martens, attack. In a moment, Seznec tries to join, envisioning the sort of sprint he likes on the incline. But the quartet's relaying succeeds in distancing the French threat. The slowest of the four, Den Hertog, launches the sprint — mainly, it would seem, to make it all the more difficult for Martens. Knetemann profits to win by a full second, his second in five days, and the 11th Raleigh stage victory in the Tour. A minute later, Bertin wins the pack sprint ahead of Esclassan.

RACE RESULTS

General classification

1	BERNARD HINAULT	
	(Renault-Gitane-Campagnolo)	108:18:00
2	Zoetemelk (Mercier)	at 3:56
3	Agostinho (Flandria)	6:34
4	Bruyère (C&A)	9:04
5	Seznec (Mercier)	12:50
6	Wellens (Raleigh)	14:38
7	Galdos (Kas)	17:08
8	Lubberding (Raleigh)	17:26
9	Van Impe (C&A)	21:01
10	Martinez (Jobo)	22:58
11	Nilsson (Mercier)	23:00
12	Martin (Mercier)	32:58
13	Maertens (Flandria)	34:26
14	Laurent (Peugeot)	40:00
15	Romero (Jobo)	49:34
16	Janssens (C&A)	51:19
17	Hézard (Peugeot)	53:20
18	Menendez (Teka)	53:28
19	Bittinger (Flandria)	53:47
20	De Schoenmaecker (C&A)	54:14
21	Bazzo (Lejeune)	55:35
22	Martins (Teka)	57:07
23	Lelay (Fiat)	57:40
24	Raas (Raleigh)	58:43
25	Den Hertog (Lejeune)	1:01:46
26	Martens (C&A)	1:02:29
27	Le Guilloux (Mercier)	1:02:40
28	Bourreau (Peugeot)	1:06:34
29	Perret (Mercier)	1:06:34
30	Julien (Jobo)	1:06:45
31	Villemiane (Gitane)	1:07:50
32	Pujol (Kas)	1:08:20
33	Rouxel (Mercier)	1:09:19
34	Kelly (Flandria)	1:10:18
35	Thaler (Raleigh)	1:10:22
36	Mollet (Mercier)	1:13:38
37	Chaumaz (Gitane)	1:15:50
38	Teirlinck (Gitane)	1:16:30
39	Oliva (Teka)	1:20:08
40	Vilardebo (Teka)	1:21:27
41	Lasa (Teka)	1:21:37
42	Legeay (Lejeune)	1:29:19
43	Knetemann (Raleigh)	1:30:10
44	Beyssens (Flandria)	1:31:58
45	Mathis (Mercier)	1:34:40
45	Alfonsel (Teka)	1:34:58
47	Wesemael (Raleigh)	1:36:14
48	De Carvalho (Fiat)	1:39:48
49	De Meyer (Flandria)	1:40:50
50	Sanders (Fiat)	1:41:26
51	Dillen (C&A)	1:41:31
52	Didier (Gitane)	1:44:44
53	Muselet (Flandria)	1:48:10
54	Patritti (Jobo)	1:50:07
55	De Cauwer (Raleigh)	1:50:12
56	Van Vlierberghe (Flandria)	1:52:03
57	Van Den Hoek (Raleigh)	1:53:13
58	Quilfen (Gitane)	1:53:46
59	Tinazzi (Flandria)	1:53:46
60	Laurens (C&A)	1:56:53
61	Esclassan (Peugeot)	2:00:25
62	Bossis (Gitane)	2:02:36
63	Chalmel (Gitane)	2:03:23
64	Vandenbroucke (Peugeot)	2:04:00
65	Hoban (Mercier)	2:06:33
66	Plet (Lejeune)	2:10:16
67	Beucherie (Fiat)	2:16:40
68	Durel (Jobo)	2:17:13
69	Gauthier (Lejeune)	2:17:16
70	Sherwen (Fiat)	2:18:34
71	Budet (Fiat)	2:20:13
72	Bertolo (Jobo)	2:25:50
73	Fussien (Fiat)	2:27:20
74	Bertin (Gitane)	2:36:31
75	Gisiger (Lejeune)	2:49:16
76	Delepine (Peugeot)	3:02:41
77	Coccolo (Jobo)	3:24:13
78	Tesnière (Fiat)	3:52:26

King of the Mountains

		POINTS
1	Martinez *(Jobo)*	187
2	Hinault *(Gitane)*	176
3	Zoetemelk *(Mercier)*	155
4	Seznec *(Mercier)*	90
5	Agostinho *(Flandria)*	73
6	Nilsson *(Mercier)*	70
7	Wellens *(Raleigh)*	68
8	Bittinger *(Flandria)*	63
9	Lelay *(Fiat)*	54
10	Van Impe *(C&A)*	53
11	Martin *(Mercier)*	41
12	Romero *(Jobo)*	41
13	Menendez *(Teka)*	40
14	Lubberding *(Raleigh)*	39
15	Galdos *(Kas)*	37
16	Bruyère *(C&A)*	36
17	Sanders *(Fiat)*	24
18	Legeay *(Lejeune)*	24
19	Fussien *(Fiat)*	21
20	Laurent *(Peugeot)*	20

Green Jersey

		POINTS
1	Maertens *(Flandria)*	242
2	Esclassan *(Peugeot)*	189
3	Hinault *(Gitane)*	123
4	Raas *(Raleigh)*	109
5	Bruyère *(C&A)*	100
6	Thaler *(Raleigh)*	91
7	Bertin *(Gitane)*	79
8	Bossis *(Gitane)*	74
9	Zoetemelk *(Mercier)*	71
10	Agostinho *(Flandria)*	70
11	Wellens *(Raleigh)*	67
12	Kelly *(Flandria)*	60
13	Seznec *(Mercier)*	56
14	Lubberding *(Raleigh)*	51
15	Martinez *(Jobo)*	50
16	De Meyer *(Flandria)*	46
17	Lasa *(Teka)*	45
18	Fussien *(Flandria)*	45
19	Martens *(C&A)*	39
20	Nilsson *(Mercier)*	35

White Jersey

1	Lubberding *(Raleigh)*
2	Nilsson *(Mercier)*
3	Bittinger *(Flandria)*
4	Bazzo *(Lejeune)*
5	Lelay *(Fiat)*

Hot-points competition

		POINTS
1	Bossis *(Gitane)*	95
2	Tesnière *(Fiat)*	60
3	Villemiane *(Gitane)*	52
4	Maertens *(Flandria)*	44
5	Laurens *(C&A)*	21
6	Fussien *(Flandria)*	18
7	Hinault *(Gitane)*	18
8	Esclassan *(Peugeot)*	16
9	Bertin *(Gitane)*	15
10	Kelly *(Flandria)*	14

Team points competition (Green caps)

		POINTS			POINTS
1	TI Raleigh-McGregor	720	7	Jobo-Superia	1656
2	Renault-Gitane-Campagnolo	933	8	Lejeune-BP	1729
3	Velda-Lano-Flandria	972	9	Fiat-La France	2347
4	Miko-Mercier-Hutchinson	1072	10	Teka	2629
5	Peugeot-Esso-Michelin	1144	11	Kas	*(non-classed)*
6	C&A	1456			

Team classification (Yellow caps)

1	Miko-Mercier-Hutchinson	562:06:38	6	Peugeot-Esso-Michelin	566:11:19
2	TI Raleigh-McGregor	562:30:18	7	Lejeune-BP	566:38:05
3	C&A	562:54:14	8	Teka	566:58:40
4	Velda-Lano-Flandria	563:21:36	9	Jobo-Superia	567:09:40
5	Renault-Gitane-Campagnolo	563:53:37	10	Fiat-La France	569:07:19

POSTSCRIPT

There have been better Tours de France, but from a neophyte's point of view, it would be hard to fault what the 1978 edition gave me. With five riders all locked within one minute of one another as late as the 16th L'Alpe d'Huez stage, it was an open multi-team race; one in which almost anything, it seemed, could happen. And what did told me a lot about character, about what a yellow jersey meant to a Bruyère, a Pollentier.

And what the race lacked in competition, it more than made up for in scandal. From the various misfortunes of the Leiden prologue, to the ground-breaking riders' strike and the Pollentier pissing fiasco, it could not have been more instructive. On the one side, there was the vast commercial apparatus of the Tour organization revolving around the nomadic army of us journalists. On the other, the 110 riders, these gladiators who had clawed their way out of a trapped life, capable of anything because they had so little to lose. Uniting the two, and the real star of the occasion, was the epic landscape the race battled through, with its 20 million spectators for whom the Tour was something else again — summer itself, a festival, a happening.

Historically, the 1978 Tour marked year one of Bernard Hinault's reign. His five Tour victories were, I suppose, predictable — who else was there? — but not the completeness of his domination, or the way he was able to pass on the baton to what would have seemed impossible at the time, an American, Greg LeMond. And LeMond, returning from a very serious injury in 1988, gave us the most emotionally satisfying of Tours in his gutsy, come-from-behind last day victory over Frenchman Laurent Fignon.

But the 1978 race marked a watershed in another sense as well for Hinault's two major rivals, Bruyère and Pollentier. Bruyère would go on to win only one more race — his hometown Liège-Bastogne-Liège — before retiring in 1980. Pollentier would ride on through 1983, winning a somewhat undeserved Tour of Flanders, but he was never the same rider again. Looking back, it is clear that both Bruyère and Pollentier in their different ways, gambled their whole career on this one race. And both lost. To me that says a great deal about the quality of the 1978 race, of how very much was at stake.

It was perhaps inevitable that Bruyère would collapse under the burden of the yellow jersey. Beautiful rider that he was, it is hard not to see him as a relic from another era, and one who a strange set of circumstances had propelled into the yellow jersey. But once in that jersey, it was as if he was possessed by something outside of himself — the greatest rider of all time, Eddy Merckx. It was Merckx's extraordinary presence (and, I suspect, Merckx's cortisone) that allowed Bruyère to rise so above himself. For a rider of his size to climb that splendidly, day after day, mountain after mountain, had something of a miracle about it. And when that great oak cracked, however momentarily, on the Luitel, that marked the end of a wonderful, not to say incredible, "last hurrah." Or rather, Bruyère had just one more race, one more gulp of cortisone, left in him — Liège-Bastogne-Liège.

Bruyère's demise, his inability to sustain the weight of the yellow jersey all the way to Paris, makes sense of a kind. A foreign antibody, whether a Merckx or a magic potion, remains a foreign antibody. But Pollentier's is harder to explain. At 27, he was hardly over the hill. Perhaps a leader's shoes did not fit him as well as I had imagined. Perhaps it was the presence of that whole supporting Flandria team, of having riders like Agostinho, De Meyer, Sean Kelly, and his great pal, Freddy Maertens, that had made him the rider he was. There was a team blank, a leadership vacancy, and somebody had to fill it, collect all those shekels. Or did he attribute all those victories of the preceding year to a few good gulps of alupin, that perfectly legal children's asthma drug that helped his breathing in the mountains? Perhaps, too, it was a mistake for a pot-bellied gnome of his sort to sign on with a beer company like Splendor. But then cycling is, above all, a sport of the will, of a rider's self-belief. And once the morale cracks, as Pollentier's clearly did, he had no choice but to become what he was in so many eyes — a clown. Popular and well paid Pollentier may have been. But that very lonely art of winning had slipped out of his grasp.

The demises of Bruyère and Pollentier stand out all the more in that the two other contenders, Zoetemelk and Kuiper, would both go on riding to a ripe, utterly credible 40. Joop became, at 37, the oldest Tour de France winner. Kuiper never figured in another major stage race. But he did win, in his late 30s, the best classic I ever witnessed, a Paris-Roubaix in appalling mud. And both of them won in their sunset years the world championship. Clean living? In cycling, I believe, there is no such thing as pure unadulterated cleanliness. But Zoetemelk and Kuiper have always been riders' riders, people who trained seriously, who treated themselves and their profession with respect.

An ill-fated bunch, Flandria. Maertens dragged on for two years without success — although he did stage a comeback in 1981 that included winning the world road championship. He then fell back into a slough, never finishing races, even at the kermesse level. Had he, too, overdosed? And what of Marc De Meyer, a Tour stage winner at Belfort, and the victim a year later of a lethal heart attack? Unluckier still was the wonderfully fit Agostinho, the owner of a big cattle ranch outside of Lisbon, who was killed at 43 in a bunch-sprint finish when a dog happened to run out. As a team, theirs was a very brief reign, but something of their spirit survived in Sean Kelly, the best day-in, day-out rider for most of the next decade.

Even more tragic in its way was the fate of the 1978 Tour's clown prince, Jean-Jacques Fussien. While out training in September near his home in the Paris suburbs — Fussien got nailed by a truck on one of those big traffic circles and died instantly.

The 1978 Tour, with its 11 teams, seemed epic enough to me. But by present standards it marks a bygone era. In 1978, the riders came mainly from four countries: the Netherlands, Belgium, France and Spain. Today, the 22 teams have riders hailing from all over the globe. In 1978, no American had even completed the Tour de France. That's how truly insular the sport was. With the emergence of Sean Kelly, the appearance of middle-class riders with different values like Phil Anderson, Greg LeMond, Fignon, not to mention the influx of "amateur" riders from Eastern Europe, the whole dynamic of cycling changed. The sport I saw took place in a social backwater, in a landscape of industrial blight. And it was the notion of that sub-proletariat, that class of the forgotten-about, the dispossessed, that gave cycling its charm, its coherence. Seen from within the ghetto, the racers had something epic, colossal, about them. They were "giants of the road," men who on their fantasy bicycles transcended the great mountains. And the mountains, as everyone knew, were not very far from the abyss with all its temptations, its criminality. It was a sport in which scandal and achievement were constantly mixed. There was this fine line and we all watched, fascinated, by how each in turn negotiated it.

This ghetto base did not keep cycling from being a sport created by writers from the sporting tabloids; people who knew their "Iliad," their classical mythology. And with the freest of brushes they painted a sport that was truly like nothing else, based as it was on sheer hyperbole. But there was a challenge in it as well. Either a race flabbergasted our imaginations, or it didn't. Those that did, like the Tour de France, or Paris-Roubaix, survived. And many did, enough to sustain an eight-month season.

It was this ghetto base and the heady verbal mix that went with it that drew us. And it was why the sport came into its own in the mountains. Here was racing that we could actually see, for an hour or so as one then another struggling member of the peloton passed us, the living myth, cartoon reality at its richest, its most haggard. And it is what I believe has most changed in recent years. The television camera cannot show the steepness of a road, what it means to be dragging your carcass uphill, against all that gravity. And it's no accident that the Tours keep being decided in time trials, on the flat, and which keep getting longer. It makes for riveting television watching. But it is not quite the same as being up there yourself, stoned, with a picnic basket, weeping, taking it all in: the melting roads, the snow, the frantic figures with their hoses and buckets and merciful hands, and the poor, gaunt, blasted figures themselves, who have ridden up into this hell, this paradise.

EDITOR'S NOTES

I n the nearly two decades since the 1978 Tour de France was held, there have been many changes in cycling — changes that have computerized the press room, modernized the Société du Tour de France, and totally transformed the peloton. Notable in the media changes has been the increase in television crews from all over the world, and the lifting of the ban on female journalists (although there are still very few among the Tour's 600-strong press corps). Meanwhile, the laptop computer and modem have almost completely replaced the typewriter and telephone.

Although the race is still organized by the Société du Tour — owned by the Amaury Group, which continues to publish *L'Équipe* and *Le Parisien* (now called *Aujourd'hui*) — the event's two directors are no longer full-time journalists. The director general is Jean-Marie Leblanc, a former Tour rider, who was the chief cycling editor of *L'Équipe* before becoming the full-time race organizer in 1989; and the current executive president is the Amaury Sport Organization's Jean-Claude Killy, the former Olympic downhill ski champion and an organizer of the 1992 Winter Olympics. As for Guy Merlin, the principal sponsor of the 1978 Tour, he did *not* succeed Felix Lévitan as a race director when, in 1987, Lévitan was dismissed by the Société for alleged misappropriation of funds. And following a 52-year spell as the race director, Jacques Goddet — who is now in his 90s — stepped down in 1988. Another major change in the Société has been its move from cramped headquarters in Montmartre to a plush modern office complex on the western edge of Paris.

Reflecting these changes, the Tour's budget has increased from $2.5 million to more than $25 million, and the race is such a commercial success that teams no longer pay entry fees. Annual multi-million-dollar sponsors include Champion supermarkets, Coca-Cola, Crédit Lyonnais bank and Fiat cars (replacing Peugeot). The co-sponsors include AGF insurance, Bose sound systems, Compaq computers, Coeur de Lion cheese, Festina watches, France Telecom, Kawasaki motorcycles, Mavic bicycle components, PMU betting, Sodexho catering, Supradyne nutrition and United

Savam trucking. And France 2-3 Television is the major media sponsor.

Stage towns still provide a significant part of the Tour's revenues. But while Leiden got the start of the 1978 Tour for about $80,000, in 1996 the Dutch city of 's-Hertogenbosch is paying about $1 million to host the Tour's opening two stages. Also emphasizing the Tour's expansion is the worldwide TV audience that has increased from 160 million to approximately 750 million.

On the competitive front, the Poulain chocolate company no longer sponsors the King of the Mountains competition; the best young rider is no longer awarded a white jersey; and tobacco and alcohol companies are no longer involved in race or team sponsorship. Instead of 110 riders on 10 teams that contested the 1978 Tour, the 1996 race has 198 riders on 22 teams. The actual times in team time trials are now counted toward individual classification, while the team time trial is no longer part of the Olympic Games — replaced by the mountain-bike cross-country. Time bonuses are awarded on the Tour's road stages that precede the mountains (20-, 12- and 8-second bonuses at stage finishes, and 6-, 4- and 2-second bonuses at the intermediate sprints). Black shorts and white socks are no longer mandatory, and teams often have color-coordinated uniforms (including green, blue, red or even denim-patterned shorts). The annual budget of a top team has increased dramatically, from around the $600,000 of a TI Raleigh in 1978, to the $10 million of a Banesto in 1996.

On the technical front, most Tour riders now use titanium or carbon-fiber bikes, which can cost up to $15,000 each, and since being pioneered by Greg LeMond in 1989, every rider now uses aerodynamic handlebars for time trials. Those bars helped LeMond become the third rider in history to come from behind to win the Tour on the final stage — when he beat Laurent Fignon in 1989. As for technical support, team cars no longer have cutaway doors for mechanics to make on-the-move equipment adjustments.

Riders prepare for the Tour far more technically in the late 1990s: Heart-rate monitors allow more intense training; rations handed up during a race are made up predominantly of nutrition drinks and not solid food; and every team has a sports doctor on its staff.

Looking at the new countries that have discovered the Tour, the first American to compete in the Tour was Jonathan Boyer in 1981. Since then, the United States has taken three overall Tour victories thanks to LeMond, while the U.S. today has 35,000 licensed road racers (and 30,000 mountain bikers), compared with a total of only 10,000 racers in 1978. And other countries new to the Tour — including Brazil, Canada, Colombia, Latvia, Mexico, Poland, Russia, Slovakia, Ukraine and Uzbekistan — have all supplied stage winners in the past 15 years.

Finally, today's professional cyclists are far better paid — with the top stars earning more than $1 million a year — while the prize money for the Tour now totals $2.5 million. This means that riders no longer have to depend on contract money from exhibition races (criteriums) to supplement their salaries — which has contributed to the disappearance of more than half the post-Tour criteriums. Among the other events that have been dropped from the calendar is the famous Bordeaux-Paris classic (last held in 1988).

SELECTED BIBLIOGRAPHY

ALDERSON, FREDERICK, *Bicycling: A History,*

  David & Charles, 1972

BASTIDE, ROGER, *A la Pointe des Pelotons,*

  Solar Editeur, 1972

BASTIDE, ROGER, *Doping, les surhommes du vélo,*

  Solar Editeur.

BASTIDE, ROGER, *Anquetil, Darrigade, Geminiani, Stablinski: caids du vélo,*

  Solar Editeur.

BLONDIN, ANTOINE, La joie de suivre le Tour,

  in *Joies de la Bicyclette,*

CHANY, PIERRE, *La Fabuleuse Histoire du CYCLISME,*

  Editions ODIL 1975

L'Équipe, Le tour à 75 ans (Paris),1978.

NICHOLSON, GEOFFREY, *The Great Bike Race,*

  Magnum, 1978

NUCERA, LOUIS, *Le Roi René,*

  Le Sagittaire, 1976

SIMPSON, TOM, *Cycling Is My Life,*

  Stanley Paul 1966

SLOANE, EUGENE A., *The New Complete Book of Bicycling,*

  Simon & Schuster (New York), 1974

TERBEEN, FRANÇOIS, *Grandeurs et misères du Tour de France,*

  del Duca, 1972

WADLEY, J. B., *My Nineteenth Tour de France,*

  J. B. Wadley (Kew), 1974

WILCOCKSON, JOHN, *Cycling: Fitness on Wheels,*

  Sunday Times/World's Work, 1977.